The Killing of Justice Godfrey

THE KILLING OF
JUSTICE GODFREY

An Investigation into England's
Most Remarkable Unsolved Murder

STEPHEN KNIGHT

GRANADA
London Toronto Sydney New York

Granada Publishing Limited
8 Grafton Street, London W1X 3LA

Published by Granada Publishing 1984

British Library Cataloguing in Publication Data

Knight, Stephen, *1951–*
    The killing of Justice Godfrey.
    1. Godfrey, *Sir* Edmund   2. Popish Plot,
    1678
    I. Title
    364.1'523'0924   DA448

ISBN 0-246-12351-6

Printed in Great Britain by
Mackays of Chatham Ltd

For Barbara Mary Land
★
Love

Contents

Acknowledgements   11

Prologue   13

Part I: The Victim and his World
1   The Man who Died   19
2   Hero in the Making   22
3   Plague and Fire   24
4   Scandal   29

Part II: Gunpowder, Treason and Plot
1   The Years of Conspiracy   37
2   The Great Plot Unveiled   41
3   Citizen Titus   47
4   The Forged Letters   51
5   The Very Honourable Friends   54
6   Limbo   57
7   The Perjurers' Progress   59
8   Lo! A Damned Crew   64

Part III: The Primrose Way to the Everlasting Bonfire
1   The Final Days   71
2   The Messenger of Death   77
3   One Day in October   82
4   Suspicion, Search and Speculation   87
5   The Man in the Grey Suit   93
6   I Find Murdered by Rogues   94
7   The Inquest   98

Part IV: The Age of Discovery
1   Panic   107
2   The Curious Flight of Mr Godfrey   112
3   The Domino Plan   114
4   God Almighty on Horseback   120
5   The Alibi   126
6   Terror   130

7   Evil Doings at the Water-Gate   134
8   The Scapegoats   140

PART V: Enigma Variations
1   The Romish Assassins   167
2   Creatures of the Underworld   171
3   Fratricide and the Grim Reaper   174
4   Oates or his Double   177
5   To Be or not to Be   179
6   Post Post Mortem   182

Part VI: The Answer
1   Peyton's Gang   191
2   The Spy from Long Island   202
3   The Mighty Giant   210

   Epilogue   221

Appendices
A.   The Godfreys of Kent   225
B.   Edmund's Childhood   228
C.   The Man with Three Names   232
D.   The Tankards   233
E.   The Inquest Verdict   234
F.   Godfrey's Will (1677)   236

Abbreviations   241

Notes and Sources   245

Bibliography   259

Index   271

Illustrations
(between pages 104 and 105)

The only portrait of Sir Edmund Berry Godfrey painted from life
National Portrait Gallery

Charles II
National Portrait Gallery

James, Duke of York
National Portrait Gallery

Anthony Ashley Cooper, first Earl of Shaftesbury
National Portrait Gallery

An engraving of Sir Edmund Berry Godfrey
Guildhall Library

The four 'discoverers' of the murder of Justice Godfrey – Oates, Bedloe, Dugdale and Prance
British Library

A selection from a pack of 'Godfrey' playing cards
Guildhall Library

A comic-strip pamphlet promoting the official version of the murder, published in London in 1679

DOCUMENTS REPRODUCED IN THE TEXT:

Minutes of the last vestry meeting Godfrey attended	79
The medical evidence that lay undiscovered for 298 years *Public Record Office*	184
Peyton's gang *Public Record Office*	193
The Petition signed by twenty-two Whig peers *Public Record Office*	219

Acknowledgements

When I was thirteen I had the idea of taking an historical mystery and 'solving' it in the form of a short story. I approached my history teacher at West Hatch Technical High School, Chigwell – an inspiring man called John Hudson – and asked if he knew a suitable case. He immediately told me to get *Who Killed Sir Edmund Berry Godfrey?* by Alfred Marks from the library. It was, he said, the greatest unsolved murder in English history. Alas, Mr Marks's turgid prose proved too much for me and I abandoned the project. But the idea stayed with me and when, ten years later, I finished my book *Jack the Ripper: The Final Solution* and was casting around for a new subject, Godfrey seemed the obvious choice: the three hundredth anniversary of his death was just three years off. If John Hudson had not hooked me in 1965 it is unlikely this book would ever have been written.

I am grateful for the support of my friend and former publisher Ken Thomson who planned to publish the book in October 1978, and who but for a series of unhappy accidents would have done so.

Others I wish to thank for their support and direct help are Prof. John Kenyon who gave generously of his time and expert knowledge of the period both during my research and after the book was complete; Professor C. Keith Simpson; Paull Harrap; Andrew Hewson; Richard Johnson; Rev. P. M. Jaquet; Christine Spillane; Norman Davies; John Back, Metropolitan Police Archives Department; Isabel Kenrick, Royal Commission on Historical Manuscripts; K. C. Harrison, Westminster City Librarian; Penny Bourne (née Godfrey); C. H. Curtis, Assistant County Librarian, Hertfordshire; Dr Levi Fox, director, the Shakespeare Birthplace Trust; T. J. Rix, Borough Librarian, London Borough of Hammersmith; Ms Sweet, Archivist's Department, Kent County Council; Rev. J. V. H. Russell; Maurice G. Rathbone, County & Diocesan Archivist, Wiltshire; the Rt Hon. the Earl of Pembroke; Elspeth A. Evans, Research Consultant, National Portrait Gallery; Sir Oliver Millar, Surveyor of the Queen's Pictures; Peter Brooks, Head of Picture Department, Lawrence Fine Art, Crewkerne; Patricia Bell, Bedfordshire County Archivist; Y. Nicholls, Assistant Archivist, Bedfordshire County Council; L. Peebles, Subscription Manager, Longman Group Journals Division; H. J. R. Wing, Assistant Librarian, Christ Church, Oxford; Charles Keeley, Archivist, Westminster School; John Cooper, former head of the Department of Metalwork, Victoria and Albert Museum; H. S. Cobb, House of Lords Record Office; the Marquess of Ormonde; R. B. Haughton, Lord Ormonde's agent in Kilkenny; H. L. Bryant Peers, Founder Secretary and Archivist, London Appreciation Society; Graham Dyer, Curator and Historian, Royal Mint; Harry Margary; Henry Hallam; Marie-Laure Prevost, Conservateur, Bibliothèque Nationale Département des Manuscrits; David F. Allen, School of History, University of Birmingham; A. N. Harrisson; J. H. H. Gaute; Mahdi and Ron McWilliam; B. M. Austin, Librarian, Longleat House; Derek Jones, Director of Old Master Paintings Department, Sotheby's; Jack Hammond; and Ms Coleman, Ms Fitzsimons and Mr Latham of the Pepys Library, Magdalene College, Cambridge.

In addition, I am thankful to the staff of: the British Library Reading Room, Manuscripts Department and State Paper Room; the Public Record Office at both Chancery Lane and Kew; Somerset County Record Office; the House of Lords Record Office; Lambeth Palace Library; Syon College Library; New South Wales State Library, Sydney; Walthamstow Central Library; Middlesex County Records Office; Greater London Records Office; London Library; Bodleian Library, Oxford; Westminster City Library Archives Department and Local History Department; the Museum of London; Hammersmith Libraries; Woolwich Branch Library; House of Commons Library; *Daily Telegraph* Information Service; and the Guildhall Library.

I must also thank the Rt Hon. Marquess of Bath for allowing me access to the Coventry Papers at Longleat.

And to Nina Martyn and Sally Slaney, my affectionate regards and thanks.

Stephen Knight
1 December 1983

Prologue

Thirteen years after the Great Plague, England was swept by a new pestilence, as virulent in its way as any strain of the Black Death. Although fewer died, many thousands sickened and lost all control of their minds and actions.

It began in the autumn of 1678. After eighteen years of domestic peace, the nation went mad with fear and hatred. The lunacy did not begin to subside for three years. At its height every Roman Catholic in the realm went in fear of his life. Many were driven from their homes and hounded like animals into the countryside. Between 100 and 200 were imprisoned. More than 20 were judicially murdered. It took a revolution and the overthrow of a king finally to restore the country to some vestige of sanity.

The event which sparked this long terror was the murder of a melancholy fifty-six-year-old London magistrate called Sir Edmund Berry Godfrey.

Godfrey left his house near Charing Cross at about nine o'clock on the morning of Saturday, 12 October. Most of his movements that morning have been traced. He was last seen alive at about one o'clock not far from home. By mid-afternoon there were already rumours afoot that he was missing and had been 'made away' – strange indeed, because it was frequently his habit to stay out all day, and sometimes all night too.

The following day his clerk went to Hammersmith, where Godfrey owned a tavern and where his mother lived, but he had not been seen there. By Sunday lunchtime all London knew of his disappearance, and whispers of 'murder' or 'suicide' were on every lip.

The gossip spread and the suspicion grew for five full days. At last, late in the afternoon of Thursday, 17 October, three men found his body face down in a ditch at the foot of Primrose Hill, then in the country about three miles from Charing Cross. His own sword had been thrust into him, his chest and abdomen had been savagely beaten, and there were signs that he had been strangled. Even though the fields all about were muddy and there had been torrential rain, Godfrey's shoes were clean and polished.

Rarely can the death of so humble a man have had such far-reaching consequences. It was instantly bruited about that the

13

upright Protestant magistrate had been foully done to death by Roman Catholics. His death was a godsend to a group of fanatics who had been seeking without much success to prove the existence of a Popish Plot to kill the king and take over the country by force. Godfrey's murder gave credence to the Plot-mongers' wild tales, and ignited the fuse for a terror that was to embroil not only many innocent people of lower rank but also the highest men in the kingdom. There was even an attempt to strike at the King's brother, James Duke of York, through his Catholic wife and his erstwhile servant Samuel Pepys, Esq.

In three hundred years the Godfrey affair has not been fully investigated. In 1972 Professor John Kenyon, the leading authority on the Plot era, observed that there was no book on the case that could be wholeheartedly recommended. This is surprising, for quite apart from its historical importance, the crime was never solved. It is justly described as one of England's classic murder mysteries. Many writers have judged it the most baffling of all unsolved murders. In 1827 Thomas de Quincey, that connoisseur of the 'art' of murder, wrote in *Blackwood's Magazine*:

> The finest work of the seventeenth century is, unquestionably, the murder of Sir Edmund Berry Godfrey, which has my entire approbation. In the grand feature of *mystery*, which in some shape or other ought to colour every judicious attempt at murder, it is excellent; for the mystery has not yet been dispersed.

For nearly a century after de Quincey's words were written, the mystery was no further clarified. Then, in September 1924, a new and plausible idea was put forward by J. G. Muddiman in the pages of *The National Review*. But the article was only seven pages long. The research upon which it was based was limited in scope, and it contained some basic errors of fact and interpretation. Although much quoted since, the theory has never been more deeply investigated.

Only one full-length factual book has appeared on the case, and that nearly eighty years ago. It was called *Who Killed Sir Edmund Berry Godfrey?* and the author, Alfred Marks, concluded like so many other writers that Godfrey had killed himself. Only now can this recurring misconception be dismissed with certainty. Newly discovered medical evidence, examined by Britain's foremost forensic pathologist Professor C. Keith Simpson, provides rich new material for establishing Godfrey's true fate.

Theories have abounded, as in Sir John Pollock's *The Popish*

Plot in 1903, John Dickson Carr's part-fact part-fiction *The Murder of Sir Edmund Berry Godfrey* in 1936, in numerous articles in magazines and books, and in the works of virtually every historian, major and minor, over the past three centuries. But with few exceptions the theories have been supported by precious little fact. Despite the industry of scores of writers, there remained a mass of undiscovered evidence. And because until now there has been no proper inquiry as to the man himself, his life, as well as his death, has remained a mystery. Fully investigated, the Godfrey legend and reality turn out surprisingly different. Facts now drawn together for the first time paint a picture of richer colour and of more fascinating detail than the grey, grim tradition.

When I embarked upon the Godfrey mystery it was scarcely my hope to discover the solution. It had, after all, defeated everyone who had tackled it in three centuries. My object was simply to produce the fullest and most accurate account of the case. But in studying it more deeply than any of my predecessors I uncovered crucial evidence that led, indeed, to the answer. From the outset, I had agreed with Kenyon's assertion that in all the many theories no convincing motive for the killing of Godfrey had ever been suggested. 'And this question of motive is crucial,' said Kenyon. 'If we only knew *why* he was murdered we would know with some certainty *who* did it.' The clues I had found, considered alongside existing knowledge, showed plainly that one particular group of men had an imperative need of Godfrey's death. Their motives, methods and the killer they employed are revealed as the true picture of Edmund Berry Godfrey's activities is brought gradually into focus.

PART I

The Victim and his World

Yet I suppose him virtuous, know him noble,
Of great estate, of fresh and stainless youth;
In voices well divulged, free, learned, and valiant,
And in dimension and the shape of nature,
A gracious person.

Twelfth Night, I.v

For you, Edmund,
Whose virtue and obedience doth this instant
So much commend itself, you shall be ours.
King Lear, II.i

1: The Man who Died

To the superstitious, Edmund Godfrey was doomed from the moment of his baptism. Thanks to the careless scribes of the seventeenth century, his middle name, variously rendered Berry, Burie or Bury, has proved an enduring problem.* But mangle the spelling how they might, they could never omit eight letters basic to the structure of the overall name, eight letters that added together spell . . . murdered. There was worse to come. In 1666, at the peak of his achievements, Godfrey was created a Knight Bachelor. Knighthood added more to his 'accursed' name than the little word 'Sir'. For without the addition of precisely those three letters, it would never have been possible, twelve years later, to twist *Edmund Burie Godfrey* into the weird but chillingly appropriate *I find murdered by rogues*.[1]

By 1678, the year of his death, Sir Edmund Godfrey was one of the best known figures in London. In the eyes of his friend Gilbert Burnet he was 'the best JP in England'. But even the most thorough historians have been able to say little of value about his life and character. Who, then, was this enigmatic gentleman whose death constitutes, in the words of Professor K. H. D. Haley, 'the most famous of unsolved historical murder mysteries'?[2]

He was, we know, a melancholy man, certainly towards the end of his life. Yet there seems also to be a gentleness, even serenity, in the few extant portraits of him. In spite of his fifty-six years, elderly in those times, he was still handsome, his dark, heavy-lidded eyes the more penetrating because of their contrast to his pale, almost sallow complexion. His nose was large and hooked and added, rather like the beak of an eagle, to the nobility of his looks. Always upon his doubtless thinning pate he wore a black, cascading periwig.[3]

According to his contemporary Roger North, 'he was a Man, so remarkable, in Person and Garb, that, described at Wapping, he could not be mistaken at Westminster. He was black, hard favoured, tall, stooping, wore a broad Hat, and sometimes a Gold Hatband, and went commonly wiping his Mouth, and looking on

---

* See Appendix C.

19

the Ground.' He was unmarried. And although he had many friends, he had a need to be alone for much of the time. He loved nothing more than wandering, alone and wraithlike, through the streets and by-ways of London, streets so narrow that in many parts the thrusting gables of the old timber and plaster houses almost met those opposite, obscuring the daylight and casting shadow everywhere. It was his daily custom, wrote North, 'to go about alone, creeping at all Hours, in Lanes and Alleys, as his Fancy, or Occasions led him'. He was never without his sword and a stout cane on these solitary walks, for the footpads and beggars who haunted the grim alleys would slide a knife between a man's ribs for a farthing. His broad hat, too, had a practical purpose. The law said that inhabitants had to sweep their streets and tip their dirt into tubs or baskets. It was rarely done. Godfrey himself, in 1672, had been involved in a plan to have the streets swept three times a week by parish 'rakers'. But it made no difference to the people. Even in the year he died it was common for filth and rubbish, including sewage, to be cast out of windows and on to the street. Unhappy was the pedestrian without a broad hat. His habitual wiping of his mouth with a handkerchief has been remarked upon before, one psychiatrist even suggesting that it indicated the presence of some unpleasant, perhaps terminal illness. Prof. J. P. Kenyon has suggested to me that Godfrey's tongue, like James I's, might have been too large. A far more likely explanation seems to lie in the foully polluted air which Londoners of Stuart times had to breathe. The capital lay under a 'hellish and dismal cloud of sea-coal' smoke and the air was heavy with soot from coal-burning fires in thousands of premises, industrial, commercial and domestic. In the words of the diarist John Evelyn, a London-bound traveller 'sooner smells than sees the city to which he repairs'. Godfrey's wiping his mouth was doubtless to remove 'those black and smutty atoms' with which the air seemed thick and which spread everywhere, insinuating themselves even 'into our very secret cabinets and most precious repositories'.[4]

As one of London's wealthiest wood- and coalmongers, Godfrey himself was at least partly responsible for disseminating the product that so impaired his comfort. He served also as a Justice of the Peace for both the county of Middlesex and the City of Westminster. His work as a magistrate, for which he received no wage, bore little resemblance to the duties of a modern JP. His office invested him with considerable powers not only to try criminal and civil cases, but made him, in effect, a senior police officer and public prosecutor as well. Conducting criminal investigations, interrogating suspects and witnesses, and having offenders arrested was as much a part of his work as sitting on the bench. Early in 1678 he did the detective work on a notorious murder case and acted as the foreman of a Middlesex Grand Jury which indicted the killer. And as a vestryman in the parish of St Martin-in-the-Fields he was concerned with issues in the Court quarter of London that are handled today by an army of local government officials. Along with his fellow vestrymen he had responsibility for tasks now divided between six departments of Westminster City Council. The upkeep of roads and footways, distribution of alms for the poor, refuse collection, rating – all this and much more was within his province.[5]

His father's diary states that 'Edmund Berrie Godfrey' was born, the seventh of twenty children, between three and four o'clock in the morning of 23 December 1621. He was baptized at the little Norman church at Sellindge near Ashford, Kent, on 13 January 1622. His father, Thomas, came from a long line of Kentish gentry stock, traceable back to the late 1300s, with a strong tradition of public service as JPs. Thomas Godfrey was active not only as a justice, but also in local and national politics. He became MP for Winchelsea in 1614 and sat in the Puritan-dominated third parliament of Charles I from 1628–9.[6]

Edmund was educated at Westminster School and Christchurch, Oxford, which he left without a degree in the summer of 1640.[7]

He spent the next few months travelling in Europe at his father's expense. An account of his life and death published shortly after his murder states with pious certainty that during his travels eighteen-year-old Edmund 'kept himself (by the aids of the Divine Grace) as well free from the contagion of the *Immoralitie* as the (equally dangerous) *false Religion* of the places in which he conversed.'[8]

Such propaganda was a product of the terror that followed the murder. It is typical of dozens of pamphlets, as truly believed as the Gospels themselves, which presented Godfrey as an unblemished Protestant martyr in order to blacken still further the names of those unjustly saddled with his murder. Several historians of later times have perpetuated the myth and led readers to believe that Godfrey remained celibate until the day he died. This is almost certainly untrue. He may even have fathered at least one illegitimate son, who bore his name, as the records of St Benet's,

Paul's Wharf indicate. In July 1716 a one-day-old girl, perhaps his granddaughter, 'a bastard child of Edmund Berry Godfrey and Ann Hudsell', was baptized at St Benet's.[9]

After returning from France, in December 1640, Godfrey entered the Inns of Court, one of a hundred and thirty-three men admitted to the Honourable Society of Gray's Inn that year.[10]

2: Hero in the Making

Edmund worked hard at his law studies, but towards the end of his teens he noticed the first signs of hearing trouble. It is known that he suffered some illness at this time, and it is more than possible that it was some sort of fever that left a legacy of deafness. It became such a handicap that he began to wonder if he could cope with the life of a lawyer. He tackled some friends about his dilemma, who agreed with him that his deafness 'might be an hindrance to him in the nice and difficult practice of Pleading, where the circumstances of debated Matters from the Mouths of Pleaders or Witnesses not being audibly received might be a great prejudice to the Clyent's Business.'[1]

He was also concerned about the delicacy of his health in other respects. He had been unwell physically for some time, and wondered if 'the laborious employment of the Law-practice might be prejudicial to him.' For both these reasons, he abandoned his studies at Gray's Inn in 1642 or 1643, and moved back to his family and friends in Kent.[2]

For some time he was uncertain what course to pursue. Eventually, with £1,000 provided by his father, he set up in business as a woodmonger with a family friend, James Harrison. They bought a wood-wharf at Dowgate, off Thames Street in the City of London, and embarked upon a profession 'known to be usually very gainful to the undertakers'.[3]

Although a kind and generous man in his personal life, Edmund proved to be a tough businessman. Within a very few years the partners had 'advanced their stocks to a very considerable increase and advantage'. To the citizens of London, coal was second only in importance to bread, and it was possible to charge inflated prices for it. Throughout the civil wars, while Cromwell and his Parliamentarians fought to overthrow King Charles I and his Royalist forces, Godfrey and Harrison extended their hold on the wood and coal market. By the end of the wars they were both wealthy men. By the age of twenty-eight, Edmund had proven himself beyond all his father's hopes. His deafness had not improved, but there was no longer any sign of the delicacy that had threatened to prevent his undertaking intense work.[4]

Some time in the next few years Harrison relinquished his part in the business to get married, and Edmund continued alone. This was probably in 1658 when Godfrey moved out of the City and took a house in Greens Lane, a road that ran between the Strand and the Thames near Charing Cross. This made him the only coal merchant outside the City boundaries.[5]

Two years later, in October 1660, while the freshly severed heads of the Regicides were being pecked to pieces by the crows on London Bridge, Edmund Berry Godfrey was sworn in as a Justice of the Peace for Westminster and Middlesex.[6]

Godfrey was severe in his dealings with the 'idle beggars and vagabonds' who appeared before him in court, but at the same time he was genuinely troubled by true poverty. There are numerous witnesses to testify to the truth of the assertion that 'he was so much a friend to those that were necessitatedly poor, and whose poverty was neither occasioned by ill Husbandry, nor continued by idleness, that such should never want his Charity.' The conscientious magistrate would spare no pains in finding work for such people or, if that failed, in making them an allowance from his own fortune. There were many families in and around Westminster who received donations from Godfrey. One family, 'religious, but suffering', were allowed ten pounds a year for several years until they were able to support themselves once more.[7]

In the courts and among his closest friends, Godfrey gained the reputation of a peacemaker. He was one 'that coveted not so much the Triumph of the Lawrel as the shadow of the Olive-bough', and was indefatigable in helping to reconcile differences between his friends and neighbours. As his reputation as an impartial adjudicator spread, so he was sought out more and more to arbitrate in private quarrels. Although his public and private business left him little spare time, he rarely refused.[8]

He was, according to Dr William Lloyd, rector of St Martin-in-the-Fields, 'a Devout, a zealous and a conscientious Christian'. He was an unshakeable devotee of Protestantism, and although he was tolerant with all manner of dissenters, 'he always declared a particular hatred and detestation of Popery'. He was unswerving in his magisterial duties, and active in the practical application of the Oath of Allegiance.[9]

Godfrey's father died in October 1664. Possibly as a result of pondering on the old man's life and work, Edmund himself entered politics that same autumn. This was the one area of public service into which he had so far not followed his father, and what heights he expected to achieve it is hard to say. But in this venture he was to be unsuccessful. On 1 December he was nominated as an alderman for the ward of Farringdon Without in the City of London. Three others also stood for election, and one of them, a scrivener called Richard Shelbury, was chosen to fill the vacancy. For a time, at least, Edmund allowed his political ambitions to slumber.[10]

3: Plague and Fire

The first new cases of bubonic plague were reported in London in the spring of 1665. Although the disease had been a sporadic visitor for centuries, this was the beginning of an outbreak worse than any since the legendary Black Death of 1348. It began in the slums of St Giles, where the warrens of rotten, half-timbered houses were infested with the plague-carrying black rat. The pestilence spread quickly all over London, and most people of means removed themselves hastily from the capital. The Court and Parliament retreated to Oxford, leaving the running of the city to the formidable Duke of Albemarle.[1]

Edmund Berry Godfrey was one of the few men of means who remained in the beleaguered capital. Previous writers have attributed this solely to his courage and his sense of public duty, but this is not entirely true. Only three types of trader flourished during the Great Plague – prostitutes, tobacconists and coal merchants. The physicians had as little idea of cures for the plague as had their predecessors in 1348 and among the myths the people invented to comfort themselves were those that claimed syphilis and tobacco smoke gave protection from the pestilence. Another protection, it was thought, was to light bonfires to fill the air with smoke and banish the 'plague venom'. Great bonfires were lit all over London and were kept blazing for weeks with seemingly endless loads of Newcastle coals supplied by Godfrey and his fellow coal merchants at nearly four pounds per chaldron.[2]

Although there was this strong financial advantage in remaining in London throughout the Plague, Godfrey acquitted himself with distinction in that year of horror. As one of the few justices of the peace left in London, he had charge of the excavations of the largest mass grave in England. With plague deaths having risen to more than two thousand a week by July, individual burials had become impossible. The death carts trundled through the streets every night, their drivers calling, 'Bring out your dead,' and newly-perished corpses would be heaved out of stricken houses and carried to the 'vaults' or burying places. Godfrey and his colleagues, as the only effective police even in normal times, had now to work almost ceaselessly to control looting, quell riots, bury the dead, clean the streets, and dispense charity to those reduced to starvation by the stoppage of all business. They had also to make house-to-house visits in the worst affected areas and to implement the laws brought in to curb the spread of the Plague. One such law ordered that any house containing a victim of the disease must be sealed up with all its inhabitants, sick and healthy, inside. A red cross was daubed upon the doors of these so-called 'pest houses', and the plaintive plea, 'Lord have mercy upon us!' inscribed beneath. There was, of course, no mercy. Even the strongest would soon break out in the plague's awful blotches and give way to agonizing spasms of retching black vomit after being locked up with their dying relatives.[3]

A light on Godfrey's character, illuminating his hatred of mean criminals as much as his courage, is seen in an incident that took place at the height of the plague. Godfrey's constables, searching for a notorious grave robber, had traced him to his hideout in a pest house. For months the felon had nightly crept into the cemeteries and churchyards of the city and dug up hundreds of corpses, 'taking from them their Dying Apparel, the Sheets and othen Linnen in which they were Inhumed, and decently covered, leaving the Poor Carcasses inhumanly Naked'.

One report says that the robber had pursued his ghoulish activities with impunity so long that he had 'furnished a Warehouse with the Spoils of the Dead'. Some people said he had collected nearly a thousand winding sheets. The constables sent by Godfrey to arrest the malefactor were terrified of following him into the plague-house. Godfrey, outraged that the wretched creature thought he could escape the law's vengeance, went to the house himself. Seemingly unconcerned by the danger of infection, he left his quailing officers in the street and walked into the house.

In a few minutes he dragged the criminal out of his sanctuary and ordered the constables to throw him into prison.[4]

When the grave-robber appeared before him in court, Godfrey declared that an example must be made of him for the benefit of anyone else 'that should be tempted to any such execrable designs'. He ordered the parish beadle to strip the prisoner to the waist and flog him around one of the churchyards he had desecrated. The sentence was duly carried out in the presence of 'a great number of Spectators, who were assembled out of Curiosity to see so remarkable an Execution.'[5]

During the worst of the plague there was a curfew of nine o'clock at night, by which time all healthy citizens had to be indoors so that the plague victims might, in the words of Pepys, 'have liberty to go abroad for ayre'. During the night hours of that long, sweltering summer, hordes of dying people would roam the streets, crying out with the agony of their suffering, and waiting for death. Unlike most uninfected Londoners, Godfrey could not lock himself up at home night after night. He had often to venture out in the course of his duties. Late on one such night, the city air filled with the smoke of the bonfires and the stink of corpses piled up ready for collection, he met the unrepentant grave robber. Recognizing the magistrate, the villain flew at him with his cudgel, aiming a savage blow at his head. But Godfrey was no mean swordsman, and managed to keep his assailant at bay until help arrived. The ruffian was seized a second time, and this time Godfrey committed him to Newgate Gaol until the next Sessions of the Peace at the Old Bailey. For this and other offences he was eventually condemned to death, but the sentence was commuted to transportation for life.[6]

The plague raged on. Still the authorities had no idea that the cause of the evil was the black rats that lived in such vast numbers in the houses and streets. The rats bred in the open sewers and in the stinking heaps of household rubbish and dung. Fleas bred upon the rats. And the fleas carried the deadly, unheard-of bacillus that caused bubonic plague. The rats were so numerous that people had come to accept them. They scurried about the rooms, ran across tables, and lived in their hundreds behind the skirting and in the cellars of the wooden houses.

People did seem to have some general notion that foul conditions were responsible for the spread of the disease. Godfrey and the other justices strove hard to keep the 'scavengers' at work, collecting rubbish and transporting it to the big garbage heaps outside the city; but the task, difficult at the best of times, was next to impossible in the state of emergency. There was even an official extermination of four thousand dogs which were thought to be carrying infection. But no one thought of the rats.[7]

The death toll increased to six thousand a week during August and seven thousand in September. It was, without exaggeration, a nightmare. Victims' glands swelled up, they burned with fever, hideous pustules appeared on their bodies and they suffered ever worsening pain. 'Death from the bubonic plague,' said one writer, 'is rated, with crucifixion, among the nastiest human experiences of all.'[8]

Still Godfrey remained at his post. And still, despite his contact with the stricken, he remained free from infection. With the onset of winter, so cold in those days that the Thames regularly froze solid, the disease began to lose its hold. By the middle of December the King was planning his return to the capital. In a handwritten report of his activities, dated 19 December 1665, Godfrey said:

> We [the JPs on duty in London] have caused all ye common sewers and Water Courses to bee cleansed against ye Kinge and Courte cominge to Town, ye better to sweeten ye places where we live, and to take away any visible cause of ye sayd Distemper.[9]

As one of the few who had not fled from the town, for whatever motive, Godfrey was severe on those who had. He was instrumental in the publication of orders condemning 'all persons who are gone out of town without paying their respective rates and taxes due on the Royal Aid'. And he supervised the breaking open of defaulters' houses and the selling of their goods 'and household stuff'.[10]

Godfrey's indignation was not without foundation. Even though he believed the stricken and the poor 'were never so well relieved in any plague time whatsoever,' he and his colleagues had undergone 'much inconvenience and censure' for the shortcomings in the assistance they were able to provide. The reason for the shortcomings was not hard to see.[11]

> I am ashamed to acquaint your honour [he wrote to the Earl of Newport], though nothing but truth, that not half our pest or poor's rate is paid by them who are charged therewith, and of right ought to pay the same, who are and have been most of them out of town all this time of visitation, and not taken care to pay anything of what is justly rated and assessed on them.[12]

27

As the frost and snow increased in severity, so the Bills of Mortality, records of the death toll in each parish published weekly by the authorities under the supervision of Godfrey and his fellow magistrates, began to tell a brighter story.

> This week's bill doth somewhat increase in Westminster [he wrote in his report to Newport], 'but abates very considerably in St Martin's-in-the-Fields, in St Giles'-in-the-Fields, Covent Garden, and other parts at our end of the town, whereby upon the whole, by the best measure we can take of things, we conclude it will be a decreasing bill, though it may not be so much as was hoped for.[13]

Valentine Greatrakes, the celebrated Irish healer who claimed to effect wondrous cures simply by stroking patients' bodies, came to London during the plague year. Godfrey met him and watched him at work 'driving the pestilence' from sufferers' bodies and curing them of ague, palsie, tumours, falling sickness, belching and twenty-year-old headaches. He was enormously impressed and often acted as intermediary between Greatrakes and his patients. He sometimes gave over his house in Greens Lane for the Irishman to use as a consulting room, and was gratified to see several 'miracle' cures take place there.[14]

The plague continued to decline throughout the winter. It flared anew when the warm weather returned but despite the long dry summer of 1666 it did not reach the epidemic proportions of the previous year. It was finally purged by the Great Fire, which started near London Bridge in September and raged for four days. In this calamity, too, Edmund Berry Godfrey distinguished himself, tirelessly assisting in the fire fighting and in conveying refugees to safety. The flames had scarcely died away before King Charles II, filled with admiration and gratitude for Godfrey's activities during the two catastrophes, summoned him to Whitehall and knighted him.[15]

On 25 September, at the crest of his popularity, Godfrey again fought in the aldermanic elections in the City, this time for the Bread Street ward. He must have been confident of victory. His chief opponent was Sir Thomas Bludworth, the Lord Mayor, and his prospects were very bleak. Bludworth, a vintner whose daughter later married Judge Jeffreys, had disgraced himself in the fire. Pepys recorded that he had lost all control at the critical moment. When the diarist arrived in Cannon Street with orders from the King that Bludworth should demolish all houses in the path of the flames, 'he cried like a fainting woman, "Lord, what can I do? I am spent. People will not obey me."' And he had been seen riding up and down with a handkerchief around his neck, 'looking like one frightened out of his wits'. This was the same cocksure Mayor who had looked out of his window when the fire began and said, 'Pish! A woman might piss it out.' What sort of threat could such a man pose to Sir Edmund Godfrey, hero of plague and fire?[16]

And so it was. Bludworth was no threat. He was roundly defeated in the election. But so was Godfrey. The new alderman of Bread Street was one Henry Partridge Esquire, a man of no great note whom Godfrey had probably barely considered. It was Godfrey's second and last attempt to enter politics.[17]

A few weeks later the King's Jewel House fashioned eight hundred ounces of white plate into an ornate wine vessel,* which was presented to Godfrey as a gift from the King in material recognition of his heroic exploits.[18]

4: Scandal

As Godfrey basked in the glory he had so deservedly won, a breath of scandal entered his public life. There was, it seems, another side to the worthy magistrate's character. Once again, historians for three hundred years have been, in general, content to take the word of their predecessors without checking facts for themselves. Thus the hardly credible image of the incorruptible 'plain and upright', almost saintlike Sir Edmund has been perpetuated. There was a sound political reason for the myth in the 1670s and '80s. It is astonishing that no one has expressed any real doubt about it since.

In 1665 Godfrey had written of the plight of London's poor, 'who crie out upon the dearness of fuel and want of employment, by reason of the King and Court having been so long out of town, and some of the courtiers, nobility, and gentry forgetting of their debts as well as their charity'. He was plainly concerned about the poor and suffering, as his actions testify again and again.[1]

How this charitable spirit accords with his actions as a businessman it is hard to understand. Godfrey was one of the few wood and coal merchants in London whose supplies had not been

---

* See Appendix D.

destroyed in the Fire. The King's remedy of blowing up houses in the path of the conflagration stopped the flames before they got further west than Fleet Street. Godfrey was fortunate indeed that he had moved from Dowgate – his old wood yard there was destroyed. Because of the great loss of coal, prices 'soared to famine heights'. The desperate need for coal in the months after the fire is said to have brought the capital close to insurrection. England was at war with the Dutch, and the enemy's navy frequently attacked the coal ships sailing around the coast from the north. The increasing need for an uninterrupted supply of coal as the winter set in contributed enormously to the hasty peace settlement.[2]

The temptations to follow the example of his fellow traders and take part in dishonest dealing must have been immense for Godfrey. He was a leading merchant in one of the most notorious trades in London. As John Ulric Nef wrote in his *Rise of the British Coal Industry*, 'the hoarding, forestalling, and engrossing of coal ... had been common in the London coal trade at least since the latter part of Elizabeth's reign.' In addition to this, coal-mongers were notorious for making extra profits by palming buyers off with anything that was 'black as coale, though it be a stone'.[3]

According to Nef, 'the frequent interruptions in the trade during the last three-quarters of the seventeenth century facilitated the practice of such tricks. It became increasingly common, not only for the ordinary dealers, but for others who were not regular members of the trade, to buy up in time of low prices quantities of fuel for which they had no immediate use, but which they knew they could dispose of advantageously in time of shortage.'[4]

So it was with Godfrey. At the beginning of January 1667 Godfrey was hauled before a committee of the House of Commons, which had been set up to investigate the supply of coal and other fuels. Godfrey confessed that he and others had sold coal to the poor at the rate of 72 shillings per chaldron, although he had paid only 41 shillings, 'or Forty-seven shillings at the most'. He had also received one chaldron in every score, and two shovels of coal to each bushel free of charge. In its report, the committee described Godfrey's dealings as 'a very great Extortion and Oppression, especially to poor People, and worthy the Consideration of this House'.[5]

In the event, no action was taken against him, probably in further recognition of his public service. The shame of exposure either persuaded him to follow his conscience rather than the example of his colleagues in conducting his business, or to be more cautious in his sharp practice, for no further word was raised against him. From the reputation he had among those who knew him best it seems likely that he came to realize that as one of the capital's wealthiest merchants he had no need to indulge in shady dealings, and as the years passed he devoted more of his time to public work and less to business.

Godfrey's courage was again put to the test in May 1669. Sir Alexander Frazier, one of the King's physicians, owed him £30 for firewood – a considerable amount, roughly equivalent to £1,130 today. Godfrey asked repeatedly for his money, but with no success. He knew Frazier was well able to pay the debt, but that he was using privilege to evade payment. The physician was secure in the knowledge that as a member of the King's household he could not in the ordinary course of justice be touched over a matter of debt. But Godfrey decided to run the risk of the King's displeasure and sue the debtor in common law, privilege or no privilege. Eventually, with a warrant granted by a sheriff, he had Frazier arrested. The King was so incensed that the privilege of one of his courtiers should be so blatantly disregarded that he ordered the immediate arrest of Sir Edmund and of the bailiffs who had carried out his orders. Pepys, an acquaintance of Godfrey, wrote that the bailiffs were 'severely whipped; from which the Justice himself very hardly escaped, to such an unusual degree was the King moved therein'. Godfrey was thrown into the porter's lodge at Whitehall. But he was not to be intimidated. A command from the King that he should cancel the warrant and have Frazier set free was met with a curt refusal. Instead he went on hunger strike until, after six days, Charles bowed to pressure from the Lord Chief Justice and several judges who supported Godfrey, and discharged him. But Godfrey, so recently knighted by a grateful monarch for his courageous work during the plague, was struck from the Commission of the Peace. He was out of office for nearly two years.[6]

In 1671, after a period away from London, he was reinstated and in 1672 took a house and woodyard next to the Thames in Hartshorn Lane. The yard, with its stacks of timber, can be seen clearly between the gardens of Northumberland House and Hungerford Stairs in Buck's View of the Thames, published in 1749. Godfrey's tall narrow three-storey house on the west side of Hartshorn Lane, the house from which he would step on the last day of his life after only six years there, is also visible. Before the construction of the Victoria Embankment in the 1860s, the Thames was about five hundred feet wider at this point. What in those days was a shingle beach sloping into the water from Godfrey's property, is today occupied by the Playhouse Theatre in Northumberland Avenue, some distance from the river. Hartshorn Lane, also known as Christopher Alley, had been the home of Ben Jonson as a child. It was demolished in 1760 and Northumberland Street built in its place, but Godfrey's house remained as late as 1860, when it was in use as a police station.[7]

The following spring, the press gangs came to London. Godfrey received a letter from the King informing him that he, his friend Colonel Edmund Warcup and a JP called Newman were appointed to assist the press masters in taking men to serve in the navy. It was a violent, unpleasant business but Godfrey had no choice but to take part, organizing 'the most active constables' in Westminster to assist in the official kidnappings.[8]

Godfrey's staunch protestantism was doubtless considered when, in July 1675, the Lord Treasurer ordered that Godfrey and ten other JPs should be commissioned to seize two-thirds of the lands of all Catholics in Middlesex. The seizure of recusants' land, made legal by an Act of James I, was reintroduced after the King was forced to withdraw his Declaration of Indulgence. However, little action was taken.[9]

About this time, a Roman Catholic silversmith called Miles Prance appeared before Godfrey at Hicks' Hall, the venue for the Middlesex County Sessions. Prance, who had worked for the Queen and other notable Catholics, begged to be freed from carrying out certain parish duties. But Godfrey, staunch parish worker, could not see why anyone should be freed from service to the community. Godfrey was known to be less liberal in pleas of this nature than several of his colleagues, and he refused Prance's request. When the appellant seemed displeased with his decision, the magistrate reminded him sharply that 'the Queen could not protect her servants'.[10]

Richard Tuke, writing in 1680, said that 'about the year 1678' Godfrey went abroad for several months on the advice of his doctors. Constant repetition of the story by later chroniclers soon eliminated the approximation of the date, and the journey abroad was placed definitely in 1678. Since an article by J. G. Muddiman in the *National Review* in 1924, in which it was stated without justification that Godfrey returned to England just before the outbreak of the Popish Plot in the autumn of that year, the myth has been regurgitated by almost every writer on the subject. Godfrey's long trip abroad was not – could not have been – in 1678. His longest absence from the St Martin's vestry meetings was thirty-five days in the whole of the year. The trip was in fact in July of the previous year, and took him to Montpelier in France.[11]

By the spring of 1678, when Samuel Pepys asked him to prepare a warrant for the arrest of his butler, discovered in bed with one of Pepys's maids, there was much talk of omens and terrible times ahead. The dire effects of a comet sighted in the previous year were expected to begin any day. There were predictions of 'frenzies, inflammations and new infirmities proceeding from cholerick humours,' and 'troubles from great men and nobles'. By August, white faces whispering in dark corners said that the Devil himself was abroad, and had presided over a great gathering of witches in Scotland.[12]

One of the men who probably took least account of the terrified ramblings, Godfrey was about to be hurled into the very heart of the nightmare. The Devil's appearance not only in Scotland but, in human form, in London marked the beginning of the end for Sir Edmund.

PART II

Gunpowder, Treason and Plot

Some truth there was, but dashed and brewed with lies
To please the fools and puzzle all the wise.

John Dryden, *Absalom and Achitophel*, 114–115

There is some strange thing toward, Edmund; pray
you, be careful.

King Lear, III. iii

1: The Years of Conspiracy

Despite the outward appearance of tranquillity in the early years, the reign of Charles II was an age of plots from beginning to end. The murder of Sir Edmund Berry Godfrey was a product of those years of conspiracy.

In the first eighteen years of the reign, the King's secret agents were continually uncovering conspiracies against his life among dissident groups such as the Puritans, the Anabaptists, the Atheists and the Fifth Monarchy Men. All had their own plans for doing away with the King and setting up their chosen leader in his place.

Less than ten months after the downfall of the Commonwealth and the long-awaited restoration of the monarchy, a wine-cooper called Thomas Venner led a Fifth Monarchy rising in London. The Fifth Monarchists, many of them Anabaptists, interpreted prophecies in the Book of Daniel to mean that the four great Antichrist monarchies of Assyria, Persia, Greece and Rome would eventually be succeeded by a thousand-year reign on earth by Christ himself. Venner and his armour-clad followers set out on Twelfth Night 1661 to inaugurate the divine millennium. After defeating a party of soldiers in a street battle they withdrew into the woods at Highgate. Three days later the capital was again plunged into confusion when the rebels, now according to some eye-witnesses three to four hundred strong, surged back into the City and engaged an entire regiment of the King's men, killing about twenty and losing twenty-six of their own number. The Royalist forces under the Duke of Albemarle put them to rout and Venner was taken. He was later executed with twelve of his lieutenants and their severed heads were impaled on spikes at London Bridge.[1]

In the autumn of the following year another Fifth Monarchy man, Thomas Tonge, led a plot to ambush and murder the King and so open the way for an invasion by English republicans exiled in Holland. Tonge's chief stratagem was a faked letter intended to be used in stirring up the populace to support the insurrection. He was run to earth and executed with five disciples.[2]

In 1663 came the Yorkshire Plot, one of whose leaders was a Captain Oates. But the conspirators' ranks had been infiltrated by government agents and about a hundred of Oates's confederates were seized on the eve of a planned attack on York. The rest, among them the arch-conspirator Colonel Thomas Blood, fled. Oates and about twenty others were executed.

Next, in 1666, came Colonel John Rathbone's plot to kill the King, set fire to London, take the Tower and establish a republic. Like all those before, it ended in disaster and its leaders were executed at Tyburn.

The plots, most of which did not progress beyond the planning stage, continued unabated year by year. Then in May 1670 the King took a step that led some of his own closest advisers to conspire against him. He concluded a secret treaty with the hated papist King Louis XIV of France. In the treaty, to which only two of Charles's ministers, Clifford and Arlington (both Catholics), were privy, Charles confessed himself 'convinced of the truth of the Catholic religion' and 'resolved to declare it and reconcile himself with the Church of Rome as soon as the welfare of his kingdom will permit'. In return he accepted £140,000 from Louis, half in advance, and the promise of French military aid to quell the inevitable rebellion when his conversion was made known.[3]

This was political dynamite. France was the traditional enemy of England. Popery was loathed and feared. One word too soon about the secret Treaty of Dover and a new civil war would be unavoidable. It was by no means hysterical for the King's most intimate advisers to foresee the King upon the scaffold like his father if the secret clauses of the treaty leaked out. Doubtless with this in mind, Charles took things slowly. But at the same time he had to act positively to assure Louis that he had signed the treaty in good faith. He needed the French King's money, and England could ill afford a war with France. It had long been Charles's aim to bring about religious toleration in England, to allow all people, not only Catholics, to observe their own religions in private. In 1672 he issued a Declaration of Indulgence which suspended the barbarous penal laws, allowed dissenters to worship in public and Catholics to worship in private houses.[4]

This was regarded with deep suspicion. The penal laws had allowed for papists to be treated as 'a sort of vermin'. Under them, it was a capital offence to be a Catholic priest or to conceal a priest. By law everyone had to attend the services of the Anglican Church once a week. If they failed they were condemned as 'recusants' and were liable to pay a fine of £20 a month or two-thirds of the income from their estate. To convert others to Rome was also a capital offence, and to be converted a felony. The death penalty could also be imposed on those who refused to take the Oath of Allegiance – which was anathema to Catholics, who regarded the Pope as their temporal as well as their spiritual master. The possession of crucifixes, missals, pyxes, rosaries, vestments and other Catholic emblems was regarded as a serious offence. Convicted recusants were forbidden from moving more than five miles from their homes without a licence.[5]

Except for brief periods of anti-Catholic fever, such as the one that followed the Gunpowder Plot, the penal laws had not been rigorously enforced. But so far as Charles's critics were concerned, there was a great difference between not enforcing the laws and deliberately suspending them. It was not long before the King was forced to withdraw the Declaration.

One of the loudest and strongest opponents of France and popery was Anthony Ashley Cooper, First Earl of Shaftesbury, whom Charles had made Lord Chancellor in 1672. He was satirized as 'the false Achitophel' by Dryden:

> For close designs and crooked counsels fit;
> Sagacious, bold and turbulent of wit;
> Restless, unfixed in principles and place,
> In power unpleased, impatient of disgrace.
> A fiery soul which, working out its way,
> Fretted the pigmy-body to decay
> And o'er-informed the tenement of clay.
> A daring pilot in extremity;
> Pleased with the danger when the waves went high,
> He sought the storms; but, for a calm unfit,
> Would steer too nigh the sands to boast his wit . . .
> In friendship false, implacable in hate;
> Resolved to ruin or to rule the State.

Shaftesbury seems to have begun to suspect the King's motives some time early in 1673, and thereafter openly opposed him in major issues. He voted in favour of the 1673 Test Act, which prevented anyone refusing to declare his disbelief in the Catholic doctrine of Transubstantiation from holding office or a King's commission. Eventually, when Shaftesbury was dismissed by the King in November 1673, he said, 'It is only laying down my gown and girding on my sword.' He promptly set himself at the head of a powerful Opposition to the Court Party.[6]

The concern of Shaftesbury and his supporters at the way the tide seemed to be turning in favour of toleration of the hated papists had been exacerbated by the conduct of the King's brother James, Duke of York – the heir presumptive. It was rightly suspected that he was a Catholic, although he had not openly admitted his conversion to the Roman Church in 1672. After the Test Act, James renounced his post as Lord High Admiral rather than receive the Anglican sacrament and deny Transubstantiation. In 1673 he married the Catholic princess Mary of Modena and opinion hardened against him.

Charles, himself married to a Catholic Queen, now had implacable enemies both in parliament and in the country.

While independent plots continued to rise up and be crushed, Shaftesbury and his ultra-Protestant followers worked in secret on some more decisive way of defeating the King and popery.

The new Opposition party, or Country Party, began to look dangerously republican. Shaftesbury began meeting certain staunch Protestants in the Commons. Their meetings were the beginning of Shaftesbury's Green Ribbon Club, the chief instrument of disseminating his republican propaganda and fomenting popular hatred of popery.

By 1677, the Green Ribboners, now meeting at the King's Head in Fleet Street, were contemplating a secret alliance with the Fifth Monarchists and the Atheists in order to forge into one viable force the dissipated power of republican feeling. Events moved apace and in October 1677, a year before Justice Godfrey's murder, a secret meeting took place between the Green Ribbon president Sir Robert Peyton and his notorious 'Gang', and other republican groups. They swore their hatred of France and popery. Their rabble-rousers had been busy stirring up their supporters in three counties, and they plotted to attack the Tower, kill the King and the Duke of York, and set up Richard Cromwell, son of the late Lord Protector, as nominal ruler. But the King's agents got wind of the conspiracy and it had to be abandoned. Except in the written reports of the secret service, many of those involved in the plot have never been named. For lack of proof perhaps, and because several of the conspirators were themselves influential or had powerful friends, they escaped to plot another day.[7]

The climax of all the years of conspiracy came ten months later with the Great Plot of 1678. The unique thing about this plot was that it did not exist. It was the figment of an astute but peculiarly sick imagination. It was the invention of a man who nursed a fanatical hatred of popery. But the republicans who had failed in their bid to foist Richard Cromwell upon the nation in 1677 saw in this imaginary Popish Plot a means to secure their end. It could be used to stir up such hatred against the Catholics that, by constitutional means, the Duke of York might be excluded from the succession and the Catholic gentry could be decimated.

Shaftesbury and his Green Ribboners stepped in and stage-managed the great Popish Plot. And the country fell hook, line and sinker for the story of a plot to kill the King, massacre the Protestants and re-establish Catholicism.

2: The Great Plot Unveiled

One of the things on Sir Edmund Godfrey's mind when he awoke at his usual early hour on Monday, 12 August 1678 was death: specifically, dead bodies.

The trouble was, some of the paupers of St Martin-in-the-Fields were being buried in linen shrouds, and it was proving too costly. As from today the twelve-year-old Burial in Woollens Act was going to be rigorously enforced in St Martin's parish, and it was Godfrey's job as magistrate to make it work.[1]

Even as he breakfasted at his imposing riverside house in Hartshorn Lane, events were taking shape that would soon bring death much closer to Godfrey than an abstract problem of other people's shrouds. Within a few hours, in a cluttered room just over a mile away, two men were to meet and discuss dark secrets, initiating a chain of dire events that in twenty-five days would hopelessly embroil the luckless Sir Edmund. Once caught up in the maelstrom, nothing and no one would be able to halt the rapid and inexorable ticking away of his life. From the moment of his waking that radiant summer morning, Edmund Godfrey had just sixty-one days to live.[2]

Parish matters, petty sessions and the routine work associated with the coal yard occupied him in the morning before the weekly meeting of the parish officers and the churchwardens at the vestry room of St Martin's Church after lunch. Almost every moment filled with industry, perhaps to compensate for the loneliness of his bachelor existence, he went about his business oblivious to the events taking shape and the dreadful nearness of his end.

At about noon a thick-set Vauxhall merchant called Christopher Kirkby paid a visit to his friend Dr Israel, or Ezerel, Tonge, who lodged at a house in the Barbican. The ageing Tonge ushered

Kirkby into his chamber, and in hushed tones promised to make him privy to an awful secret.[3]

Tonge, probably a brother of the Fifth Monarchy man Thomas Tonge, executed for his part in the republican plot of 1662, was a shaggy, unkempt ex-Puritan in his late fifties. He had graduated as Doctor of Divinity at Oxford in 1656 when Oliver Cromwell's mailed fist held the reins of power. With the overthrow of the Commonwealth and the restoration of Charles II in 1660, Tonge had little hope of a lucrative living in the re-established Anglican Church. In the fiercely anti-Puritan period that followed the Restoration, he did his best to disguise his true leanings. But they were frugal years, and after a spell abroad as an army chaplain he finally took a meagre living as a country minister in Hereford-shire.[4]

In 1666 things began to look up, and thanks to his patron Sir Richard Barker, a respected City of London physician and an acrimonious anti-Catholic, Tonge became vicar of St Mary Stay-ning in the City. But in a matter of weeks his church and most of his parish were destroyed in the Great Fire.[5]

An already weak mind snapped under the blow, and the deranged Tonge became unalterably convinced of what he had long suspected: that the Roman Catholic Church was determined by fire and sword to reassert itself in England. The fact that the Fire, if deliberate, was far more likely the work of republicans than papists, did nothing to calm men such as Tonge.[6]

Since the abolition of the Roman Church in England by Henry VIII the greatest bogey to have haunted the establishment was popery. The slaughter of Protestants during the reign of Mary and the subjugation of Protestants by certain Catholic monarchs in Europe, seemed to justify the country's obsessional hatred of Rome. And although from the beginning of Charles's reign the biggest threat was the uprisings by men of Tonge's ilk – republi-cans and Puritans – Tonge felt that after the Fire no God-fearing Protestant worthy of the name could now deny that the followers of the Old Religion were a legion of the damned. There was no question in his mind but that they stood ready to set up Satan's kingdom on earth at a single word from their demonic leader the Pope. The Vatican's terrorist force, he now decided, was the Society of Jesus. Tonge charged the Jesuits not only with starting the Great Fire, but also with masterminding the Civil War and the execution of Charles I!

He waged his solitary war for twelve long years. Except for the odd hare-brained ally like Kirkby he found little positive response to his propaganda. People were on the watch for republican, not Popish, conspiracies. For twelve years he was ignored or denounced as a raver. For twelve years he derived a masochistic pleasure from being a still small voice crying in the wilderness. 'He was hardly ever without a plot in his head and a pen in his hand,' wrote a contemporary pamphleteer. 'The one held the maggots and the other vented them.'[7]

By 1678 the mood of the nation had changed. Under Louis XIV France had become the most powerful nation in Europe. James, Duke of York, had openly embraced the 'One True Faith'. And Charles's motives for signing the Treaty of Dover, and indeed the true nature of that treaty, were being called into question by the turbulent Shaftesbury and his followers. Could it be, the rumours flying around the capital demanded, that Charles had secretly united with Louis to re-establish the Church of Rome in England? By August 1678 the country was willing at last to listen to the crazy little clergyman and his talk of plots.

A plot such as no one had previously imagined was the crux of the secret story that Tonge imparted to Christopher Kirkby in his shadowy chamber at twelve o'clock on 12 August.[8]

There was, he said, a conspiracy against both the Protestant religion and the life of the King himself. In support of his story he produced a handwritten document of forty-three articles which set out the exact nature of the alleged plot.[9]

Kirkby listened wide-eyed as Tonge ranted his way through the various points. Pope Innocent XI, he said, had instructed the Jesuits to overthrow the King and his government and to replace them with a Roman Catholic administration under James. The Jesuits had already appointed Catholic clergymen, noblemen and gentlemen to all the highest offices in church and state, and these villains stood ready to take over. The Papists had already burned down London once, said Tonge, climbing on to his favourite hobby-horse, and they had tried to do so again in Southwark in 1676. At that very moment they were plotting to set fire to all the shipping in the Thames. The King, he claimed, was to be murdered either by stabbing, poison or being shot with silver bullets. After that every Protestant in the land was to be massacred. Twenty thousand Presbyterians and eight thousand Catholics stood ready to rise in Scotland. The Irish were ready to rise at ten days' notice and had twenty thousand infantry and five thousand cavalry to bring into the field. They were also ready to allow the French king to land a force in Ireland. Sir George Wakeman, the Queen's physician, was to be offered £10,000 to poison the King.[10]

Horror-stricken, but at the same time delighted that his own anti-Catholic ravings had at last been vindicated, Kirkby declared that matters of such magnitude ought not to be concealed. It did not seem to occur to him to ask Tonge the source of his information. Kirkby was a dabbler in chemistry, exactly how successful no one knows, but he had managed somehow to ingratiate himself sufficiently in the right quarters to obtain access to the royal laboratories. He was thus in the fortunate position, if not of being known himself, at least of knowing the King by sight. Kirkby told Tonge that he would confront the King and tell him man to man of the peril in which he stood.[11]

This was the gratification for which Tonge had been waiting since his little world of St Mary Stayning had been reduced to ashes twelve years before. Now at long last retribution was to fall upon those responsible for the evils done him. He agreed eagerly to Kirkby's plan, but earnestly petitioned him to tell no other person than the King. Kirkby agreed.[12]

At about two o'clock Kirkby went to Whitehall and spent the afternoon haunting all the places in which he thought it most likely he would encounter the King. Although he once caught sight of Charles, he was strolling with the papist Duke of York, and Kirkby dared not approach. At the end of the day he scurried back to his psychopathic comrade and told him the frustrating news. Then he sat down and penned a note to the King, which he said he would slip into his hand during his walk in St James's Park the next day:

> If Your Majesty would be pleased to give me a quarter of an hour's audience, I should make known something that, as it is of the greatest importance, so it is only proper for Your Royal Ear, and not to be delayed without eminent danger.[13]

Accordingly, next morning, Kirkby was lurking in the outer gallery of Whitehall Palace, the King's residence, and awaiting the coming of His Majesty once more. When Charles appeared with his entourage, Kirkby darted forward from the shadows and pressed the note into his hand. Charles read it as he walked slowly down the stairs to the exquisitely landscaped royal garden. At the bottom he stopped. Beckoning Kirkby to approach, he asked him what he had to say for himself.[14]

'Your Majesty's enemies have a design against your life,' he said, and humbly begged the King not to wander off alone. 'For,' he added gravely, 'I know not but that you might be in danger in this very walk.'

Intrigued at this unexpected talk of assassination, the King asked, 'How?' and Kirkby, casting sidelong glances into the shrubbery of the great garden, replied in a whisper, 'It might be by being shot at.'

By now Kirkby was relishing his role as secret agent and royal adviser, and told the King that he had said enough, and that 'a privater place was necessary for a more particular account'.

The King commanded him to go inside the palace at once and present himself to his servant William Chiffinch, who would conduct him to the royal Bedchamber. He said he should wait there for him to return from his stroll in the park.[15]

There now followed the briefest Whitehall farce. Kirkby obeyed the King, but Chiffinch, dubious about his version of the King's command, refused to take him to the Bedchamber. If he must wait, Chiffinch said curtly, it would have to be in the gallery. The King, returning from his walk, came back up the stairs to the gallery. Preoccupied with his own thoughts, he did not notice Kirkby waiting there and proceeded to his Bedchamber for the meeting. Surprised at not finding him there as he had commanded, he came out and bumped into him in the gallery. Without further ado he called him into the chamber and asked him to tell what he knew. This was Kirkby's cue to reel off the salient points of Tonge's conceit.[16]

There were two men, he said, by name Thomas Pickering and John Grove, who had been sent to watch for a chance of shooting the King. Pickering was a Benedictine monk and Grove a Jesuit. He added that Sir George Wakeman had been employed to poison the King if Grove and Pickering failed. Asked how he knew all this, Kirkby said it was all in writing and that he himself had learned of it from a friend the day before.[17]

'My friend is near at hand,' he said, 'and ready with the papers to be brought before Your Majesty, should you so command.'[18]

Charles's reaction to the tales of Kirkby and Tonge is described by most historians, from Roger North onward, as highly sceptical. Looking at the facts, this is hardly tenable. Charles, an over-worked statesman, not only agreed to interview Kirkby as soon as he returned to the palace after his walk, he now appointed to see both Kirkby and Tonge in the Red Room of the palace that same night between eight and nine. There can be no doubt that whatever his private judgment of Kirkby's character, the inscrutable Charles was taking no chances.[19]

Tonge busied himself during the afternoon copying out the forty-three articles, explaining to Kirkby that he would keep the original document 'for [my] own security'.[20]

At the appointed hour they arrived at the palace and were shown into the King's presence. He was alone. Tonge handed over the duplicate screed, then joined with his accomplice in asking the King to keep it secret and safe.

'Otherwise,' nattered Tonge, 'the full discovery will be prevented, and our lives in hazard.'[21]

Relishing the cloak-and-dagger world they had invented, they now proposed that they should have continued access to the King, but that they should come disguised as chemists to divert suspicion arising from frequent visits. Charles, however, was going on holiday to Windsor the next morning and thought it best if he sent Tonge's papers to his Lord Treasurer, Thomas Osborne, Earl of Danby, with whom he said he 'would entrust both his life and Crown'. Together with Danby, said Charles, he would answer for the lives of the two informers. Thanking them for their information, he ordered them to see Danby first thing in the morning.[22]

They spent all Wednesday morning and most of the afternoon waiting for Danby to get up. His son was seriously ill and he had sat up with him all night. It was four o'clock in the afternoon before he finally stirred out of bed at his lodgings in the Cockpit, and admitted Tonge and Kirkby to his chamber.[23]

When the two fanatics went in, Danby had Tonge's papers in his hand. He had received them sealed up from the hand of Lord Plymouth, a Gentleman of the King's Bedchamber. He judged them, he said, to be 'of the greatest concern imaginable'. Whether he placed much faith in their authenticity is uncertain, but he saw in them a way of diverting the Opposition's baleful attention away from himself when Parliament met again in October. He had already foiled one attempt by his enemies to impeach him, but he was so disliked by the Shaftesbury group for his adroit handling of Charles's financial problems that it would take something big to save him next time, and he knew 'next time' could not be far off. Nothing could be more useful to him than evidence of a new popish terror.[24]

Danby asked Kirkby to withdraw, and grilled Tonge about the genesis of the information contained in the forty-three articles.

Here the story took an unexpected turn: Tonge confessed that he was not the author of the papers.[25]

He told a fanciful yarn of having found them 'under the wainscot at the farther end of Sir Richard Barker's gallery in his house at the Barbican', near to his own chamber door. In fact Tonge had arranged for the true author to 'hide' the papers and for he, Tonge, to 'find' them. It was all part of his mania. The papers had been deposited outside Tonge's door on 11 August, the day before Kirkby had been summoned from Vauxhall.[26]

The real brains behind the 'discovery' of the non-existent Popish Plot was that same devil whose appearance in London coincided with the diabolical goings-on in Scotland. His name: Titus Oates.

3: Citizen Titus

Late in life Titus Oates's mother confessed that while he was in her womb she seldom slept; and when she did 'I always dreamt I was with child of the Devil'. He was born in 1649 at Oakham in Rutland. As a child he suffered from a constantly running nose. His school fellows called him Filthy Mouth, and his father, an unpleasant Anabaptist 'dipper', knew him as Snotty Fool. Dull at learning and unpleasant to look upon, Titus had to cope in adulthood with the added disadvantage of being homosexual when homosexuality was considered an atrocious crime.

At the age of fifteen, in 1664, he was sent as a free scholar to Merchant-Taylors' School in London. A year later he was expelled for misdemeanours unknown. For the next two years he was taught at a small village school in the remote community of Sedlescombe, six miles from Hastings. In June 1667, just eighteen, the bow-legged, bull-necked youth was admitted to Caius College, Cambridge. A fellow student, Adam Elliot, wrote later:

> During my stay there I remember Titus Oates was entered in our Colledge; by the same token that the Plague and he both visited the University the same year.[2]

Titus did not do well at college, and after only two terms he was 'spew'd out'. Somehow, doubtless by some imaginative duplicity, he got himself admitted a servitor at St John's College. It was while at St John's in 1669 that he tricked a poor tailor out of a coat.

Despite the polished lies he told his tutor in a hopeless bid to defend himself, Titus was sent down in disgrace.[3]

His antecedents notwithstanding, he managed to 'slip into orders' through the good offices of the Catholic Earl of Norwich. How he obtained the earl's goodwill is uncertain, but by means of that connection he became curate of a church at Sandhurst in Surrey. It was here that his psychotic loathing of Papists first gained serious hold upon him. It was at Sandhurst in 1670, he later lied, that he first got wind of the dreadful Romish plot to overthrow Protestantism in England. From this time on, he led his listeners to believe, priests and Jesuits poured out the dark secrets of their religion to him. Why they should feel impelled to commit such a blunder he never explained.[4]

Physically, the promise of his childhood had been fulfilled. Oates's biographer, Jane Lane, wrote:

> His complexion is variously described as 'rainbow-coloured', 'vermilion', 'coffee-colour' and 'purple'; the truth would seem to be that he suffered from high blood-pressure. His eyes were abnormally small and sunken, and on one eyebrow was a large wart. But his most striking feature was his chin; it was so long that his mouth . . . was four inches above it.[5]

Roger North said that 'His Mouth was the Center of his Face; and a Compass there would sweep his Nose, Forehead and Chin within the Perimeter'.[6]

In 1673 he became vicar of Bobbing in Kent, but even as a parson he proved to be a troublemaker, a drunkard and a thief. At the end of 1673 he was sacked by the Archdeacon of Canterbury and went home to Hastings, where his weird father was now a professed Anglican and Rector of All Saints. He made Titus his curate. At Easter 1675 Titus took his first faltering steps in his career of perjury. In an impressively detailed slander he informed the Mayor of Hastings that he had seen a local schoolmaster, William Parker, buggering 'a young and tender man-childe' in his father's church porch. Although the charge seemed unbelievable to those who knew Parker, he was thrown into prison to await trial. Titus's genius for malevolent talk now led him to attack his first victim's father, Captain William Parker. The incredulous Mayor was assured that Parker senior had uttered treasonable and seditious words. Both father and son now stood indicted for capital offences that had never taken place outside the rancid milieu of Titus's mind. At the same time the perjurer had a less serious case proceeding against one of his father's churchwardens, who, he said, had threatened to thrash him. All three cases were eventually thrown out and Titus, not for the first or last time in his life did a moonlight flit to escape his just deserts.[7]

This time he secured a job as a naval chaplain and went to sea. He left England aboard Sir Richard Rooth's ship *Adventure*, bound for Tangier, in late May or June 1675. Despite the known prevalence of homosexuality aboard His Majesty's ships in the solitary weeks and months at sea, Titus's behaviour aboard the *Adventure* made him notorious, and he 'narrowly escaped a hanging at the yardarm'. After a single voyage he was drummed out of the navy. In 1676 he surfaced in London.[8]

The authorities at Hastings, who still wanted Oates to face two counts of perjury for his pre-naval escapades, tracked him down about the beginning of September. He was taken to Hastings and thrown into prison. Shortly afterwards he was moved to the dungeons in Dover Castle. From that formidable stronghold, incredibly, he somehow managed to escape, and he fled back to London. In late 1676 he was introduced to a club at the Pheasant Inn in Fuller's Rents, Holborn. Many members of the club were Catholics. As a result of his connections there he was reintroduced to his old patron Lord Norwich, and in 1677 became chaplain to the Protestants in his London household.[9]

There were now less than eighteen months to go before his account of the imaginary Popish Plot would be unveiled by Kirkby and Tonge.

At this point the lives of Titus Oates and Israel Tonge came together for the first time. The link between them was Sir Richard Barker, in whose house in the Barbican Tonge was living and who was a patron of Oates's father. Within three months of entering Norwich's household, Oates was dismissed, the reason unknown.[10]

Immediately, on 3 March 1677, the fanatical anti-papist became a papist. He claimed later that he had become a convert to Catholicism merely to infiltrate the ranks of the Jesuits as a spy for Tonge. True or not, Oates spent the next thirteen months gathering intelligence which, in the summer of 1678, he and Tonge would fashion into their notorious Plot.[11]

Soon after being received into the Church, Oates gained admission to Richard Strange, the English Provincial of the Society of Jesus. How a man like Oates managed even to meet an eminent man like Strange is in need of explanation. Far more mysterious is the fact that Strange was undeterred by Oates's murky past, and promptly despatched him to the English College at Valladolid in Spain to train as a novice.[12]

One writer suggests that Oates and Strange, and possibly even Lord Norwich, were members of a homosexual group, perhaps based at the club in Fuller's Rents, pledged to helping each other in adversity. Certainly this might explain Norwich's patronage of Oates in the past, and Strange's otherwise illogical championing of him now.[13]

It is also odd that Strange should send Oates to Valladolid just as the term there was ending. He thus had to kick his heels for six months waiting for studies to recommence in October. When they did, his total ignorance of Latin and Spanish, the only languages in use at the college, meant that he was packed off home at once. He arrived back in London at the end of November. In his six months abroad Oates had picked up little of use against the Jesuits, and to make matters worse he lost ten pieces of eight to a confidence trickster called William Bedloe, who was on a journey through Europe with his brother James, posing as an English aristocrat and his valet. 'Captain' William Bedloe, though he did not yet know it, was destined to play a decisive part in the story of Oates's plot, second only in importance to Titus himself. And he would achieve national fame as a 'discoverer' of the murder of Justice Godfrey.[14]

For a week or so Oates stayed in London with Tonge, but determined to have another crack at prising open some Jesuit secrets, he turned again to Richard Strange. On 10 December 1677, armed with letters of introduction from the Provincial, he arrived at the Jesuit College of St Omers in northern France. His name, he told them, was Sampson Lucy. In keeping with his past record, his period at St Omers, characterized by drunkenness and blasphemy, ended in disgrace. In June 1678 he was expelled by Strange's successor Thomas Whitebread, and returned yet again to London.[15]

At Cambridge, revealing himself 'a great dunce', Oates had seemed capable only of 'a plodding Industry, and an unparallel'd Assurance'. His one distinction, it seems, was 'a tenacious memory'.[16]

That singular ability was now put to fearful use. His hatred of the Jesuits now fermenting within him even more furiously, he teamed up once more with Tonge. His experiences with the Jesuits abroad, details of individuals he had met or seen at a distance, places, events and the idlest gossip were now frantically rewritten into the forty-three articles purporting to blow the lid off the great popish conspiracy. He could hardly have guessed that he was on the eve of being hailed the Saviour of the Nation.[17]

He deposited the papers outside Tonge's door, as arranged, on 11 August. Within three days Lord Treasurer Danby was gravely concerned, and demanding to know more.

4: The Forged Letters

After Kirkby had withdrawn, Danby asked Tonge if he knew where to find the author of the forty-three articles. The doctor replied that he did not, but that he had lately seen him two or three times in the street and thought it likely they would meet again before long. Tonge of course knew very well where Oates could be found, but at this stage in the subterfuge Citizen Titus thought it prudent to stay in the background.[1]

Apart from the personal benefit he could derive from a shrewd manipulation of Tonge's information, Danby was in no doubt that the King wanted it thoroughly investigated. But before he could launch a serious inquiry, the Lord Treasurer needed more concrete evidence. He agreed that Tonge's informant should preserve his anonymity on condition that he should obtain further details of the Plot. Danby arranged for Lloyd, one of his servants, to act as secret messenger between himself and Tonge.[2]

Within two or three days, Oates had invented further details. At Tonge's behest they were copied out by Kirkby and passed to Lloyd. It was now known, the Lord Treasurer learned, that Grove and Pickering, the popish assassins, were to kill the King at Windsor. The exact day of the murder had been discovered. Grove and Pickering, like many another innocent man accused by Oates, were personally known to him. He bore some trifling grudge against most of those named in his accusations. Pickering, for example, had turned him away during the summer of 1678 when he went to him begging. Thomas Whitebread would eventually pay for expelling Oates from the Society of Jesus with his life.[3]

According to the papers already in Danby's hands, Pickering and Grove had proven singularly inept in their roles as would-be assassins. They had 'dogged' the King for eight years, but at every attempt to kill him something had gone wrong. Once Grove had a cold. At another time Pickering had fired at the King in St James's

Park but missed. On yet another occasion he had forgotten to load his pistol. The story of their blunders was later embroidered still more. Lurking in the bushes of the park, Pickering had once tried to shoot the King but the flint of his pistol had been loose. Once he had no powder in the pan. Once he had loaded with bullets only and forgotten to bring his powder. Now 'Four Irish Ruffians' had been appointed to stand by at Windsor to execute the deed if Pickering and Grove failed again. It was not explained at any stage why plotters of such diabolical cunning as the Jesuits had appointed such clowns to perpetrate the first and most crucial deed in their intended revolution.[4]

The story of Pickering and Grove's past exploits was enough to strain any man's credulity, but Danby agreed on a plan to capture the assassins. He would ride to Windsor while Tonge would arrange for Lloyd to travel in the same stagecoach as the ruffians. They could then be arrested on arrival. The coach was waylaid at the prearranged spot, but there was no sign of any ruffians. A solitary and frustrated Lloyd explained to Danby that some accident had prevented the ruffians' taking the coach. A day or so later, with new plans laid to catch the traitors, they again failed to arrive. The reason this time, according to Tonge, was that one of their horses had fallen and injured its shoulder.[5]

The Plot had begun to sicken. Danby was losing patience, and the King himself was now openly incredulous. He refused to report such suspect allegations to the Privy Council. 'It would only create alarm and may perhaps put the design of murdering me into the head of some individual who otherwise would never have entertained such a thought,' he said.[6]

Oates was in trouble. If he and Tonge were to escape being thrown into Newgate for falsely accusing men like Sir George Wakeman, some convincing evidence would have to be invented.

So they set about forging some treasonable letters that purported to be from four Jesuits and a papist physician whom Oates had once consulted after contracting venereal disease. The letters indicated that the five men were involved in just the conspiracy Oates claimed to have uncovered. They were despatched by Tonge to Father Thomas Bedingfield, the Duke of York's Jesuit confessor at Windsor, on 31 August. Tonge then wrote to Danby informing him that he had learned of five letters containing treasonable designs which should be intercepted.[7]

This was bold indeed. If they could secure the downfall of Bedingfield, it would seriously harm the Duke of York. The Duke had powerful enemies who quailed at the prospect of a papist succeeding to the throne when Charles died. James had already made himself unpopular by refusing to submit to the Test Act. If by means of the forged letters it was believed that his confessor was engaged in treason, his fate would be sealed. Shaftesbury, the Country Party and the Green Ribboners, who were already candidly discussing the possible exclusion of James from the succession, would ride high on a wave of popular acclaim.[8]

But things went awry. Danby's minions in the Post Office let him down and the letters got through to Bedingfield. By the time the Lord Treasurer had ridden triumphantly to Windsor to announce Tonge's latest 'informations' to the King, the cat was already out of the bag. Realizing the letters were forgeries, and alarmed at their content, Father Bedingfield had taken them to James, who had shown them directly to the King.[9]

The handwriting on all the letters, whether Oates's or Tonge's, was remarkably similar. The paper on which they were written, which bore an identical watermark on each letter, appeared to have been cut from a single sheet. Every signature was misspelled and the same errors of spelling and style appeared throughout.[10]

James had so far heard nothing of Oates and Tonge. But clearly somebody was intending to incriminate Bedingfield, and through Bedingfield to strike at him. He told Charles the whole matter should be formally investigated by the Privy Council but, knowing the prime mover in the case was a madman, Charles resisted. As far as he was concerned the plot was fiction and he refused to consider it further.[11]

The misfiring of the forged letters ploy made Tonge desperate. The King and Danby knew nothing of Oates. To them Tonge was the sole source of the infuriating rumours which now seemed incapable of verification. Oates's name had been mentioned to nobody, and unless he came forward and revealed his true part in the matter, Tonge might well find himself in Newgate. So he persuaded Oates that he should swear to the truth of his allegations before a magistrate. Titus unflinchingly agreed.

Sir Edmund Godfrey now had thirty-eight days to live.

5: The Very Honourable Friends

On the evening of 4 September, while Sir Edmund Berry Godfrey sat with fifteen of his fellow vestrymen discussing parish matters, Dr Israel Tonge called upon one of the two Secretaries of State, Sir Joseph Williamson, the country's chief magistrate after the Lord Chancellor. Williamson, who well knew Tonge and was under no illusion about his state of mind, was not at home. As Sir Edmund sat in the vestry room of St Martin's describing how he had spent £33 of parish money on the relief of the poor, Israel Tonge scuttled back to his hole and determined to try again in the morning.[1]

He rose early next day and returned to Williamson's lodgings. But all that awaited him, as he wrote later, was 'a rude repulse and noe admission'. Williamson sent a servant to tell Tonge that he was 'by noe means' to bring Oates before him, 'but rather to have him sworn before some Justice of ye Peace'.[2]

The next logical step for Tonge would have been to recruit the help of a justice who shared his own extreme hatred of the Catholics. There was just such a man in the person of Sir William Waller, a zealous Protestant described as 'a great Inquisitor of Priests and Jesuits, and Gutter of Popish Chapels'. But Waller, better known as the Priest Catcher and one of the more extreme Green Ribboners, was ignored by Tonge. The doctor wrote in his journal that he was 'at a losse because he knew noe justice of ye peace in or about Westminster'. But there can be little doubt that he knew Waller. Instead he 'advized with some very honourable friends', who turned him in the direction of Justice Godfrey.[3]

Who these 'very honourable friends' were, and why they recommended Godfrey, are crucial points in the solving of the mystery of the magistrate's subsequent murder. The answers shine a light where for three centuries there has been darkness.

Most writers, in telling Godfrey's story, have relied on Christopher Kirkby's account, which omits vital details of the course of events.

Kirkby tells how Tonge presented Oates to Godfrey on 6 September. According to the merchant, his friends 'would not permit [Godfrey] to read the particulars of the Information, telling him that His Majesty had already had a true copy thereof; and

54

that it was not convenient that it should be yet communicated to any body else, only acquainting him in general, that it contained matter of treason and felony, and other high crimes'. At this, says Kirkby, Godfrey 'rested satisfied without reading them, and underwrit Dr Oates his affidavit, that the matter therein contained was true; and at the same time Dr Tonge made oath that it had been made known to the King'.[4]

Most historians have accepted that this is what actually happened, even though it is clear from Kirkby's known movements that he was not even present at the interview with Godfrey, but in Windsor. Several writers have remarked that this behaviour was hardly consistent with the magistrate's character, but have failed to explain the inconsistency.

Godfrey was noted for his public spirit, his courage and strict sense of duty. It is inconceivable that this exemplary officer of the crown could receive affidavits attesting the truth of certain written allegations about treason and other crimes, and not insist on reading them.

Or is it?

Writers baffled by this episode have sought to explain it in one of two ways: either that Godfrey did read the articles, and concluded from their fanatical nature and his own assessment of the men who brought them that they were false; or that he did not read them, and accepted the word of Oates and Tonge that the King knew their contents.

Neither answer is tenable. If he had read the articles, an upright magistrate would never have allowed his own judgment of their authenticity to prevent him doing what was his plain duty. Failing to report them to the Lord Chief Justice or the Lord Treasurer would lay him open to a charge of Misprision (concealment) of Treason, a heinous offence. The suggestion that he had no need either to read the articles or report the meeting with Oates because the latter had assured him the King already knew, at first seems more plausible. In fact it is as flawed as the first explanation. The registers of the Privy Council show that a copy of the depositions *were* left with Godfrey on 6 September. In addition to this, Godfrey later made it clear that he knew Oates was a liar. As Oates and Tonge were his only source for the claim that the King had been told, and on his own admission he knew Oates was a perjurer, why did he remain silent?[5]

The answer goes back to those 'very honourable friends' of Dr Tonge. There is an episode linking this shadowy group's recommendation of Godfrey with the 6 September interview. It has so far never found its way into print.

In his journal, Tonge wrote that after his friends had told him to approach Godfrey he replied that he did not know him, 'and feared he would not take ye depositions with necessary precautions'. He would agree, he said, only if his honourable friends would mediate with Sir Edmund on his behalf, and get the magistrate to promise to take the depositions. The friends 'promised to intercede with ye justice in this businesse and gave ye doctor leave to acquaint ye justice that they desired to speake with him in that affaire'.[6]

Tonge went immediately to Godfrey's house in Hartshorn Lane and 'acquainted him with ye weight and moment of ye affaire and the extreame necessity of haveing ye witnesse sworne.'[7]

But Godfrey, true to his character, objected. No matter. The ace up Tonge's sleeve was his very honourable friends. He told Godfrey about the friends and asked him to confer with them about the matter. Godfrey agreed and accompanied him to the house of the friends. All Godfrey's scruples in the matter were overcome in a single conversation with one of the friends, and he 'condescended to ye Doctor's request, who appointed ye next day to bring his informant with ye information before him'.[8]

The identity of these powerful friends, who held such sway with Godfrey that he was persuaded by them to lay aside his doubts and deliberately to fail in his duty, will be shown to be central to the solution to the riddle of Godfrey's death.

The deposition sworn before Godfrey on 6 September has never been found. Its exact contents are unknown. It is fairly certain that it consisted of the original forty-three articles accompanied by whatever embroidery and expansion had occurred to Oates in his three weeks of lying low since Kirkby's approach to the King.

Tonge's account of the meeting at Godfrey's house on the sixth is much fuller and more reliable than Kirkby's. By the next day, it seems, Godfrey was again concerned at the compromising position in which he stood. He was 'not very forward' in taking the depositions and urged Tonge to take Oates 'to some other'. But Tonge again impressed upon him the dread weight of the matter, *and reminded him of 'ye Recomendations of his honourable friends'*. Godfrey relented. He could not defy the wishes of the honourable friends, whatever danger was involved in complying.[9]

He asked, 'What are these felonious matters contained in the information?'

'Firing houses and towns,' replied Tonge.

Oates chipped in and told the magistrate that among other subjects the depositions concerned the fire of Southwark in 1676, and told him, 'Groves was one of the incendiaries.' He referred, of course, to poor slandered John Grove the Jesuit.

Sir Edmund said he knew Grove very well, and that in fact Grove had been active in 'saving and securing the poor Southwarkers' goods', to which Tonge added the wry comment that 'whether for their or ye Jesuits' use will not be much question'.[10]

6: Limbo

The letters forged by Oates and Tonge to give credence to their story had completely misfired. Far from increasing confidence in their wild allegations, they had weakened their position even more. For three weeks the Plot was in limbo.

In the days after the interview with Godfrey, Christopher Kirkby tenaciously shadowed the Lord Treasurer. But Danby was still fuming over the embarrassment the informers had caused him. It seemed that he would not be able to use the story of the Plot to any purpose, and his mind was filled with the predicament facing him when Parliament sat again on 1 October. Kirkby trailed Danby back and forth between his country house at Wimbledon and his lodgings at Windsor, but although on one occasion Danby saw his erstwhile informer, he swept past without even speaking to him.[1]

On Monday, 9 September it rained for the first time in months. Danby again left Windsor on his way to Wimbledon. Kirkby, frustrated and perplexed, hung around the castle at Windsor for the anticipated summons from the King. But by midday even the numbskull merchant was beginning to realize that he and his cronies were no longer in favour. The King remained obstinately aloof and Kirkby made his way back to town, where he joined Oates and Tonge at the doctor's temporary lodgings at the Flying Horse in King Street, Westminster that evening.[2]

Oates, incapable of speaking the truth even to his own closest associates (perhaps to them least of all), regaled Kirkby with a fanciful story about a Jesuit having lain in wait for him at his lodgings in Cockpit Alley off Drury Lane when he returned there on Saturday. The Jesuit, said Oates, had abused and assaulted him, and kept him there all night 'in great terror'. Hanging on the imposter's every word, Kirkby advised Oates to accompany him to Vauxhall for safety. It was a timely invitation. Mrs Hutton, mistress of the Flying Horse, had already asked Tonge to remove Oates, who had sought refuge at the inn since the imaginary encounter with the brutal Jesuit. He was now in a 'sad condition'. Penniless, and uncertain where to find money for his next meal, leave alone enough to pay his rent, Oates seized the chance of indefinite free accommodation, and all three took the ferry for Vauxhall that night.[3]

At about the same time Sir Edmund Berry Godfrey's tall, stooping figure was to be seen walking along Hartshorn Lane to a routine meeting at St Martin's Church. There was a discrepancy in the parish accounts and Sir Edmund was due to see Dr Lloyd, the rector, and four other vestrymen to clear the matter up.[4]

At Vauxhall, Oates devoted himself to writing out copies of his 'informations', and to instilling the fear of the devil in his two gullible friends. Tonge went several times to Wimbledon but had no more success than Kirkby in passing on 'the needful and occurring informations' to Lord Treasurer Danby. Tonge and Kirkby were 'much perplexed, both in regard of the danger they were in, and the seeming neglect of the Discovery they had made'. Oates pretended to have a similar fear of attack by Jesuits, but his real anxiety was that, having revealed himself as the author of the forty-three articles, his perjury might be discovered and he would end up at Newgate, or perhaps even Tyburn.[5]

For nearly three weeks there was no contact between the conspirators and the Court. At last Tonge could contain himself no longer. On 26 September he went to Gilbert Burnet, a young clergyman and good friend of Sir Edmund Godfrey. Burnet had met Tonge before. When the doctor told him about the Plot, Burnet was amazed. As he wrote later, he did not know whether Tonge was crazed, or whether he had come to him with the intention of involving him in concealing a treason. Anxious not to be guilty of misprision, Burnet went to Dr Lloyd at St Martin's and sent him to one of the Secretaries of State with an account of Tonge's disclosures. Lloyd was told that Tonge's story was already known and that he was 'making discoveries there' in order that he might 'get himself to be made a dean'.[6]

It is unlikely that anything would have come of the Plot had not the Duke of York continued to press for a full inquiry. In order to clear the Jesuits named in the forged letters, and exonerate his confessor and himself, he urged his brother and the Lord Treasurer to bring the matter before the Committee of Foreign Affairs, the forerunner of the modern Cabinet. He maintained this pressure upon his brother all through September. Charles at last relented shortly before he left for the autumn race meeting at Newmarket on 28 September.

The matter was raised at a meeting of the committee, the most confidential of the Privy Council, in Whitehall on the night of the 27th. Only the King, the Lord Chancellor, the Lord Treasurer, the Lord Privy Seal and the two Secretaries of State were present. They looked at an affidavit received by Danby from Tonge, calling for the arrest of prominent Jesuits. They also had the latest version of Oates's deposition, which in his sojourn at Vauxhall he had extended from forty-three articles to eighty-one.[7]

Once again, while events crucial to the course of the Plot were taking shape at Whitehall, Sir Edmund Godfrey was contentedly engaged in financial discussions with fellow vestrymen. St Martin's parish was preparing for a visit by auditors.[8]

The Lord Treasurer sent his man Lloyd to Vauxhall to summon Tonge before the committee. Kirkby and Tonge returned with Lloyd, but before they arrived at Whitehall the committee had already risen and left orders that they should attend a special meeting of the Privy Council in the morning at ten o'clock.[9]

This was the chance they had been awaiting. That night they resolved to get the final version of Oates's depositions sworn before Sir Edmund Godfrey.

7: The Perjurers' Progress

Tonge rose early next day. Rousing his two friends, he collected all the papers they had amassed in their weeks of frantic copying and re-copying and took to the river. Landing on the beach next to Godfrey's yard, they clambered up to the timber stacks and piles of coal and picked their way through to the magistrate's house. Sir Edmund again went through the legal rigmarole of taking Oates's oath that his articles concerning the Plot were true. The conspirators had brought two copies of the new, expanded version. Both were signed by Oates and Tonge and countersigned by Godfrey. One copy was left with the magistrate as an insurance against the possibility that the Privy Council would try to hush up the Plot.

This was a shrewd move, doubtless planned by Tonge and his very honourable friends. Godfrey was not only courageous and conscientious, he was also quite unafraid of the King, as he had shown in the sensational confrontation over Frazier's debt nearly ten years earlier.[1] Tonge knew that if the Privy Council decided to suppress Oates's evidence, Sir Edmund Berry Godfrey was a brave enough man to take it upon himself to report the 'discoveries' to Parliament.

The three men left Godfrey poring over the eighty-one articles, written in dirty brown ink in Oates's straggling hand and covering many pages. Having asked Oates to repair to Vauxhall until called upon, Tonge and Kirkby sped to the Council Chamber at White-hall for the meeting of the Privy Council at ten o'clock.[2]

It was a most illustrious gathering. The King was in the chair. Around the council table were ranged eighteen of the most powerful men in England. There were the elderly Prince Rupert, veteran of Edgehill, Marston Moor and Naseby; the Archbishop of Canterbury, William Sancroft; Sir Heneage Finch, Earl of Nottingham, the Lord Chancellor; Lord Treasurer Danby; Arthur, Earl of Anglesey, Lord Privy Seal; two dukes including Monmouth, Charles's illegitimate son by Lucy Walter; six other earls; Lord Viscount Newport; the Vice Chamberlain; Secretary of State Sir Joseph Williamson; the Chancellor of the Exchequer; and the Speaker.[3]

Williamson presented the bundle of papers he had received rolled up the night before, and announced to the councillors that information had been received that there existed a Jesuit conspiracy against the life of His Majesty. When the first buzz of interest had died down, Charles told the councillors about his meeting with Tonge in the Red Room of the palace on 13 August, and of how he had referred the matter to Danby. He then summarized the short history of the Plot since then – touching on Danby's inquiries and the tiresome business of the Bedingfield letters. Charles was bored with the whole affair. The letters had confirmed him in his opinion that the Plot was a hoax. He was in the council chamber now only to please his brother, and while he wearily trotted out the details of the case, his mind wandered to the hunting and horse racing at Newmarket, where he was bound that afternoon.[4]

The five letters were passed among the members of the council. Several of the lords present noted that 'the writing in most of them seemed to be forced and by the ill spelling of names and other suspicious marks, thought to be a counterfeit matter'.[5]

60

Tonge was then called in. His first move was to present the King with 'a short writing' naming several Papists. Chief among these was Thomas White (Whitebread), inserted at Oates's insistence for the 'wrong' he had done him in expelling him from St Omers. These men should be seized as hostages for the King's life, said Tonge. Asked what he knew of the Plot, the doctor replied that he would like to refer to the papers already presented to their lordships, 'which gave the narrative of all things'.[6]

'Of my own knowledge I know little or nothing,' he said. 'I have my information from one Mr Oates.'[7]

The Oates papers were then read aloud. They comprised a brief general account of the alleged conspirators and their plans, taken chiefly from the documents handed to the King on 13 August, followed by 'a long writing of many sheets said to contain forty-three articles, but it contained seventy-one'. This was the intermediate document between the first version of August and the final one sworn before Godfrey that morning.[8]

The councillors were plainly impressed by what they heard, and it is neither surprising nor questionable that they were. During his association with the former Provincial, Strange, and in his periods at St Omers and Valladolid, Oates had learned the names of scores of Jesuits of the English Province. Many of them he had come to know personally. Their names and functions had been easily retained by the perjurer's 'tenacious memory', and were now woven into the fabric of his story to lend it verisimilitude. It was, indeed, a masterpiece of mendacity. The statements capable of verification were without exception true. The lies were restricted to the evil designs of the Jesuits, which no one expected Oates to be able to prove. Bolstering the entire structure was Oates's ice-cool style of recording the Papists' fell designs. Trifling misdemeanours were noted among the most horrible treasons, the haphazard effect of which was to convey the impression of being an honestly constructed catalogue written from memory. Memory's erratic harvest also neatly explained the seemingly endless expansion of the 'discoveries'.[9]

Oates claimed that he had been employed as a messenger by the Papists, and had carried letters between them detailing the plans for killing the King and taking control of the country. He did not now have the letters because it had been vital to preserve the Jesuits' trust, and after painstakingly opening each letter and devouring its contents, he had resealed and delivered it.[10]

The lords were courteous to Tonge, and he was 'encouraged for his care in so weighty a matter'. Then came the real test of their feeling. So that he would not walk in fear of attack from the Jesuits for his part in exposing them, he was granted both food and lodging at the expense of the Court. They then directed him to bring Oates before them with all possible haste, and appointed to continue their sitting in the afternoon so that the chief witness could be examined.[11]

Meanwhile, Sir Edmund Berry Godfrey had become seriously alarmed by what he had been reading in the expanded depositions. After studying them thoughtfully for a long time he fell into a state of nervous indecision. His conscience bade him take a positive course of action; his concern for his own welfare bade him do nothing. On the one side was the life of a man in mortal peril. On the other were the very honourable friends. At length he decided on a courageous step. Just as he had faced up to the danger of defying the King in 1669, so he now decided to run the risk of a far graver danger from the honourable friends. Some time that morning he sent an urgent message to a man called Clarke. At the end of the Privy Council's morning sitting the King left for Newmarket with Monmouth and two of the earls present. The Speaker and Lord Privy Seal were also absent in the afternoon, but the thirteen remaining councillors were joined by the Earls of Oxford and Stafford, and the Lord Bishop of Durham.[12]

The session began with a statement about the Bedingfield letters by the Duke of York, confirming what the King had said in the morning. Having described in detail how the letters were discovered, James expressed his hope that 'their lordships would be able to find out the truth of all things,' and withdrew to join his brother at Newmarket.[13]

The council had been fed stories of a subtle, intrepid spy who single-handed had laid bare the darkest secrets of popery. No one expected the comic figure who waddled into the chamber when Oates was eventually called:

> Sunk were his eyes, his voice was harsh and loud,
> Sure signs he neither choleric was nor proud.
> His long chin proved his wit; his saint-like grace,
> A church vermilion and a Moses face.[14]

Oates asked that he might speak on oath, which instantly strengthened the less sceptical councillors in their sympathy for the witness. Having taken the oath, he launched into a minutely detailed tirade against the Jesuits. Those who were hugely impressed that his impromptu testimony coincided exactly with the written depositions were presumably unaware that he had been doing little else but copy and re-copy the articles for six weeks. It would be astonishing if he had not known them by heart.[15]

He was then shown the Bedingfield letters one by one. The official record of the Privy Council conveys the feeling of confidence that Oates's performance inspired:

> He did positively affirm the handwriting to be one of Nicholas Blundel's, another of John Fenwick's, another of Dr Fogerty's, who some writ Fogarthy, another the writing of Thomas White, and another the writing of William Ireland, not doubting or mistaking in any, though the writing was showed him with curiosity, and sometimes only the sight of a very few lines.[16]

At this their lordships 'were very much changed in their opinion, and began to apprehend that there was some danger and mischief contrived against His Majesty'. It did not occur to them that Oates was able to identify each letter so readily because he had written them himself.[17]

The council instantly directed the issue of warrants for 'the seizing of the bodies and the papers' of Fogerty, Ireland, Grove, Pickering and Fenwick. Another warrant was issued for the arrest of a Benedictine monk named John or George Coniers, who, according to Oates, had bought a dagger with a blade a foot long with which to kill the King, and wagered £100 that Charles would eat no more Christmas pies.[18]

The tide had turned. Oates was given command of a force of officers and ordered to seek out and arrest the men he had condemned. Oates, so lately starving in his garrett at Cockpit Alley, swept out of the council chamber like an avenging angel, with all the power of the state behind him, and a luxury apartment with full board thrown in.[19]

Less than a mile away, Sir Edmund Godfrey sat impatiently waiting for the reply to his message of the morning. At last, when Godfrey was engaged in his parlour with some visitors, it came. A man called Samuel Idells, servant to Godfrey's friend George Welden, knocked on the door. Godfrey's clerk opened the door and let him in. He asked him to wait in the passage while he told his master of his arrival. Moor, the clerk, then showed Idells in. He. told Godfrey that 'Clarke would speak with him'. The magistrate made hurried excuses to his visitors and left the house.[20]

That night Secretary of State Williamson jotted down some rough notes of the day's proceedings. 'Why not call to Sir E. Godfrey what he did?' he wrote as a memo to himself.[21]

But before Williamson got around to implementing the idea, Sir E. Godfrey was called upon by the very honourable friends.

8: Lo! A Damned Crew*

Oates and his men spent all night raiding houses and dragging Jesuits from their beds. It rained ceaselessly and a biting wind howled through London's winding lanes and narrow, cobbled streets. The wind carried off the sounds of soldiers' boots crunching on the gravel, of brutal men hammering on doors in the small hours and plundering private homes for evidence of treason. It dampened the cries of pain from those poor ill-treated souls the guards had come to seize. But it could do little to soften the harsh, braying voice of Titus Oates, clad in his sober parson's gown and bellowing his godless orders to the troops. In short, the closest modern parallel to the regime of fear and hatred which Oates was doing so much to establish, was in the early days of Nazi Germany, when Jews took the place of Jesuits. Citizen Titus was a flamboyant Himmler.[1]

By morning Ireland, Fenwick and Pickering were all in Newgate.[2]

Before the council adjourned on Saturday night, Danby had sent a rider to Newmarket to beg the King to return to London. This was too dangerous for the jaded men of the council to handle alone. Reluctantly, Charles had turned around and trundled back along the uncomfortable road to the capital. He was once again seated at the head of the Council Table when the proceedings resumed at three o'clock that afternoon. It was Michaelmas Day.[3]

The mild panic of the councillors did nothing to banish Charles's cynical view of Oates and his tales of terror. Some of the most persuasive members, after all, had their own reasons for supporting Oates. Danby, for instance, held out renewed hope

---

* A contemporary anagram of *Edward Coleman*.

64

that Citizen Titus could after all be used in deflecting Parliament from its bid to impeach him. Danby had received a brief reprieve. On 25 September Charles had prorogued Parliament (due to reassemble on 1 October) to 21 October. The Duke of Lauderdale, another councillor, was a voluble opponent of Popery. And of those with no great axe to grind, the majority were weak or junior men easily swayed by their more committed colleagues. Charles tried in vain to show the Council that Oates was a liar. He challenged him on his claim that he had once met Don John of Austria, whom he said had been present when the money to bribe Sir George Wakeman had been handed over. Charles asked what sort of man Don John was.

'A tall man,' hazarded Oates, unaware that the King had met him. When he was informed that Don John was in fact 'a very short man', Oates replied that 'it was one they called Don John, and he could say no more than as he was told.'[4]

The King tripped him up on two other points. In his evidence, Oates claimed to have taken letters to Père François La Chaise, the confessor to the French King. Why, then, did he persist in spelling the confessor's name 'Le Shee'? Oates could not answer. Charles, who knew Paris well, asked him where in the French capital Père La Chaise lived.

'In the Jesuits' house just by the King's house,' replied Oates, again hopelessly guessing. Charles said in exasperation that the Jesuits had no house within a mile of the Louvre, but the perjurer brazened it out, doubtless making a mental note to be far more circumspect in his use of gratuitous detail in future.[5]

Oates continued unabashed, and new perjuries resulted in the issue of warrants for the arrest of twenty more Papists that night – among them the former Provincial, Strange, and Whitebread's *socius* or secretary Father Edward Mico. Oates told the council that he thought he could name two hundred more English Jesuits.[6]

Apart from Sir George Wakeman, physician to Charles's Catholic queen Catherine, Oates had mentioned only one other man directly associated with the royal household, a foolish, meddling Catholic dreamer called Edward Coleman. Coleman had not appeared at all in the first version of Oates's articles, but he had been named as a conspirator in the very first article of the final, expanded version. Coleman had formerly been James's secretary and was now secretary to James's wife the Duchess of York. Oates was now closely examined about Coleman's alleged part in the Great Design.[7]

'Mr Oates testified much touching the activity and concern of Mr Coleman in these matters,' says the official report of the Privy Council, 'and particularly of his corresponding with Mr Le Chese [La Chaise], confessor of the French King, and that if his papers were well looked into there would appear that which might cost him his neck.'[8]

The response was immediate. A warrant was issued for the seizure of both Coleman and his papers, and an armed guard was despatched at six that evening to his house behind Westminster Abbey.[9]

Oates's plan was undoubtedly to secure the private papers of as many Jesuits as possible. The re-imposed penal laws made the mere presence of Papists in England illegal. It seemed a safe bet that in the masses of papers now being seized there would be something that could be construed as confirmation of a Plot.

Somehow, despite the secrecy that had attended Oates's revelations to the Council, Edward Coleman had learned that he was on Oates's blacklist. He had burned his most private papers and fled. As his wife stood helplessly by that Michaelmas night, the whole house was ransacked by the guards. Furniture was overturned, drawers and cupboards were rifled. If he had burned everything, Coleman would have been safe. If he had burned nothing, the true picture of his activities would have been plain, and it is just possible that no real harm would have come to him. But in his fright and haste he had destroyed only his correspondence for the past two years. He had forgotten an old deal box with its lid nailed down, hidden away in a secret recess behind one of the chimneys. It contained letters written and received in 1674, 1675 and a part of 1676. Along with several bags full of innocuous papers and a packet of his wife's letters, the deal box was delivered to the Privy Council.[10]

While Oates sallied forth at the head of his armed guards for the second night in succession to lay violent hands upon the men who had once given him food and shelter, Edward Coleman cowered in his hideaway and reviewed his position. He had never participated in the treason of which Oates had accused him. But because of his zeal for the popish religion – he was a convert, the son of a Suffolk clergyman, and had all the convert's fiery devotion – he eagerly awaited the day when James sat on the throne. He had faith, even, that Charles's ardent wish for toleration, and his suspected sympathy for catholicism, might lead England peacefully back into the Vatican's fold during the present King's lifetime. But some of his references to this hope in his letters to La Chaise were indiscreet in the extreme. There was much in the letters 'to prove the restless and intriguing spirit of the man'.[11]

But flight would be taken as a sure sign of guilt. And he was confident of his own ability to extricate himself from Oates's snare. The search for Coleman went on all night but, early on Monday morning, he went to the house of Sir Joseph Williamson and surrendered himself. Williamson summoned a messenger, who took Coleman into custody. Coleman was confident still that there would be nothing proven against him, and wrote as much in a letter to M. Paul de Barillon, the French ambassador.[12]

In the afternoon, Coleman faced the lords of the council. Excessive fasting had weakened his constitution. He stood, surveying the mighty lords with his 'sad, sunken eyes', his gaunt face looking deathly white beneath his jet black peruke. Under questioning, he admitted that he had travelled to France without a pass, and that he had met Père La Chaise, but only by accident. He was asked if he ever used cyphers in his letters, and frankly confessed that he did, and that he assumed they were all among the papers that had been seized. 'If not,' he told the lords, 'I shall send them in.' Coleman still had not remembered the deal box behind the chimney piece, and so far the councillors had had no opportunity to have the papers read.[13]

The defendant's coolness of manner was impressive. He made 'so good a discourse for himself' and the King 'seemed to be so far satisfied with what Mr Coleman said', that the blank warrant written out in advance to commit him to Newgate 'was respited', and he was placed back in the hands of the messenger. He had candidly admitted several misdemeanours, but with the greater charges hanging over him these were of little moment either to him or the councillors.[14]

On Tuesday morning Charles left again for Newmarket, having appointed a special committee to examine the papers seized from Coleman and the Jesuits.[15]

When the lords of the special committee turned their attention to the deal box, they were, according to Sir Robert Southwell, clerk to the council, 'amazed'. They signed a warrant without delay and sent Coleman in chains to a rat-infested cell at Newgate.[16]

Oates had struck gold. In his letters to La Chaise, copies of which were found hidden in the deal box, Coleman had allowed his papist zeal to run away with him. There was nothing in them that confirmed the existence of the bloody, murderous Plot described by Oates. But there was enough Catholic fervor in Coleman's words to delude the lords of the Privy Council, in their doubt and panic, into believing that there was.[17]

An unbiased reading of the letters makes Coleman's ambitions clear: he placed all his hopes in Charles's toleration and the eventual succession of the Catholic Duke of York. There was one great obstacle in the path of Charles acting in accordance with his wishes. The Opposition. That same body of powerful, papist-hating men were now also talking about banning James from the succession. Without money, Charles was powerless. And Parliament, riddled with the enemies of popery, held the purse strings.[18]

In one letter Coleman begged La Chaise's help in getting the French king to send money secretly to King Charles so that, in defiance of Parliament, the Duke of York could be restored to his post as Lord High Admiral. And greater still, freed from his financial dependence upon Parliament by a sizeable handout from Louis, Charles would be able to establish the liberty of conscience of which he dreamed.[19]

In the present climate these were dangerous sentiments. But Coleman's rhetoric was his undoing. 'We have here,' he wrote in one letter, 'a mighty work on our hands, no less than the Conversion of three Kingdoms, and by that the utter subduing of a Pestilent Heresie, which has domineered over great part of this Northern World a long time.'[20]

This was the crowning folly, a product of Coleman's inflated view of his own importance. Observations like 'there were never such hopes of success since the death of our Queen Mary, as now in our days,' and 'Success would give the greatest blow to the Protestant Religion that it has received since its birth,' were enough to damn him.[21]

When Oates had first been faced with Coleman in the Council chamber he had been asked whether he knew him. Genuinely not knowing him, he had replied that he had never seen him before. That blunder was now forgotten as Coleman was dragged off to Newgate.[22]

PART III

The Primrose Way to
the Everlasting Bonfire

A fair attempt has twice or thrice been made
To hire night murderers and make death a trade.
When murder's out, what vice can we advance,
Unless the new-found poisoning trick of France?
And when their art of rats-bane we have got,
By way of thanks, we'll send them o'er our Plot.

John Dryden, Prologue to *The Spanish Friar*, 1681

Edmund, farewell.
                    ★
        Edmund, I think, is gone,
In pity of his misery, to dispatch
His nighted life.
                    ★
Edmund is dead.

                        King Lear, III. vii, IV. v, V. iii

1: The Final Days

From the moment he began to read Oates's expanded version of the statement about the Plot when the perjurer and his two associates visited him on 28 September, Sir Edmund Godfrey was observed by many people to be in a state of confusion and alarm. After he had made his fateful decision to contact Mr Clarke, his state of mind deteriorated rapidly into a terrified expectation of murder.

Oates himself spoke about Godfrey's condition early on the morning of the 28th when the unholy trinity presented themselves at his door. 'He was a cowardly rascal,' Oates told his old schoolmaster William Smith, 'for when I went with my depositions to him, he was so frightened, that I believe he beshit himself; for there was such a stink I could hardly stay in the room.'[1]

Oates's coarse sarcasm reveals the first sign of alarm in the magistrate. Why should he have been so frightened? Of whom? Certainly not Oates himself. The chief cause of his fear at this stage was the new additions to Oates's depositions. Exactly what unnerved him will be seen presently.

Immediately after Oates, Tonge and Kirkby had left Hartshorn Lane – Oates to return to Vauxhall and the others to Whitehall – Godfrey fell to carefully reading every word of the document left with him. His clerk, an elderly man called Henry Moor who had been with him about eighteen months, noticed a change in him from that time. He observed his master to be 'under great discontent, and in disorder many times, and wished they [Oates and company] had never come to him'.[2]

Evelyn recorded the following Tuesday, 1 October, the general consternation all over London when details of the Plot began to leak out. At about this time, the exact day is uncertain, Godfrey met his friend Gilbert Burnet in the street. Burnet, formerly the King's chaplain, was a staunch Whig and a supporter of Shaftesbury. He saw a great change in the magistrate.[3]

'It is certain,' he wrote later, 'Godfrey grew apprehensive and reserved. For meeting me in the street, after some discourse of the present state of affairs, he said he himself should be knocked on the head. Yet he took no care of himself, and went about according to his own maxim, still without a servant. For he used to

71

say, that the servants in London were corrupted by the idleness and ill company they fell into, while they attended on their masters.'[4]

This was the first time Godfrey had confessed to anyone that he was afraid he was going to be murdered. To the chagrin of investigators of the case, he never told Burnet the reason for his fear.

It was almost certainly during this week that Sir Edmund took to his bed for several days. The source of this information is Mrs Mary Gibbon, the wife of an impoverished kinsman of Godfrey and one of his closest friends and confidants. According to Mrs Gibbon, Godfrey sent a servant to tell her he was ill and to ask her to make him some jelly. A day or two afterwards Mrs Gibbon went to visit Sir Edmund and found him drinking whey with brown bread in it. She said to him, 'Sir, I make jelly for you one day and you drink whey another.'

'Oh cousin,' said Godfrey, throwing the pot one way and the spoon another, 'my father's dark melancholy hath seized me. It is hereditary and I cannot get it out of me.'[5]

It is this reference to inherited melancholy that has led a number of writers to suggest that Godfrey committed suicide. Apart from the fact that suicide is ruled out by newly discovered medical evidence, examined later, it is perfectly clear that, wretched as he was, Godfrey was not suicidal. It was death he most feared, and murder he expected. Without doubt he had received plain intimation that his days were numbered, and it was this threat that plunged him into the paroxysms of despair witnessed by Mrs Gibbon and many others. Fear that death awaited him at every step led him into the deepest misery, exacerbated almost certainly by the melancholy he had suffered all his life. It is therefore no surprise that Mrs Gibbon should have observed him 'very sad and pensive some time before his death', nor that he should say to her, 'Oh! Cousin, I do inherit my father's deep melancholy. I cannot get it off. I have taken away a great many ounces of blood, but I cannot get the victory.'[6]

Blood-letting was then a recognized method of curing many diseases, among them mental depression. If, by applying leeches or opening a vein, Godfrey could relieve the incapacitating depression he was suffering, he might hope, perhaps, to work upon ways of eluding those who threatened him. But above all Sir Edmund Godfrey was a practical man. He knew the danger in which he stood. He knew from whence it came. He had indeed set in motion of his own volition the chain of events that had led to his present predicament. But there was now no escaping his fate and he knew it. Had it been otherwise his deep melancholy would probably never have descended upon him. It was the utter hopelessness of his position that brought him, courageous as he was, into the very depths of despair. As he lay in his bed fretting, one thought must have rolled endlessly around and around in his brain. *There can be no escaping the wrath of the very honourable friends.*

By 4 October Godfrey had managed to stir himself from the worst of his depression. Perhaps his lifelong habit of banishing evil humours with intensive work was reasserting itself. He was thought by many, wrote Burnet, to take too much upon himself, and was at this critical moment of his life launching an ambitious project of taking up all beggars in his quarter of the city and putting them to work.[7]

Some time on the 3rd or 4th, Godfrey met Richard Mulys, an auditor who worked for several wealthy families, as he walked in St James's Park. Mulys questioned Godfrey about the Plot and about his examination of Oates. The magistrate gave his friend an outline of his contact with Oates and the essence of the Plot, most of which Mulys already knew from 'the common discourse of the Town'.

After some moments, Godfrey said, 'I pray that God will preserve your master, for he is in danger.'

'Which of my masters do you mean?' asked Mulys in alarm.

'My Lord the Duke of Ormond,' said Godfrey.

Mulys took him by the hand and begged him to explain.

'The Duke of Ormond is to be destroyed,' said Godfrey, shaking his head. 'But I must not talk much, for I lie under ill circumstances. Some great men blame me for not having done my duty, and I am threatened by others, and very great ones too, for having done too much.'

'He then pressed to leave me,' testified Mulys later, 'and without saying much more we parted.'[8]

On the evening of the 4th, Sir Edmund left his house and walked slowly along to St Martin's Church to attend a vestry meeting, but there was precious little there to take his mind from his troubles. Part of the discrepancy in the parish accounts was now finally settled, and a memorandum to that effect was placed in the minute book. Godfrey and another vestryman, James Dewy, listened to a complaint by the vestry that the Overseers of the Poor for 1676 had failed to turn up at a meeting with their auditors the previous

Wednesday. The overseers, among them a man named Henry Bradbury, held between them £70 14s 4½d which should have been paid in to the vestry long since. There seems to have been some doubt about Bradbury's part in the case – the chief offender being a man called Nicholson – but Godfrey and Dewy made no exception in summarily sentencing all the overseers for the year in question to a fine of forty shillings apiece.[9]

On the 5th or 6th, Sir Edmund at last felt unable to go on without reporting his part in the taking of Oates and Tonge's depositions. After a great deal of thought, he decided the best person to approach was the Lord Chief Justice, Sir William Scroggs. He went to Scroggs, gave him his own version of his actions (as opposed to that which was flying in rumours around the town) and handed him his copy of the depositions. Scroggs told him he would have the document copied and that he could collect it from him in a week.[10]

On 7 October, while the King sported himself at Newmarket, while Titus Oates supervised the arrest of more Jesuits, and while Edward Coleman languished in Newgate, Godfrey attended the Westminster quarter sessions. There he met fellow magistrate Thomas Robinson, who had been his friend for more than forty years, since their days together at Westminster School. Robinson, chief prothonotary of the Court of Common Pleas, joined Godfrey after the morning session of the court and they dined together with the head bailiff as was their custom. Talk turned to the Plot, which was now the subject of the moment and the source of excited debate in all the coffee houses and taverns of the capital.

'I understand you have taken several examinations about this Plot that is now made public,' said Robinson.

'Truly, I have,' replied Godfrey. 'But I think I shall have little thanks for my pains.' He fell silent a moment and then said, 'I did it very unwillingly, and would fain have had it done by others.'

'Why?' said Robinson. 'You did but what was your duty to do, and it was a very good act. Pray, sir, have you the examinations about you? Will you please let me see them?'

'No, I have them not,' said Sir Edmund. 'I delivered them to my Lord Chief Justice Scroggs. But as soon as I have them, you shall see them.'

'But I should be very glad to understand, Sir Edmundbury, that the depth of the matter were found out,' pursued Robinson.

'I am afraid of that, that it is not,' said Godfrey gravely. Again he became silent. After a while he emerged from his sombre introspection and exclaimed, 'Upon my conscience, I believe I shall be the first martyr.'

'Why so?' asked Robinson in bewilderment. 'Are you afraid?'

'No,' said Godfrey, 'I do not fear them if they come fairly, and I shall not part with my life tamely.'

'Why do not you go with a man if you have that fear upon you?' asked Robinson, echoing Burnet's sentiment of the week before.

'Why?' said the justice. 'I do not love it. It is a clog to a man.'[11]

In this dialogue, too, is a clue to Godfrey's killers. From whom did he expect to receive no thanks for his pains? It was in fact unreasonable in a normal sense even to raise the question of thanks. The taking of affidavits was part of the daily course of events for a JP. He could not easily have refused his services. What, then, made his part in this deserving of thanks? It will be remembered that there was something out of the ordinary about these depositions as far as Godfrey was concerned – and until he had been prevailed upon by the very honourable friends he had refused to swear Oates. It was, of course, the very honourable friends who might in other circumstances have thanked him for his pains. But as things had turned out he knew that would not happen.

The following afternoon, after the morning sitting of the quarter sessions at Westminster, Godfrey called on Mary Gibbon at her house in Old Southampton Buildings, behind Chancery Lane. The atmosphere at the house was hateful to the magistrate. Captain Thomas Gibbon, Mary's husband, had been ruined by the civil wars, during which he was 'sequestered, imprisoned, often plundered and decimated'. The calamities of fighting for the losing side combined with domestic troubles such as a fire at home had reduced the Gibbons' 'plentiful estate' almost to nothing. And while Godfrey doubtless did what he could, the family nevertheless lived under 'very necessitous circumstances'. To make matters worse, Mrs Gibbon's mother was on her deathbed and the family wore looks of misery. Godfrey went into a room with Mrs Gibbon alone, bolting the door behind him.[12]

'Have you not heard that I am to be hanged?' he asked her, beside himself with anxiety.

'The Lord bless us!' she said. 'Sir, what d'ye mean? For what?'

'All the town is in an uproar about me,' he persisted.

'For what?' said the practical Mrs Gibbon, calmer now.

'I took Oates's and Tonge's examinations a month ago,' he whispered, eyeing the door. 'And though I have often been at dinner since at my Lord Chancellor's and at Sir William Jones, the

Attorney-General, yet I have never discovered [i.e. told them about] the Plot they hath sworn to.'

She peered at him through her tiny, round spectacles. 'What Plot?' she said. Since the onset of her mother's illness she had been cut off from the gossip of the outside world.

'Oates has forsworn himself,' said Godfrey, 'and it will come to nothing.'[13]

He again called at Old Southampton Buildings after court the next day, Wednesday. She showed him into her parlour and asked him to wait for her there while she fetched her hood. She was away only a few moments, but when she returned to the room, he had gone.[14]

The paralysing depression that had gripped Godfrey the week before now seemed to be waning a little. He was still very frightened and unhappy but the diversion of work and the company of friends seemed to fortify him. His ability to cope with his troubles fluctuated considerably. At times he seemed his old self, at others he was as disconsolate as before and his behaviour in the presence of several acquaintances became markedly eccentric. Once or twice he seemed almost flippant about the threats that had been made.

His friend and fellow vestryman Rector Lloyd observed little change in him. Once he overheard Godfrey say, 'I am told I shall be knocked on the head,' the self same words he had used in such terror to Burnet the previous week. But according to Lloyd he now spoke of the death threat 'without any great visible concern'. Whenever Lloyd encountered him in the week leading up to his disappearance, he seemed 'the same he ever was'. He saw him 'serious in business, but cheerful and pleasant at other times. Thus he used to be alway.'[15]

Godfrey had earlier contracted with his intimate friend Thomas Wynell of Cranbrook, Essex to buy some of the latter's houses in Brewer's Yard, close to Hartshorn Lane. Godfrey was acting in the transaction on behalf of another friend. Some business concerning the deal had to be completed before a counsellor at law, and now Sir Edmund walked with Wynel to the house of a lawyer, Goodwin, near Temple Gate. On the way he was sufficiently in command of his emotions to speak with apparent ease about the Plot.*

---

* In a statement made some years later, Wynell mistakenly dated this conversation towards the end of October, when Godfrey was already dead.

'Oates is sworn and is perjured,' said Godfrey.

'Speak the truth,' said Wynnel. 'Tell me the meaning on't.'

Godfrey told something of what he knew about the Plot. At the end of it he said, 'There is nothing against the King. But there is a design upon the Duke of York. And this will come to a dispute among them.'

Before Wynnel could ask the inevitable question, 'A dispute among whom?', Godfrey said, 'You may live to see an end on't, but I shall not.'[16]

At another time, Wynnel asked Godfrey why he had been so melancholy. Sir Edmund said, 'I am master of a dangerous secret that will be fatal to me.'[17]

After that day, Godfrey again sank into his state of depression. On Thursday, 10 October he sent for Mary Gibbon. As she was unable to leave her mother's bedside, her husband called round to Hartshorn Lane instead. He found the magistrate in 'great disorder' in his dress, looks and actions. Finding his presence causing Godfrey unease, he soon took his leave and went home. He told his wife about it, 'expressing great trouble for his condition'.[18]

When Thomas Wynnel saw him again he was 'very much disordered and troubled in his mind'. Godfrey told him once again 'that he had not long to live'.[19]

He had never spoken a truer word. In fact, he had just two days left.

2: The Messenger of Death

After a fortnight of uncertainty, the vague threats that had been made against the life of Justice Godfrey at last took tangible form. By the evening of Friday, 11 October he knew the end was at hand.

Some time during the day, he collected his copy of Oates's depositions which he had left with Lord Chief Justice Scroggs the week before.[1]

That afternoon, between four and five o'clock, he was seen walking along Drury Lane towards the Strand by an acquaintance, Edward Birtby. Birtby was in the company of his wife and a friend. Godfrey had his eyes fixed upon the ground and he seemed 'extremely pensive and melancholique'.[2]

Birtby and his companions were about to pass along the narrow path by the side of the Kennel, but stopped so that Godfrey could pass by. Birtby saluted the magistrate with his hat. At that, Godfrey paused suddenly and stamped on the ground. Then he caught hold of the brim of his hat with both hands and stared into Birtby's face without speaking. The trio passed him by as he stood thus. They looked back and saw him in the same position for 'a little while after'. He then continued on his way by the side of the Kennel. As they turned into an alley off Drury Lane, Birtby said, 'This is Sir Edmund Berry Godfrey. This looks strangely. Pray God bless him.'[3]

On his way home, he called on his friend Lady Margaret Pratt and spent some time there. At about five o'clock he arrived at the home of Henry Bradbury in St Martin's parish. According to Bradbury, he came through the house 'in a very unusual manner', showing signs of 'trouble and discontent'. Godfrey told him he was going to the vestry and that he would send for him from there.[4]

As soon as he got home, Godfrey threw himself into his work. After a short time a private messenger called at the house. He was not known by anyone in the magistrate's household. Elizabeth Curtis, Godfrey's maidservant, answered the messenger's urgent rapping.

'Is Sir E. Godfrey within?' the man asked. He held a letter, tied with string or ribbon, which he showed to Curtis. She told him her master was at home, but that he was busy. She then offered to carry the letter to Sir Edmund for him. The messenger agreed, and waited in the passage while Curtis tapped on the parlour door and entered. She appeared a moment or two later, but the messenger said he would stay for an answer. Curtis went back into the parlour and told Godfrey that the man required an answer.

'Pr'ythee,' said the magistrate in confusion, 'tell him I don't know what to make of it.'[5]

Indeed, he did not know what to make of some of the instructions contained in the letter. But there can be little doubt that he knew the senders of the letter and what their summons presaged. The very honourable friends were moving at last.

Godfrey was late in leaving home for the evening meeting of the St Martin's parish officers. He arrived shortly before the end of the meeting, entering the vestry hastily and taking his usual place. In the words of his colleague Richard Wheeler he was 'commonly the mouth of the board', but tonight he sat leaning with his face upon his hand, hardly speaking.[6]

At a Vestry y: 11:*th of October 1678.*

Present.

D:n Loyd S:t Thomas Clarges S:t William Pultney S:t Edmund Godfrey, Mathew Lock Esq:. James Denry Esq:. Doc:t Clarke, Cap:t Bindall. M:r Crump, M:r Leames, M:r Wheeler. M:r Cooke, M:r Morgan /

M:r Monk   } Church Wardens
M:r Parsons }

Ordered that the Sravengers of the last Yeare 1677. have notice to attend at the next Vestry. /

Memorand: That M:r Kempe have notice to receive the Poores money of Majo:r Brookhurst, due from the Duke of Buckingham. /

That the Overseers of the poore doe meet the last Sunday in every Month in the Church after Divine Service to Consider of the affaire of the parish in reference to the poore according to the Law, and give a particular Accompt in Writing to the Church Warden of their Extraordinary Disbursments of the Month then last past, and to whom they dispose the same, and for what, And the Church Warden to present the same to the Vestry then next following. /

That the Accompt of the Overseers for 1676. has beene Audited and it appeares that they are in Generall Accomptable for 6 : 5 : 0 to ballance their Accompt, besides 15 : 02 : 08 which is particular only due from M:r Nicholson one of the said Overseers. /

That the Orders concerning the Overseers of the poore for the Yeares 1673. and 1674. be looked out against the next Vestry. /

That M:r Hughes have notice to attend at the next Vestry being on Wednesday next by 3 in the Afternoone. /

That there be raised Thirteene hundred Ninety and One poundes in Six Monthes from the Feast of S:t Michael the Archangell last past and that the same be rated according to the Bookes of Assessment for the present three Monthes, Assessing on every person three times the proportion that hee or shee is rated for the Assessment to the King /

And that the ten Bookes of Assessment for the Montly Tax be transcribed into five Bookes for this purpose That is the Assessment on the high streete upper Division and Lower Division into one Booke, the Divisions for Long Acre East, Long Acre West and Dirtty Lane into one Booke, The Division of S:t Martins Lane into one Booke, The Divisions of Soho and Pikadilly into Two Bookes And the Divisions of the Pall-Mall and the out Brooke in one Booke. /

Minutes of the last vestry
meeting Godfrey attended

79

The case of the defaulting overseers was being discussed, their accounts having at last been audited. Although several of the officers were at fault, the main blame had been traced to Nicholson, who was found to be owing the board £15 2s 8d. Bradbury, as Godfrey had come to realize, had been wrongly fined.[7]

'That will not do,' said Sir Edmund, lifting his head and speaking for the first time.[8]

After the meeting most of the vestrymen adjourned to a nearby tavern. Godfrey, however, beckoned to his friend Joseph Radcliffe and asked him to accompany him to the house of George Welden. This was the same Colonel Welden whose servant had been used a fortnight since to summon Godfrey to the meeting with the mysterious Mr Clarke.[9]

Captain Bridall and the other parish officers were full of talk of Sir Edmund as they supped their ale in the tavern. It was generally agreed that he must be ill, 'his countenance and behaviour being very much altered'.[10]

Meanwhile, Radcliffe and Godfrey trudged along the windswept lanes to Welden's house in York Buildings, by the Thames. It was bitterly cold. Noticing another vestryman, James Heames, walking some way behind them, Godfrey turned and invited him to join them.

'I have done a wrong to Bradbury,' said Godfrey to Radcliffe, 'and I am resolved to right the matter tonight.'

Once indoors, Sir Edmund asked Radcliffe to help him off with his coat. Despite Radcliffe's protests about the coldness of the night, he insisted. Throwing his coat down on to the window shelf, he went to the other end of the room and sat down in his waistcoat and shirtsleeves.

Radcliffe, an oilman, asked how Bradbury had been wronged.

'I made him pay forty shillings for a fault which was not his,' was the reply. 'Bradbury must be repaid out of parish funds, if you agree.'

Radcliffe agreed, and a servant was sent to fetch Bradbury. Godfrey explained that he was holding some parish money which, as Radcliffe was handling some of the St Martin's accounts, he would pay to him. Bradbury soon arrived and the two pounds was paid back to him.

'Sir Edmund,' said Radcliffe, 'you are in a very good mind.'

'Yes,' said the justice. 'I am resolved to settle all my business tonight, and the accounts shall be brought in your name, and not in mine.'[11]

Now that the hand of the enemy had been revealed, Godfrey seemed calmer. Welden described him that evening as 'in good humour', although the sensitive Bradbury still detected the earlier 'disorder' in his looks. Somehow the magistrate had managed to detach himself from the horror of the situation. Perhaps in the days since his secret meeting with Mr Clarke he had lived psychologically through every atrocity the honourable friends might perpetrate upon him, so that now the reality was infinitely preferable to the continuation of that dreadful state of unknowing. Whatever the explanation for his improved condition, Godfrey now went about arranging his affairs with a coolness that would have been unnerving to his companions had they only realized he was expecting to die on the morrow.[12]

He passed from one subject to another, scarcely pausing for breath. At last, Radcliffe asked him if he had done.

'I have not done yet,' he said, and spoke about the ten shillings a week which he gave in bread to the poor. He said he wanted to change the baker.

'Might I bake the bread, Sir Edmund?' asked Bradbury, who was a baker. Godfrey asked Radcliffe what he advised.

'You are master of your own charity,' said the oilman, at which Godfrey consented to Bradbury taking the job and told him that he had arranged in his will for the money to be paid from the rent of some houses he owned in Westminster.[13]

Again Radcliffe asked him if he had done. He had never known business 'done in so sudden a manner before'.[14]

'No, I have not done yet, for the parish is now in my debt,' he said. He jotted down a few figures and told Radcliffe that he was owed thirteen shillings. Radcliffe paid him immediately and asked him a third time if he had done.

'Yes,' said Sir Edmund, clapping his hand upon his breast, 'now I am at quiet. My conscience is clear.' He rose and asked Radcliffe to help him on with his coat, repeating as he heaved himself into it that his conscience was clear. He then joined his friends at the table and they drank a glass of beer together.[15]

'What news?' said Radcliffe, turning to more general matters. But Godfrey's thinking could not be turned from the channel in which it was running. 'In a short time you will hear of the death of someone,' he told them. Radcliffe later said that the word Godfrey used might have been murder. Either way, he was confident that he himself would be the first victim.[16]

Heames asked him why he went abroad alone if he feared being murdered. He said again that his conscience was clear, and that he cared for no company and that he feared nobody. To Colonel Welden he said, 'There will be no bloodshed or cutting of throats, but there will be alteration of government.'[17]

As he was leaving about nine o'clock, Welden asked Godfrey whether he would be dining with him on Saturday. Godfrey already had arrangements to meet his friend Wynnel at Welden's for lunch, but he replied enigmatically that he 'could not tell'.[18]

When he got back to Hartshorn Lane that night, Godfrey's fears had again seized him. He was, recalled his elderly housekeeper Mrs Judith Pamphlin, in great disorder. To the alarm of his household he spent a great while in his private chamber, tumbling over drawers and trunks, and eventually came downstairs with an armful of documents – enough, as Mrs Pamphlin thought, to fill her apron – and burned them in the parlour fire. The letter delivered by the messenger that evening was doubtless among the papers he destroyed, for it was never found.[19]

The night was cold and wet.[20]

3: One Day in October

Godfrey rose earlier than usual on Saturday morning. It was still bitterly cold and he dressed accordingly, donning three pairs of stockings and a pair of socks, his drawers and black breeches. He then put on a flannel shirt and a waistcoat and went down to the parlour.[1]

When Elizabeth Curtis carried in his breakfast, a man she did not know was with Godfrey. She went upstairs about her chores and returned later to collect a bunch of keys she had left on the parlour table. The man was still there. She busied herself making up the fire and the stranger remained there 'a good while'.[2]

It is uncertain what time Godfrey left home, but he had already gone out by the time his friend Richard Adams, a Lincoln's Inn lawyer, called on him between six and seven o'clock. Adams, like Godfrey a staunch Protestant and opponent of popery, went on to Westminster, intending to call back later in the morning.[3]

At about eight o'clock Godfrey was seen walking northwards along St Martin's Lane by three acquaintances – Richard Cooper,

Cooper's sister Mary Leeson and their friend James Lowen, keeper of Hatfield Park.

'There comes Justice Godfrey,' said Leeson.

'So he does,' replied Cooper. The magistrate was all in black, from his hat to his stockings and shoes. He was clearly preoccupied and walked 'with his cane dangling before him'. Cooper greeted him as they drew together, saying, 'Good morrow, Sir Edmund.' Leeson had already noticed a change in Godfrey's humour since the last time she had seen him.

'Good morrow, Mr Cooper,' he replied gravely.

They waited until he was out of hearing. 'The justice is melancholy,' said Leeson.

'No,' replied Cooper, 'he is studying.'[4]

The route taken by Godfrey after that is unknown, but he must have made his way slowly back home.

Some rather doubtful testimony turned up six years later from two men who claimed to have seen Sir Edmund talking to a milkwoman in the country near Paddington at about nine o'clock. The honesty of the two men, William Collins and Thomas Mason, has not been called in question, but their memories have. It has been generally accepted that they did see Godfrey, but not at that hour. By nine he was certainly back in Hartshorn Lane, for according to the more certain testimony of his clerk, Henry Moor, he left home again between nine and ten.[5]

It has not been realized before that the departure from home described by Moor was the second of the morning. He had been out, possibly on the business of the court or vestry, and returned to prepare for another kind of business altogether. Before he left this last time, Godfrey and Moor were together in the parlour of the house in Hartshorn Lane. The magistrate asked his clerk to help him on with his new camlet coat, which he did. Soon after, however, he changed his mind, took off the coat and asked Moor to help him on with an old coat of the same fabric.

'This will serve the day well enough,' he said, and went immediately from the house. At the gate between the woodyard and the lane he suddenly stopped and turned back towards the old clerk. He 'looked seriously' upon him, 'as if he would have said something' to him, and 'in that posture he stood a small time, but immediately went his way, not speaking'. He was wearing his wide-brimmed hat with the gold band and a lace cravat around his neck. It was the last time Moor saw him alive.[6]

His probable route lay once again along St Martin's Lane,

northwards past Cock and Pye Fields and along Hog Lane, now the upper part of Charing Cross Road. From there he passed into the fields which began where Oxford Street, Tottenham Court Road and Charing Cross Road now converge in the shadow of Centre Point. All the evidence suggests that it was getting on for ten when Collins and Mason sighted him near Paddington talking to the milkwoman. Mason, who lived at Marylebone, saw him again about an hour later. He was 'coming toward London, in the fields, betwixt Mary-bone Pound and Mary-bone Street.' They passed the time of day.[7]

Not long afterwards, it was written later, he was seen passing by Lady Cook's lodgings near the Cockpit.[8]

Towards eleven, Richard Adams called again at Godfrey's house. The servants, he later swore, seemed to be in great consternation.

'What is the matter?' asked Adams.

'We have cause to fear Sir Edmund is made away,' said one of the servants.[9]

It was two hours at most since Godfrey had left home. It was customary for him to be away for hours at a time, and it was not uncommon for him to stay away all night. Yet as early as eleven o'clock on this Saturday morning the magistrate's servants already thought he had been murdered. Why? The only clue to Godfrey's fate was the strange letter of the night before, and the curious effect it produced on him.[10]

Godfrey was seen again about noon, back in town. Thomas Snell lived in Holborn 'over against Turn-Style'. He had no personal knowledge of Sir Edmund but he knew him by sight. He saw him for the last time ever passing his house and walking into Red Lion Fields about noon. Later, having heard of Godfrey's death, he reflected that he had looked melancholy.[11]

Sir Edmund had arranged to dine with Thomas Wynnel at the house of Colonel Welden in York Buildings, a short walk from Hartshorn Lane.* After dinner they had intended to visit Goodwin, their lawyer, to complete their property deal. Wynnel, who had received no word that Godfrey had changed the plans, arrived at Welden's in good time. When Godfrey failed to turn up, he

---

* York Water Gate, an attractive stone arch that used to stand at the top of a flight of steps leading from the river near York Buildings, is now in a deep hollow at the *foot* of ten steps at the back of Charing Cross Gardens, about 500 feet from the river. The river, not the Water Gate, has been moved.

asked Welden to send his servant to Hartshorn Lane. It was then past noon. The servant, Idells (the same man who had gone to summon Godfrey to the meeting with Mr Clarke on 28 September), returned with the news that Godfrey was not at home. Wynell continued to wait, expecting Godfrey to arrive at any moment. Eventually he told Welden that he would go to the magistrate's house himself and discover what was amiss.

Approaching the big house at the end of the lane, he saw Judith Pamphlin, Godfrey's housekeeper, leaning on the rail outside the door. Moor was also there, leaning against the doorpost. Both of them looked 'sad and surprised'. Wynell asked them where their master was. One of them said that he had gone out about two hours before. Wynell asked where he had gone, but they said they could not tell.

'Your master promised to dine with me today at Colonel Welden's,' said Wynell. 'Will he not be there, think ye?'

Moor replied that he could not tell. Wynell bade him tell his master when he returned that he had gone to the colonel's, and expected him there according to his appointment.

'Aye, sir,' said Moor. 'When I see him, so I will.'

Wynell thought there was 'so much disorder in their countenances, their manner of speaking and their behaviour,' that it made 'an impression of heaviness' upon him. He went his way and returned to York Buildings at about one, telling Welden that he could not find Sir Edmund and that they had best dine without him.

'Ah! Mr Wynell!' said Welden in obvious distress. 'You will never see him more.'

Startled, Wynell asked what grounds he had for saying so, adding, 'You and I know very well that 'tis a common thing for Edmund to go out in a morning so soon as his Justice business is over, and not come home till night, and no apprehension all this while of any hurt to befall him. Why should you be so suspicious then of any ill for two hours' absence, and at this time of the day?'

Welden replied, 'To tell you the truth, his brothers have been with me, and are just now gone. And they say the Papists have been watching him for a long time, and that now they are very confident they have got him.'

'Why should the Papists do him any hurt? He was never observed to be an enemy to them.' But Welden could not be shaken.[12]

Michael and Benjamin Godfrey were both merchants in the

City. From this day on they were to play a prominent part in the story of their brother's death. Already, within two hours of his departure from home, someone had sent them the information that he had been murdered by Papists. Plainly, the mysterious message came from those who knew what was to be Godfrey's true fate. It came from the same source as the letter that had sent Godfrey into such a passion the night before.

It came, without doubt, from the honourable friends.

At about the same time as Wynell and Welden were debating whether or not Godfrey had been 'made away', the subject of their speculation was in fact walking only a few hundreds yards away. His friend Joseph Radcliffe was taking delivery of some goods at the door of his house in the Strand. He looked up and saw Godfrey walking past. He greeted him and Godfrey stopped. Taking his friend's hand, Radcliffe invited him in to dine, but Sir Edmund said he was in haste and could not stay. So saying, 'he took away his hand, and went hastily away, speaking very earnestly'. The incident, witnessed by Radcliffe's wife Eleanor, left Radcliffe wondering, Godfrey 'having been usually freer and easier' with him.[13]

Radcliffe's was the last certain sighting of Godfrey. There was a report, by no means certain, that he was seen in the Back Court of Lincoln's Inn. He was seen, it was said by two gentlemen, to make a sudden turn and to go out at the back door. Two men later claimed they had seen him walking in the country near Hampstead about two or three o'clock, but their evidence is unsatisfactory. The men were Thomas Grundy and James Huysman. According to Grundy, they espied a tall person walking alone towards the White House tavern near Primrose Hill.

'There goes Dr Barwick,' said Grundy to his companion. But when they drew closer he changed his mind and said it was not Dr Barwick. He said that he 'wondered a little with himself to see a person alone thereabouts', having often walked that way himself but rarely seen anybody there. This really does not make sense. The White House was a well frequented tavern, and later evidence showed that many people walked in the fields there at all times of day. Grundy said he took it into his head to follow the man he had mistaken for Barwick, and did so at a distance of twenty yards for nearly a quarter of a mile. He observed that the man's stockings were 'a kind of rusty black and his shoes seemed to be old, and his coat of a dark coloured mixed chamblet'. Later, hearing of Godfrey's fate, he concluded the man he had seen was he.[14]

Huysman, a painter, described the man they saw as 'a person in a very melancholique posture and way of walking . . . He was a tall, slender man in a black or dark coat, which I took to be chamblet. I wondered within myself to see a person of his appearance walking in so lonesome a place.'[15]

By now the rumour of murder by Papists was all over town. At about two or three o'clock, a Papist named Thomas Burdet met Thomas Wynell in the Strand not far from Greens Lane, where Godfrey had once lived.

'What have your people done with Sir Edmund Berry Godfrey?' cried Wynell. 'The town says you have murthered him.'

Burdet said he did not know what Wynell meant. Wynell told him he had been at Godfrey's house and at Colonel Welden's where they were to have dined, and that Sir Edmund's brothers were saying that he had been murdered by Papists.[16]

Such talk spread quickly. Long before dusk it was the chief topic of discussion all over London. At Mrs Duke's coffee house next to Northumberland House at about three or four o'clock, one Captain Thomas Paulden overheard talk of Godfrey's disappearance. Someone said that when the justice had gone out in the morning he had said, 'If I live, I shall be home again by one o'clock.' He had not arrived home, said the raconteur, and it was believed that he was killed by the Papists.

'Why should the Papists have murdered him?' asked Captain Paulden. The reply was that it was 'so believed'.

'I am confident,' said Paulden, 'that if he be killed, that it is either by thieves, or he has done it himself.'[17]

So the speculation about how Godfrey had died began. It was still only six or seven hours since he left home. It was by no means certain he was missing, far less proven that he was dead.

But London cared nothing for proof. The word was out: Godfrey was dead and the Papists had done it.

4: Suspicion, Search and Speculation

Sir Edmund Godfrey did not return home on Saturday night. Early on Sunday morning one of his servants went to Hammersmith, where the magistrate's aged mother lived. It was thought he might have heard she was ill or dying and flown to her in panic. But he was neither there nor at his tavern in Hammersmith, the Swan.

Later, Henry Moor trudged into the City to tell Michael Godfrey of his brother's continued absence.[1]

'God have mercy upon us!' exclaimed Michael. 'I pray God we hear good news of him.' He then despatched Moor back to Hartshorn Lane, warning him to keep silent about the affair and to await the coming of himself and his brother Benjamin in the afternoon.[2]

Moor got back to his master's house at about nine o'clock, and joined the other servants in making ready for morning service at St Martin's. Before they set out, Judith Pamphlin asked him about Godfrey. He was loathe to deceive her, but the request of Michael Godfrey that he should keep the disappearance 'very private and secret and not to communicate it to any person' allowed no exceptions. Leading her to believe that Godfrey had returned the night before, he said that he had got up and gone abroad two hours earlier. But Mrs Pamphlin was not deceived. Later in the day she called on Mrs Gibbon. She arrived at Old Southampton Buildings weeping and asking where Sir Edmund was.[3]

The town was now ringing with excited gossip about the strange case of Justice Godfrey. New versions of his fate were appearing in all quarters of the city. One story, first recorded by a regular at the Feathers tavern at Charing Cross, was to grow to alarming proportions. William Collinson called into the Feathers for his morning draught as usual on Sunday. Seeing several neighbours there and bidding them good morning, he asked, 'What news?' One of a group engaged in excited chatter turned and said, 'Here's brave news for you Papists. Sir Edmund Berry Godfrey went from his house yesterday, and did not come home last night.' According to Collinson, 'It was in all people's mouths in that quarter that he was murthered by the Papists at Somerset House.'[4]

Here was brave news indeed. Somerset House in the Strand was the residence of Charles's Catholic Queen. Catherine had surrounded herself with priests and Catholic servants, rendering Somerset House one of the few places in England where Papists could live unmolested. The source of the Somerset House rumour was probably a man called John Oakley, a servant of one of Godfrey's neighbours in Hartshorn Lane. Oakley believed he had seen Godfrey at a gate of Somerset House known as Somerset Water Gate. This led to a road that passed along the west side of the palace and its garden, down to the river's edge. Oakley said Godfrey had been standing still, and 'there was a man or two' near him.[5]

After evening service on Sunday night, Michael and Benjamin Godfrey called at their brother's house. They told Moor that they would make inquiries at all the places Sir Edmund frequented, 'to make discovery of him'. They renewed their request for secrecy.[6]

One of the first places the brothers visited in search of Godfrey was the house of Captain and Mary Gibbon, where they went with Moor first thing on Monday morning. Moor waited for them outside while they entered and spoke to Mrs Gibbon. From her account of the interview, it seems the brothers were in a belligerent mood. They told her that Godfrey had dined with her the day before, and that he had lain there all night. Michael said, 'I am sure he is here.' Mrs Gibbon declared that he was not there. 'Why should I deny it if it were otherwise?' she said. He then interrogated her about when she had last seen Sir Edmund, and what they had spoken about. She told them of the day he had come to her, locking the door behind him and talking of threats to his life. At this, 'Mr Michael fell to stamping and crying out, "Oh Lord! We are ruined. What shall we do?"'

Brother Benjamin lifted up his eyes, 'wringing his hands and breaking out into exclamations'.

'What will become of us?' he cried. Mrs Gibbon asked them what was the matter. They looked at her and said, 'Nothing.'[7]

After they had left, Captain Gibbon went to Colonel Welden's and asked him what he thought of Sir Edmund's disappearance. 'I dare not tell you my thoughts,' said Welden, 'for I have observed him to be much out of his ordinary temper, ever since his examination of Oates.'[8]

From Old Southampton Buildings, the brothers Godfrey went to the Lord Chancellor, Sir Heneage Finch, and reported their brother's absence, telling him they thought he had been murdered by the Papists. Finch told the Privy Council of their fears the same morning. Sir Robert Southwell, clerk to the council, recalled that 'his Lordship told it in such a sort (seeing the man had beene then wanting but two nights) that little notice was taken of it and noe order given'.[9]

Before ten o'clock on Monday morning, Henry Moor went out to scour the fields north of London where his master was wont to wander. He searched the fields where rumour had it the justice had been seen, and made inquiries of anyone he met, but found no sign of him. Eventually, it became too dark to carry on, and he turned his steps homeward.[10]

Meanwhile, Michael and Benjamin were continuing their

inquiry in town. They visited Lady Pratt, a friend of their brother whose house near Charing Cross he had visited on Friday. They also visited several other houses, but found no clues.[11]

They searched all day, charging Moor once again to keep all secret before taking their leave of him and returning home at night. After their departure, Moor learned that a great funeral was to take place the following night, Tuesday, at St Martin's Church. He penned a note to Michael Godfrey, suggesting that such a large gathering of local people would be an ideal opportunity to make the true picture clear and to appeal for news. He sent the note into the City by messenger. Before he retired that night, the troubled old clerk received word from Michael that he could announce Godfrey's disappearance just as he suggested.[12]

On Tuesday morning, however, Michael sent another message to Moor, telling him not to divulge details to anyone until they had again seen the Lord Chancellor. The brothers' concern about keeping the story quiet was futile. All London knew Godfrey was missing. They were, of course, anxious to avoid scandal and to squash the more outlandish rumours. A properly-worded announcement by Moor might at least still some of the wilder tongues and bring in new information at the same time.[13]

They saw the Lord Chancellor again that morning, and again he reported the situation to the lords of the council. The brothers were now summoned to attend the committee.[14] Southwell wrote:

> They were called in and there made such a story to the Lords as I had order presently to draw up a forme of enquiry concerning Sir Edmond to be printed and dispersed about. And this I did, and read it to the Board, and after gave it to Newcomb the printer of the Savoy.[15]

Mrs Gibbon arrived at Hartshorn Lane during the morning and again found Judith Pamphlin weeping. 'We shall never see Sir Edmund more,' said the housekeeper.

'Why? What has become of him?' asked Mrs Gibbon. But Pamphlin's cryptic reply was that 'she durst not trust her,' and would say nothing.[16]

Mrs Gibbon then left Pamphlin and went downstairs, where she saw Henry Moor. She asked him to tell her the truth of how Sir Edmund fared, and whether he was alive or not. If Godfrey was truly murdered, Moor's future security lay in the hands of the brothers. He dare not risk alienating them. So far he had not received their final permission to speak openly, so he turned to

Mrs Gibbon and said with a false lightness that his master was as well in health as himself.[17]

When Mrs Gibbon had gone, Pamphlin came downstairs. She could hold herself back no longer. She went to Moor, her eyes red with weeping, and asked him to tell what he knew of their master's fate. Surely, he must have thought, surely he could trust Pamphlin to keep silent.

'To tell you the truth,' he whispered, 'we are afraid he is murdered.'[18]

Captain Gibbon called later and asked for news. Mrs Pamphlin said she could not tell him, but invited him to go into the kitchen, where Moor was, and he would tell him more. What passed between the two men was never recorded.[19]

Late in the morning, the Lord Chancellor's mace bearer arrived at Hartshorn Lane to question the servants. He was still talking to Moor when Richard Wheeler, the vestryman, called for news about noon. Shortly afterwards, a report reached Sir Robert Southwell's ears that Sir Edmund had appeared melancholy on the previous Friday while at Lady Pratt's. Southwell sent an immediate note to the Savoy printer to delay printing the handbills until further order. The Godfreys soon heard about the move, and went to Southwell to protest.[20]

'I told them it would next morning be Councill day,' wrote Southwell, 'that I was very tender of the honour of the Board, and would then represent what I had heard of their brother's melancholly, who perhaps was but stept for a few dayes into the country; and herewith they seemed to acquiesce.'[21]

Before evening, Moor received the brothers' consent to his announcing Sir Edmund's disappearance at the society funeral that night. He carried out their wishes, appealing for anyone who knew anything to come forward. A coachmaker called John Parsons, one of the churchwardens of St Martin's, did step forward. He had what might be a clue. He said that he had met Godfrey in St Martin's Lane between eight and nine o'clock on the morning of his disappearance, and that they had walked together for a short distance. During the walk the justice had asked him the way to Primrose Hill. And before they parted, he had pressed him three times to tell him the whereabouts of Paddington Woods.

'Are you buying a parcel of land?' asked Parsons.

'No,' said Sir Edmund.[22]

It was an extra piece in the jig-saw, but a baffling one. Why should Godfrey ask the way to Primrose Hill? It was known that he often used to walk in the country around Hampstead and Paddington, and must certainly have known the whereabouts of such a landmark.

The suicide theory was now also gaining ground among those who did not know Godfrey. For those who did, the idea was unthinkable. When the suicide idea was brought to Hartshorn Lane, Moor's wife said, 'Oh! That ever it should be said that such a man as Sir Edmund should murther himself!'[23]

In later years it was suggested that Godfrey's brothers feared Sir Edmund had committed suicide. This was quite wrong. The evidence shows that Michael and Benjamin were convinced he had been murdered. One man, William Fall, testified later that the brothers 'came several times to the Lord Chancellor Nottingham's house in Queen Street, to speak with his lordship.' Fall, a member of Finch's household, asked the brothers what had become of Sir Edmund. Their exact reply is unknown, but Fall took it that they were 'in some apprehension that he had made himself away'. This goes against the testimony of a dozen other witnesses including Moor, who had most contact with the brothers, Welden, and Southwell's written account of their visits to the Lord Chancellor. Whatever Fall's interpretation of the brothers' fears, it is clear that the family and household of the missing magistrate believed he had been murdered. Richard Adams met Godfrey's nephew, Edmund Harrison, in Lombard Street. Harrison said that 'he doubted the report [of murder] was too true, and that he was murthered by the Papists'.[24]

The stories were coming thick and fast. A woman told Mary Gibbon that Godfrey 'was certainly murther'd by the Papists. They had a spleen at him, and they had done it.' A man called Robert Whitehall heard the same from 'a considerable citizen' at George's coffee house in Freeman's Yard. When the Westminster coroner, Robert White, heard the rumours he went to question Colonel Welden. Rumour and speculation had added detail to Welden's fears. He told White that he 'did very much suspect him to be murther'd by papists between Pall Mall and Arundel House'.[25]

On the Wednesday morning the brothers again attended the Privy Council. But before the council sat the Duke of Norfolk rushed in with the story that Sir Edmund had been secretly married to the widow of a lawyer called Ofley. That, according to Southwell, 'putt the matter into laughter for that day'.[26]

While the Privy Council laughed, the rumour mongers seized on the latest morsel. It was already being suggested by some that Godfrey had been last seen near Arundel House, the Duke of Norfolk's London residence. Surely Norfolk, a known Papist, must have had a hand in it? Others said Godfrey had been found in bed with a whore, or that he had 'stepped aside for debt'. He had been seen at the Lord Treasurer's lodgings, at St James's, the Duke of York's residence, even at Whitehall Palace. The light of day disappeared, and with it, seemingly, the last vestiges of reason.[27]

Tomorrow was Thursday. The day the terror would begin.

5: The Man in the Grey Suit

Two bizarre incidents, which have never been explained, occurred before the discovery of Godfrey's body on Thursday afternoon.

The first was in a barber's shop on Tuesday morning. William Goldsborough, a clerk in the House of Commons, reported later that he was 'under the barber's hands, and while he was a Trimming, comes a person into the shop, open-mouth'd.'

'Sir Edmund Berry Godfrey is found,' said the man.

'Where?' said barber and customer in unison.

'He has killed himself upon Primrose Hill.'

Neither Goldsborough nor the barber knew the man.[1]

The second incident happened at the shop of Mr Chiswell, a bookseller at St Paul's Churchyard, at about one o'clock on Thursday. A clergyman called Adam Angus, curate of St Dunstan's in the West, had dined early at the Woolsack in Ivy Lane with his friend John Oswald, a minister. They went to the bookshop directly from the Woolsack. Angus stood for a time, leaning over the counter next to the street and reading some printed papers. Oswald was further inside the shop. At about one o'clock, 'a young man in a grey-coloured suit' clapped Angus on the shoulder and said, 'Do you hear the news?'

'What news?' asked Angus.

'Sir Edmund Berry Godfrey is found.'

'Where?'

'In Leicester Fields, at the Dead Wall, with his own sword run through him.'

Before Angus could reply the man disappeared. The curate looked so surprised at the news that Oswald asked him what was wrong. He told him of the man in the grey suit, and then went immediately to Bishop Burnet, whom he knew to be Godfrey's friend. Angus had been taking notes for Burnet for his *History of the Reformation*. Burnet, who lived in Lincoln's Inn Fields, listened to his story, and then sent him by coach to Dr William Lloyd at his house in Leicester Fields. Lloyd knew nothing of the story. He sent a servant to Hartshorn Lane, but Godfrey's household had heard nothing.

Angus said he did not know the man in the grey suit, or his name. And he never saw him again.[2]

That afternoon Godfrey's body was found at Primrose Hill, run through with his own sword.

6: I Find Murdered by Rogues

At about two o'clock on Thursday afternoon two men were walking across the fields north of London. It was raining, the ground underfoot was muddy, and they were eager to reach the White House tavern at what is now Chalk Farm. The men were John Walters, a farrier, and William Bromwell, a baker. As they skirted a dry ditch on the south side of Primrose Hill, within two fields of their destination, they noticed a cane, a belt and a pair of gloves 'lying within a thicket upon a green bank near the ditch'.[1]

Primrose Hill, now lying on the north side of Regent's Park and surrounded on three sides by the streets and houses of Hampstead, was at that time completely in the country. Since Elizabeth's day it had been used as grazing land, and its gentle slopes were famous for their primroses. On its western side lay Barrow Hill, formerly Greenberry Hill, which had once been the scene of a battle and a burial place for the slain.[2]

Walters and Bromwell decided that the cane, belt and gloves must belong to some gentleman who had gone into the ditch to urinate. They passed on to the White House where they spent some time drinking together and talking to the landlord, John Rawson. Eventually they told him of the articles they had seen near the ditch.

'Why did you not bring them hither?' asked Rawson.

'We did not know but there might be somebody hard by to own them,' replied one of the men. Rawson told them that some soldiers had been hedgehog-hunting in the area during the week, and the articles might have been left by one of them. After further discussion, they agreed to accompany Rawson to the spot as soon as the rain stopped. He promised to pay them a shilling for a drink if they found the articles, and told them he would take charge of them until they were claimed. He was doubtless not averse to selling them at a fair profit if no one did claim them.[3]

The rain was so bad they waited for three hours. The sun had already set when they left the White House at five o'clock. Walters and Bromwell had little difficulty in leading the innkeeper to the bank. The cane, belt and gloves were still there. Rawson stooped to pick them up, but suddenly stiffened.

'Lord bless us!' he said, looking straight ahead of him into the ditch. 'There's a man murthered!'[4]

They approached the bramble-covered ditch and saw a man's body lying face down. A sword had been driven into him from the front and seven or eight inches of the blade were sticking out between his shoulder blades. At first they did not know what to do. Under the rudimentary legal system of their day, it was common for the discoverers of a body to become the prime suspects. They did not dally long. After 'a very little stay, and without touching the body, or meddling with the gloves, and stick that lay by', they hurried off to the churchwarden of the parish to report their find. The churchwarden was sick, so they set off for the house of John Brown, a constable who lived about two miles away at St Giles Pound. On the way, they met a cowkeeper called Jennings and told him about the body.[5]

'I take you for neighbours and friends,' said Jennings. 'I do e'en advise you to say nothing on't, but let somebody else find it out, for you may bring yourselves into a great deal of trouble.'[6]

Rawson rebuked Jennings for talking in such a way, and they left him. The three men arrived at the constable's house between six and seven o'clock and told their story.

'I wish it be not Sir Edmund Berry Godfrey,' breathed Constable Brown.

He roused a dozen or more of his neighbours. Some came on horseback and others, including several watchmen, on foot, and they set off for Primrose Hill. The place was

... surrounded with divers *Closes*, fenced with high Mounds and Ditches, no road near, only some deep dirty Lanes made only for the conveniency for driving *Cows* and such like *Cattle* in and out

95

of the Grounds; and those very Lanes not coming near 500 Yards of the Place.

According to Brown, the place

... was so covered with bushes and brambles, in and about the ditch, that it was a hard matter to see the body, till one were come just upon it.[7]

He gave a detailed description of how the body lay: it was lengthways in the ditch, in a crooked posture. The left hand lay under the head in the bottom of the ditch. The right hand was 'a little strecht out, and touching the bank on the right side'. The knees were touching the bottom of the ditch, but the feet were not – they rested upon the brambles. The pommel of the sword did not reach the ground beneath the body, and the periwig and hat lay at the bottom of the ditch a short distance away.[8]

Brown bestrode the corpse and felt underneath it with his hands to find how the sword was placed. Then he turned to the men nearby and asked them to help him lift the body out. As they dragged it about five or six yards into the open, someone remarked that it was a tall man.[9]

'Pray God it be not Sir Edmund Berry Godfrey, for he hath been for some time missing,' replied Brown. Other men echoed his prayer. The constable later testified that 'there was no blood at all, there was no blood in the ditch'.[10]

'It was then very dark,' said Brown. He knelt down 'to take the best view of the face' that he could. He 'continued in the suspicion, but could not be as yet positive, that it was the body of the said Sir Edmund.'[11]

'It was a tempestuous night,' said one of the men present, and the wind howled so madly across the dark hillside that it was impossible to keep a lantern alight.[12]

Brown discussed with his men how best to get the body up to the White House. They concluded 'that it would endanger the breaking the sword, to carry the body all the way with the sword in't.' So Brown resolved to withdraw the sword, but before doing so, 'cautioned the company to take particular notice of every circumstance how the sword and body were.' He took out the sword, 'which was somewhat hard in the drawing, and crashed upon the bone in the plucking of it forth.' No blood appeared to flow when the blade was pulled from the body.[13]

Two other points struck Brown. Despite the foul weather the

96

dead man's shoes were 'very clean'. It was obvious he could not have walked to the place. Secondly, the sword had made no impression in the soft earth, as it would have done if he had thrown himself upon it.[14]

They laid the body across two watchmen's staves and carried it up the hill to the White House, where it was placed upon the floor. Brown had someone take notes in duplicate of the money, papers and other items found on the corpse. It was then lifted on to a table. There could no longer be any doubt that it was the body of Sir Edmund Berry Godfrey.[15]

They now got a clearer view of the wounds. The sword had been driven through the heart just beneath the left nipple. Near this wound, which went clear through the body, there was another, shallower, wound where the first stabbing attempt had been foiled by a rib. There was also some mysterious bruising on the breast. 'He did look black about the breast,' said Brown. Finally, it seemed to the constable that Godfrey's neck had been broken. 'It was very weak, and one might turn his head from one shoulder to the other.'[16]

Brown ordered the watchmen to stay with the body, 'and not suffer any meddling with it' until further orders. Then, with about seven horsemen, he rode away to Hartshorn Lane. On the way, two of the riders stopped at Mrs Duke's coffee house, a short distance from Godfrey's house. Captain Thomas Paulden and Sergeant Ramsay, mace-bearer to the Lord Treasurer and a friend of Sir Edmund, were among those gathered at the coffee house who ran downstairs to the street to hear the news.

'Have you found Sir Edmund Godfrey's body?' asked Captain Paulden.

'Yes,' said one of the horsemen, 'at Primrose Hill.'

Sergeant Ramsay rushed off to Hartshorn Lane before anything else could be said.

'In what place and posture?' said Paulden.

'We found him in a ditch, run through with his own sword, which appeared a handful out of his back, with his head downward, and his heels upward, and as if he had fallen upon his own sword.'[17]

By this time a large crowd had gathered around the horses. When the horseman said it looked like suicide, 'there was a muttering among the people that, "These are the rogues that murdered him themselves, and would make people believe that he did it himself."'[18]

97

Meanwhile, Brown and his men had arrived at Hartshorn Lane a moment or two after Ramsey. A woman servant, probably Pamphlin, answered their blows on the door. She said the magistrate's brothers were upstairs. The constable asked to speak to them, and presently they came down along with Ramsey and Christopher Plucknet, Godfrey's brother-in-law and Surveyor of Highways. Brown informed them that the body of Sir Edmund had been found with a sword through it in a ditch near Primrose Hill, and that they had removed it to the White House. It was a shock, but hardly a surprise. Benjamin and Michael asked Brown how he was sure it was the body of their brother. 'I know him very well,' said Brown.[19]

After some discussion between the family and Ramsey, it was decided that Plucknet would go with Brown to see the body. The mace-bearer said he would immediately inform the King, and appointed to meet Brown at the Chequer Inn at one o'clock. It was already ten o'clock, and the rain had turned to snow, when Brown and Plucknet rode away to the White House.[20]

7: The Inquest

The corpse of the murdered magistrate remained on a table in a downstairs room at the White House all night, guarded by Brown's watchmen. The tavern, formerly Lower Chalcot farmhouse, was a mean place. There was 'no accommodation there, nor hangings, nor scarce a glass window in the house'. Maps of the time show its remoteness. It was the only house in the vicinity of Primrose Hill and stood on the site of the present Chalk Farm Tavern at the corner of Erskine Road and Regent's Park Road.[1]

On Friday morning, a new clue was discovered by Gilbert Burnet, who rode out across the snowy fields with Dr Lloyd to see the body of their friend. The two clerics entered the room where the body lay. Burnet later recorded what he saw: 'There were many drops of wax-lights on his breeches, which he never used himself. And since only persons of quality, or priests, use those lights, this made all people conclude into whose hands he must have been.'[2]

The Papists! The cry resounded from one end of England to the other. But, as Burnet indicated, it was not only priests who used wax candles. As 'persons of quality', the very honourable friends would have used them too.

When Godfrey's servants were shown the sword that had been withdrawn from their master's body, they testified that it was his own.[3]

Coincidence was weaving a lunatic pattern. The man in the grey suit had reported the finding of Godfrey's body run through with his own sword hours before the event. And the mystery man who had spoken to Goldsborough at the barber's shop on Tuesday morning – very possibly the man in the grey suit – had said the magistrate was dead on Primrose Hill. Coincidence? Or was it, perhaps, something more sinister?

The coroner for Middlesex, John Cowper, arrived at the White House after ten o'clock and impanelled a jury of eighteen local men. They filed into the room and viewed the body, which was still fully clothed and lying on its back as it had been left by Brown and his men the night before. They then went to see the ditch and the spot where the sword had been withdrawn.[4]

During the morning, the tavern was besieged by men, women and children, some of whom had tramped from the centre of London in the hope of glimpsing the butchered corpse. One such idle ghoul was a carpenter named Fisher. He had been on his way from town to the house of Lord Wooten, where he had been engaged to carry out some work. Passing the White House and seeing the crowd outside, he had decided to linger. Unlike most of the curious, Fisher managed to slip inside the tavern and found his way to the body. He removed the hat with the gold band and saw the two wounds in the breast. Then somebody came into the room. To Fisher's surprise, he was not thrown out, but seconded to strip the corpse in preparation for the surgeons, who were due at noon. 'They asked me if I would give an hand,' said Fisher later, 'and I told them, "Yes".'[5]

Fisher, too, noticed how clean the shoes were. Strange indeed, for the constable and his men had been 'dirty'd and moil'd up to the very saddle-skirts'.[6]

The carpenter stripped the lower part of the body, then with the help of another man he sat the corpse upright 'with his breech upon the table and his feet hanging down'. They unbuttoned his coat and waistcoat and pulled them off. But they were unable to bend the arms, so they tore his flannel shirt in order to remove it. According to Fisher, there was no sign of blood on any of Godfrey's clothing. 'Upon his back there was some blood, but upon his flannel there was none.'[7]

Fisher said later, 'There was a place, black, round about his throat, which looked as if he had been strangled, and his neck was weak and loose, and he had no strength in it [at] all, by which it's evident he was murdered.'[8]

The King's apothecary, John Chase, also saw the body on Friday morning. As well as the sword wounds, he noted a swelling upon the left ear, as if a knot had been tied. Chase's son James saw 'a great contusion on the left ear, and his whole face was very much bruised'. The apothecary thought that Godfrey had been beaten from the neck to the stomach. 'I never saw any man beaten so in my life,' he said. The son concluded that Sir Edmund had been strangled, 'for I don't believe those injuries that were offered about him, could be after he was dead'.[9]

The bruising was also observed by Lazinby, the King's surgeon. He said Godfrey's entire chest and abdomen was 'very much discoloured and black'.[10]

Zachariah Skillard and Nicholas Cambridge, the surgeons appointed to conduct the post mortem examination, arrived at the White House before midday and opened the body. There has been a lot of argument whether the body was opened or not. Both Roger L'Estrange in 1688 and Alfred Marks in 1905 stated positively that the body was not opened. They were wrong. Skillard testified unequivocally that the corpse was examined internally. 'And when we ripped him up,' he said, 'he began for to putrefy.' In a signed statement by Skillard, newly discovered at the Public Record Office in London, the surgeon says that when he went to open Godfrey, 'the Lean of his body was soe putrid, that it hung upon the Insision knife'.[11]

There is no complete record of the inquest proceedings. Only the depositions of the fourteen witnesses examined by the coroner and a full report of the verdict have survived. But just over three months later, at the trial of three men unjustly accused of Godfrey's murder, some of the inquest witnesses testified before the Lord Chief Justice as they had before the coroner.[12]

There was a suggestion in 1681 that the jurymen were first of the opinion that Godfrey had committed suicide. True or not, they rapidly changed their minds after hearing the medical evidence.[13]

Skillard's evidence, as given at the trial of the three men later accused, was as follows:

'His breast was all beaten with some obtuse weapon, either with the feet, or hands, or something.'

'Did you observe his neck?' asked the Attorney General.

'Yes. It was distorted.'

'How far?'

'You might have taken the chin and have set it upon either shoulder.'

'Did you observe the wound?'

'Yes, I did. It went in at one place and stopped at a rib. The other place it was quite through the body.'

The Attorney General then reached the crucial part of the medical evidence. 'Do you think he was killed by that wound?'

'No,' said Skillard, 'for there would have been some evacuation of blood, which there was not. And besides, his bosom was open, and he had a flannel waistcoat and a shirt on – and neither those nor any of his clothes were penetrated.'

Skillard said he was sure the neck had been broken. 'There was more done to his neck than an ordinary suffocation,' he said. 'The wound went through his very heart, and there would have appeared some blood, if it had been done quickly after his death.'

'Did it appear by the view of the body that he was strangled or hanged?'

'He was a lean man, and his muscles, if he had died of the wound, would have been turgid. And then again, all strangled people never swell, because there is a sudden deprivation of all the spirits, and a hindering of the circulation of the blood.'

'How long do you believe he might be dead before you saw him?'

'I believe four or five days. And they might have kept him a week, and he never swelled at all, being a lean man. And when we ripped him up, he began for to putrefy. We made two incisions to give it vent, and the liquor that was in his body did a little smell. The very lean flesh was so near turned into putrefaction, that it stuck to the instrument when we cut it.'

Nicholas Cambridge confirmed Skillard's evidence and agreed that the sword wound had been inflicted after death.[14]

Lazinby, and another surgeon called Hobbs who had examined Godfrey's corpse before Skillard and Cambridge arrived, noted other points. Both were convinced that he had been murdered. Hobbs said the face was 'blotted', and 'the bloody vessels of his eyes were so full, as if he had been troubled with sore eyes.' Lazinby referred to two great creases on the neck, which had swollen below and above the collar, caused by 'the strangling with a cord or cloth'.[15]

The medical evidence confused rather than clarified. How had

101

Godfrey received those mysterious black bruises all over his chest and abdomen? What was the bruise under his left ear? Had he been strangled or hanged? Why, if he was already dead, had the sword been driven into his heart? And, above all, who had done the deed?

The jury listened all afternoon to witnesses describing the finding of the body, its removal to the White House and its examination by surgeons. Constable John Brown explained his part in the affair, and again remarked that Godfrey could not have walked to Primrose Hill because his shoes were so clean. Henry Moor swore on oath that his master had been wearing a lace band around his neck when he left home the previous Saturday. The band had been removed by the time Brown arrived at the scene.[16]

The jury was told that the pockets of the dead man had contained a great deal of money – seven guineas, four broad pieces and four pounds in silver. He also had three rings on his fingers.[17]

Coroner Cowper announced an adjournment towards the end of the afternoon, but after a short rest the jury returned for a second sitting at five o'clock. Mary Gibbon told the court of the death threat Godfrey had described, and two men called Caleb Winde and Richard Duke explained that they had seen Sir Edmund talking with Joseph Radcliffe in the Strand on Saturday about one o'clock. Then a new and crucial piece of evidence was introduced. The tracks of a vehicle had been discovered near the ditch where Godfrey's corpse had lain. They were at first thought to be the tracks of a coach, but a thorough examination by Sergeant Ramsey revealed that they had been made by a cart. And 'though the owners of the ground and neighbours knew of none since haytime', the tracks were obviously fresh.[18]

An acquaintance of Godfrey, William Griffith, who was secretary to Henry Coventry, Secretary of State, wrote from Whitehall the day after the inquest:

> The bars through the grounds to the place where they [the murderers] flang him were likewise forced . . . and hay also was found scattered upon ye grass, with which they had either fed ye Carthorse, or hid his Body in carrying it thither.[19]

Yet the body had not been in the ditch all week. A man called Robert Forset or Fawcett said that on the Tuesday he had been hunting with his hounds at the place where the body was found. There was no sign of body, gloves or cane either then or on

Wednesday when a friend of Forset's beat in the same area with the hounds.[20]

The coroner himself had been near the ditch on Tuesday, and had even stopped to wash his hands in a pond near the ditch. He had seen nothing. A Mrs Blyth testified that her man 'had been upon Wednesday up and down thereabouts looking for a calf newly fallen', but no dead body had been in evidence. Finally, there was the perplexing testimony of Thomas Morgan, who said that he was at the pond near the ditch as late as noon on Thursday. Morgan believed that if the belt, gloves and cane had then lain where they were later found, he should have seen them.[21]

If Morgan spoke the truth, the body had been dumped in the ditch between twelve and two o'clock, when Bromwell and Walters came along. It seemed inconceivable that such a daring task should have been undertaken in daylight, but the idea seemed to be supported by the observations of the surgeon Lazinby, who had examined the body on Friday morning.

'I felt upon his clothes,' said Lazinby. 'I admired that his clothes were not wet, there having been so great a storm the afternoon before . . . His clothes were as dry as mine.'[22]

Even as the inquest progressed, the latest tit-bits were being carried back to town. All evening there was a constant to-ing and fro-ing between the White House and the capital.

By late Friday night almost no one entertained the thought of suicide any longer. The evidence so far disclosed had virtually all London believing that, in the words of William Griffith, the magistrate 'had been strangled some-where privately about Town', and then carried to Primrose Hill. There, his murderers had 'thrust his sword through him after he was cold, hoping he might not be found in that by-place 'till after putrefaction had taken away all marks of any other violent death, than what his own sword (being so found in him) should by his own means seem to have been occasioned.' But what would the jury think?[23]

They sat until four o'clock on Saturday morning. Then, almost exactly a week after Godfrey rose from his bed at Hartshorn Lane for the last time, the jury delivered its verdict.[24]

Sir Edmund had, they decided, been set upon by persons unknown. These persons, 'moved and seduced by the Instigation of the Devil', had, on 12 October strangled Godfrey with a piece of linen cloth, 'of no value'. The cause of death, they said, was strangling, of which Godfrey died instantly. No explanation was made of the sword wound, the bruising on the chest and abdomen, the presence of the body at Primrose Hill or the motive for the murder.[25]

The cry rose to a terrified falsetto, first in London and soon across the length and breadth of the realm: 'The Papists are rising!'

Titus Oates was made.

Sir Edmondbury Godfrey Kn.^t mur^d. A.D. 1678.

The only portrait of Sir Edmund Berry
Godfrey painted from life. His murder
launched the Terror

Charles II – Protestant King with a
Catholic wife

LEFT James, Duke of York (the King's
brother and heir presumptive): prime
target of the Plot mongers

Anthony Ashley Cooper, first Earl of
Shaftesbury: 'In friendship false,
implacable in hate'

VERITAS EX CINERIBVS REVIVISCIT

ÆTATIS SVÆ 57

P. Vanderbanc Sculp.

Are to be Sold at Thomas Cherets in James Street Couent Garden

The true Effigies of that worthy and never to be forgotten
S.ᵗ EDMOND-BURY GODFREY· Knight and Iustice of the Peace who
was MURTHERED by Papists the 12.ᵗʰ day of October Añ. Dom. 1678.

An engraving of Sir Edmund Berry
Godfrey, described by his friend Gilbert
Burnet as 'the best JP in England'

OPPOSITE The four 'discoverers' of the
murder of Justice Godfrey – Oates (chief
architect of the Plot), Bedloe ('a
villainous countenance . . . full of malice
and revenge'), Dugdale, and Prance
(vacillating liar, or the most astute and
audacious of the Jesuit agents?)

TITUS OATES. D.D. *Cap.* WILLIAM. BEDLOE.

M^rstephen Dugdale. *Mr Miles Prance.*

S.r E.B. Godfree takeing
D.r Oates his depofitions.

The Clubat y.e Plow Alehousefor
the murther of S.r E.B. Godfree.

S.r E.B. Godfree dogg'd by
S.t Clements Church.

A selection from a pack of
'Godfrey' playing cards,
numerous versions of which
were among the many
gruesome souvenirs which
flooded the market before
and after Christmas 1678

S.r E.B. Godfree is perfwaded
to goe down Somerfet houfe Yard.

S.r E.B. Godfree Strangled
Girald going to ftab him.

S.r E.B. Godfree Carying
up into a Roome.

The body of S.E.B. Godfree
is shewn to Capt. Bedlo and
Mr. Prance

The dead body of Sr. E B Godfree
Convey'd out of Sommerset
house in a Sedan.

The body of Sr. E.B. G. carry'd to
Primrose hill on a Horse.

The Murtherers of S.E.B. Godfree
are diverting themselves at
Bow after the Murther.

The Funerall of
Sr. E B Godfree

The Execution of the mur:
:therers of Sr. E B Godfree

A comic-strip pamphlet promoting the official version of the murder, published in London in 1679

PART IV

The Age of Discovery

Now to our perjury, to add more terror,
We are again forsworn, in will and error.

Love's Labour's Lost, v.ii

1: Panic

In the week before Godfrey's disappearance, belief in Oates's Plot had again started to wane. Even after the opening of Coleman's deal box, there was little evidence of organized Catholic activity. Coleman's intriguing with foreigners was established to everybody's satisfaction, but that activity bore no resemblance to the conspiracy of regicide and general massacre described by Oates.

Secretary of State Henry Coventry had been impressed with Oates's performance before the Privy Council, but he did not really believe his allegations. 'If he be a liar,' wrote Coventry, 'he is the greatest and adroitest I ever saw, and yet it is a stupendous thing to think what vast concerns are like to depend on the evidence of one young man who hath twice changed his religion – if he be now a Protestant.'[1]

Thousands of papers had been seized from the Jesuits, but none of them was found to contain matter confirming the Plot. 'Amongst the many bags of papers that have been seized there doth not appear one line relating to this matter,' wrote Lord Chancellor Finch in disgust, 'so that all depends upon what one witness will swear he saw, or heard read, without any concurrent circumstance to confirm his testimony.'[2]

The lies in which Charles had discovered Oates, and the perjurer's failure to recognize both Coleman and Sir George Wakeman, whom he had claimed to know, when faced with them in the council chamber, were now beginning to tell against him. And even though the secret committee played safe by throwing Richard Langhorn, a Papist lawyer who had acted for the Jesuits, into Newgate without any evidence of treason against him, there is no doubt that the Plot had begun 'to reel and stagger again in its Credit'.[3]

The King returned from Newmarket on Wednesday, 16 October, the day before the finding of the body. He was still cynical about Oates, now lodged with Tonge in Charles's own rèsidence. He would not countenance any action against the Papists in custody. He was 'not willing to have these men hurried off, or their blood taken in a case so improbable.'[4]

The body of the murdered magistrate turned Titus into a saviour. The 'persons unknown' of the inquest verdict was instantly translated into 'the Papists'. Suddenly, unreasoningly, the populace believed every word uttered by Oates and his crew. 'The murder proved the Plot, the Plot the murder.' Godfrey's death was seen as the prelude to the mass murder of Protestants predicted by Citizen Titus. The murder, said Burnet, 'contributed more than any other thing to the establishing the belief in all this evidence'.[5]

Godfrey's corpse was carried first to Dean Lloyd's house in Leicester Fields on Saturday morning and thence to Hartshorn Lane, where it was embalmed. It was then dressed and exposed to public view for twelve days until the funeral on 30 October. The anti-popish faction swung rapidly into action, extracting every last ounce of political capital from the murder. Never was there such an opportunity for swinging public opinion in favour of the Opposition's latest design: the exclusion of the Duke of York from the succession.[6]

'The capital and the whole nation,' wrote Macauley, 'went mad with hatred and fear.'[7]

The effectiveness of the anti-popish propaganda at this time can be judged from a handwritten document now at Somerset Record Office. Entitled *An Account of the Variety of Popish Torments That Have Been Practised on the Bodies of Protestants*, it declares:

Children have been cast to dogs and swine to be devoured.
　　Women great with child hanged up, their bellies ripped up so that the infants hath dropped out and been thrown into a pile.
　　Infants put to suck their dead mothers' breasts.
　　Some driven into rivers and if they swim, shot or knocked down.
　　Some put into nasty dungeons full of mice and dung with balls on their legs and starved with cold and hunger.
　　Some had their eyes plucked out and hands cut off and left to pine in misery.
　　Some stoned to death.
　　Some driven stark naked into mountains and woods in the extremity of snow and frost and so starved.
　　Some forced to carry their own parents to execution, to give fire to the wood, mothers to throw their children into the waters, wives to hang their husbands, children their parents in hopes and on promises of life, and afterwards themselves to be barbarously murdered.
　　Some boiled to death in cauldrons.
　　Some put in a hole in the earth all but their heads and there to die.

. . . and so on in like manner for twenty-five articles.[8]

James, Duke of York, was already feeling the danger of such

propaganda by Friday, 18 October, when he wrote to his son-in-law the Prince of Orange reporting the discovery of Godfrey's body:

> This makes a great noise and is laid against the Catholics also, but without any reason for it, for he was known to be far from being an enemy to them. All these things happening together will cause, I am afraid, a great flame in the Parliament, when they meet on Monday, for those disaffected to the government will inflame all things as much as they can.[9]

Southwell wrote that 'the indignation of this murder was so great abroad that 'twas found necessary to repair the neglect of doing nothing concerning it at the council . . .' So on Sunday, the day before Parliament reassembled, the King issued a proclamation offering a reward of £500 'for the discovery of the murderers of Sir Edmund Berry Godfrey, with a pardon to any of the murderers that shall discover the rest'.[10]

On Monday morning the Opposition was exultant, the government disconsolate. The first public statement about Oates and his allegations was made in the King's Speech. 'I now intend to acquaint you, as I shall always do with anything that concerns me,' said Charles, 'that I have been informed of a design against my person by the Jesuits, of which I shall forbear an opinion, lest I may seem to say too much or too little. But I will leave the matter to the law.'[11]

There was no specific mention of Godfrey's murder either by Charles or the Lord Chancellor, who spoke obliquely of 'a concurrence of ill accidents', and 'malicious men'. But London was resounding with news of the murder and Parliament would not be fobbed off. The Commons wasted no time in electing a committee to investigate the Plot and drafting an Address requesting Charles to banish all Papists from within a radius of twenty miles around the capital city.[12]

Meanwhile, the panic increased. Hundreds of people visited Hartshorn Lane to see Godfrey's corpse lying in state, and all that saw it 'went away inflamed'. Silver medals were struck depicting the murder on one side and the Pope blessing the killers on the other. 'Godfrey' daggers began to appear, three thousand of which were said to have been sold in one day. On the blades was engraved, 'Remember the murder of Edmund Bury Godfrey. Remember religion'.[13]

The King handed all the papers seized from the Jesuits to the

House of Lords, which appointed a committee on 23 October to sort them. On the same day the Commons sent for Titus Oates, and again his memory had undergone a wondrous improvement. As a result of his deranged accusations, the five Catholic peers Arundell, Belasyse, Petre, Powis and Stafford were committed to the Tower and orders were issued to apprehend the Benedictine monks at the Savoy, a crumbling tenement in the Strand near Somerset House.[14]

The trained bands, London's citizen soldiers, now patrolled the city day and night. Cannons were placed around Whitehall and posts and chains erected in the main streets. Houses were broken into and searched by troops, and suspected plotters carried off to prison. 'I beseech God to prepare us, everie daye, for the worst of times,' wrote the father of the Dean of Norwich on 27 October.[15]

Evelyn recorded that 'men were now very angerey with the *papists*, & violently transported, by reason of the late plot, & especially the *Murder* of Sir E: Godfrey'.[16]

The Commons and Lords committees sat every day debating all the ramifications of the Plot, examining witnesses, listening to Oates and Tonge expand their testimony indiscriminately. Now nothing could restrain the perjurers: all Protestant England was behind them. A strange 'knocking and digging' sound was heard in Old Palace Yard. The Lord Chamberlain was ordered to shift some timber stored next to the Parliament House lest the Papists should use it to burn the House down. There was renewed panic when a French Papist was reported to have a store of gunpowder in the street next to the Palace of Westminster. His house was searched and found to contain empty rocket and serpent cases set aside for a royal fête. No one seemed happy with the simple explanation that the Frenchman, Choqueux, was the royal firework maker. The Commons had the cellars of the Parliament House scoured after reports of a new Gunpowder Plot, and funeral processions were halted while armed guards searched coffins for hidden arms.[17]

On 28 October the main Lords Plot Committee set up a special sub-committee 'to enquire into the business of Sir E. Godfrey'. It consisted entirely of the enemies of the Duke of York – Shaftesbury, Buckingham, Essex, Halifax, Winchester and the Bishop of London.[18]

A second royal proclamation, promising not only the pardon and £500 reward but also security for anyone naming Godfrey's killers, set the stage perfectly for the entrance of the first of the 'discoverers'.[19]

By now the propaganda machine of the Opposition was working

at full stretch. Lord Shaftesbury and his infamous Green Ribbon Club, assisted as always by Peyton's Gang, were bruiting the lie of Godfrey's murder by Catholics all over town. Titus Oates had struck gold, and was now secure in the bosom of Shaftesbury and the other Whig peers. Godfrey's funeral, behind which is discernible the cunning and imagination of Shaftesbury, was the climax of the last week of October.

No man can have had his last wishes more blatantly defied than Justice Godfrey. In his will, drafted in 1677, he had asked for his body to be interred 'in the meanest place of burial belonging to that parish wherein I shall die, but not in the Church, this to be performed without pomp or pageantry, not to be accompanied with numerous attendants either of friends or relations – the which as I asserted not in my life time I would not have imposed on me being dead'. This strange, secretive and humble man had wished 'to avoid being troublesome to the world and especially to the streets when dead'. He begged to be buried 'very early in the morning or very late at night with as much privateness as may be without any solemn invitation of my acquaintances or kindred as also without any funeral sermon or other harangue which I do hereby forbid'. He also forbade the erection of any kind of monument or memorial, 'hoping that my failings will be buried with me in the grave without any partial remembrance of evil or good actions . . .'[20]

Not one of Godfrey's requests was met. His funeral on 31 October was one of the most spectacular and appalling ever to take place in London. The mob was whipped into a frenzy. Seventy-two clergymen preceded the coffin from Bridewell to the church of St Martin-in-the-Fields, and more than a thousand 'persons of quality' followed behind. The route was lined with angry, frightened Protestants. 'The Crowd,' wrote North, 'was prodigious, both at the Procession, and in and about the Church, and so heated that any Thing, called Papist, were it Cat or Dog, had probably gone to Pieces in a Moment.'[21]

The Papists locked themselves indoors as the raucous pageant moved through the streets, for the Protestants 'would endure nothing which was not carried with the uttmost Violence against all persons of that church'.[22]

Dean Lloyd gave a long and inflammatory funeral oration from the text 'Died Abner as a fool dieth?' in which he extolled Sir Edmund's virtues, abused the Catholics and fuelled the now uncontrollable fires of loathing that burned in every Protestant

111

heart. An unsubtle but effective touch of theatre, doubtless also attributable to the Green Ribboners, was for the worthy dean to be accompanied to the pulpit by two 'thumping Divines', who stood either side of him as bodyguards while he preached.[23]

'A most Portentous Spectacle sure!' said North. 'Three Parsons in one Pulpit! Enough, of itself, on a less Occasion, to excite Terror in the Audience.'[24]

And so the poor corpse of Sir Edmund Godfrey was finally committed 'with strange and terrible ceremonies' to the grave of a martyr in the churchyard of St Martin's.

2: The Curious Flight of Mr Godfrey

For a week after the discovery of Godfrey's body no real clues came to light. The Plot mongers and their dupes continued the merciless pursuit of Catholics – laymen as well as priests and Jesuits. The more sober of Charles's servants, the few, watched for suspicious activity in all quarters, not just the popish. But even the republicans and Green Ribboners were still not pointing an accusing finger at individuals. It was still 'the Papists'. After a week of frantic but useless inquiry, it seemed inescapable that the actual murderers had long since fled the capital. In case they should try to escape overseas, all the ports were closed and Admiralty officers maintained a round-the-clock surveillance. The man in charge of the watchdog operation was Samuel Pepys, Secretary to the Admiralty.

Late on the night of 25 October Pepys received an urgent memorandum from James Pearse, Surgeon-General to the Fleet, at Gravesend. It reported the suspicious behaviour of a man, looking like a highwayman, who had ridden furiously from London on the night after the discovery of the body, and who had arrived in Gravesend on the 19th. On the spur of the moment, when challenged, the man had given his name as 'Godfrey'. Surreptitious inquiries revealed that he had been lodging since the summer with a Presbyterian milliner called Paine in Cannon Street, London. His true identity was unknown, but it was realized he was an active member of the criminal-political underworld. On 15 October, a few hours after the mysterious man in the barber's shop had spoken of the finding of the missing magistrate's corpse, 'Godfrey' had told Paine he was leaving London forthwith. He was plainly anxious to set as great a distance as possible between himself and the capital, and he said he would return in a month. But something had happened to change his plans, because he was still in London the following day. Except that he was in town, his whereabouts and doings for the next two days were unknown. Then, while the jury sat at the White House debating bloody murder, 'Godfrey' had finally left London under cover of darkness and ridden to Gravesend.[1]

In order to confuse possible pursuers he had written to Paine telling him he was at Bridgwater in Somerset. He also took the precaution of carrying two periwigs – one dark brown, the other light in colour – to effect, if necessary, an immediate change of appearance. According to Pearse's report, 'Mr Godfrey' was 'a tall, thin faced man, squinting with both eyes', and aged about fifty. In another report from Gravesend, Pepys was informed that the suspect was

> . . . a proper well sett man in a great light colour'd perriwig, rough visag'd, having large hair on his eyebrows, hollow eyed, a little squinting, or a cast with his eye, full faced, about the cheeks, about 46 years of age, with a black hatt, and in a straight bodyed coate, cloth colour with silver lace behind . . .[2]

He should never have escaped. He had been shadowed by navy officials since his arrival at Gravesend. But, eluding them, he managed to get aboard a small vessel bound for the Downs. All ships embarking from Gravesend had to be cleared in advance by navy 'Searchers', but a ship called the *Assistance*, heading for Lisbon, had sailed earlier that day without the usual formalities. When it was discovered that 'Godfrey' had bribed a Searcher to clear the ship hurriedly without telling his associates, the navy agents assumed he had been intending to sail on the *Assistance* but had somehow missed her. It seemed probable that he now aimed to catch up with her in the faster vessel, and board her as she lay off the Downs.[3]

Pepys immediately fired off express letters to Sir Richard Rooth, Commander-in-Chief of the fleet in the Downs, and Captain Griffith, his counterpart at Portsmouth, begging them to stop the *Assistance* and arrest the fugitive. He sat up to the small hours working on plans to bring the suspect back in chains, convinced he was on to one of Edmund Godfrey's killers. In his instructions to Rooth he did not hesitate to invoke the name of the King, stressing that 'so great is the importance of it to His Majesty that this person do not escape away', that not only the *Assistance*, but 'every vessell great or small that shall came out of the River for some time' should be stopped and searched. Captain Griffith was to 'cause strict search to be immediately made upon every ship or vessell which now is, or shall for some time, come from the eastward' in case 'Godfrey' slipped through Rooth's cordon.[4]

That same night, Pepys wrote to the office of Secretary of State Coventry, urging prompt action in alerting the governor of Plymouth and the chief magistrate of Falmouth.[5]

A second express was sent to Rooth the following day, in which Pepys pressed home the vital importance of the mission, entreating him again to use 'all possible dilligence'.[6]

'Godfrey', however, was a seasoned trickster. The suspicious circumstances surrounding the departure of the *Assistance* had been a blind to divert the Admiralty's attention from his true plans and the ruse had succeeded. While the progress of the *Assistance* was followed by every navy official along the south coast, 'Godfrey' sailed only as far as Margate in the smaller vessel. From there, he got by horse to Folkestone, and at Folkestone he slipped aboard the pacquet boat to Dieppe.[7]

As soon as it was certain the suspect had escaped Titus Oates felt secure in asserting, with no likelihood of contradiction, that 'Godfrey' had been 'Father Simons, a considerable instrument in the . . . Plot'.[8]

Pepys had been correct in his belief that the man was a prime mover in the murder of Sir Edmund Godfrey. But the squint-eyed villain was no Papist. He was one of the most cunning and dangerous men in the pay of the very honourable friends.

3: The Domino Plan

A matter of hours after Pepys launched the hunt for the suspect calling himself Godfrey, the republicans set in motion a plan to implicate Pepys in the murder.

The first accusation came on 27 October, when a Captain Charles Atkins, son of the governor of Barbados, was interviewed by Secretary Coventry. There can be little doubt that the Opposition lords, 'Shiftesbury' Shaftesbury prominent among them, were behind Atkins's 'discoveries'. If not in firm control of Oates and his Plot, the lords were using both to the utmost advantage.

The forged letters had failed to bring the downfall of Bedingfield, the Duke of York's confessor. Coleman, the Duke's former secretary, still awaited trial, and it looked as if the Duke would be able to escape the worst effects of Coleman's downfall. Now some brilliant Opposition schemer had contrived a new way of striking at James – through Pepys, his faithful servant, known to have been his devoted and indispensable ally in the Navy Office during his years as Lord High Admiral.[1]

There was a stumbling block. Pepys had an unassailable alibi for the weekend of the murder: he had been at Newmarket with the King and Duke of York. Clearly, then, he could not be accused of direct involvement in the murder itself. But if he could be shown to have been in on the planning ... Atkins's story implicated a young clerk of Secretary Pepys called Samuel Atkins – no relation to the captain.

By striking at a humble employee like Atkins, the Opposition men were operating an early, human variant of the now famous domino theory. If Samuel Atkins fell, Pepys would follow. And in his own downfall, even perhaps to save himself, Pepys might well drag the Duke of York to his destruction. The cynical Green Ribboners, it seems, had little knowledge of Pepys's resourcefulness.[2]

On 30 October Captain Atkins related his fanciful tale of young Samuel's misdeeds to the Privy Council. Two days later he made a full statement under oath before his uncle Sir Philip Howard, one of Godfrey's fellow JPs in Middlesex. The captain said that before the disappearance of Godfrey he had been talking to Samuel Atkins at Derby House, where the Admiralty offices were located. The clerk, he claimed, had told him that Sir Edmund Godfrey had 'very much vilified his master, and that if he lived long would be the ruin of him'.[3]

The captain said that young Atkins had then questioned him about a seaman they both knew called Child, asking him if he thought him 'a man of courage and secrecy'. Captain Atkins had replied that Child had behaved himself very well at sea, so far as he knew. At this the clerk had bid him send Child to Mr Secretary Pepys. He had stressed that the sailor should not come to him, Samuel Atkins, 'for that he would not be seen to know anything of it'. The captain had seen Child the next day at the Three Tobacco Pipes in Holborn, and had sent him to Pepys. The next time he had seen Child after that, the seaman had tried to persuade him to join him in 'the murder of a man'. Captain

Atkins added that the discovery of the Popish Plot had brought about the difference between Pepys and Godfrey.[4]

Samuel Atkins was arrested on the evening of 1 November and hauled before the Lords Committee, then sitting at the Marquis of Winchester's house at Lincoln's Inn Fields. Lord Shaftesbury was there with Winchester, the Duke of Buckingham, Halifax, Essex, Compton the Bishop of London and Sir Philip Howard. Shaftesbury began the interrogation.[5]

'Pray, Mr Samuel Atkins,' he said, 'do you know one Mr or Captain Charles Atkins?'

'Yes, my lord,' said the clerk.

'How long have you known him?'

'About two or three years, I think.'

'Are you related?'

'No, my lord, only for name's sake have called cousins.'

'Do you know, or believe, he has any reason to do you a prejudice?'

'No, my lord, I know of none, nor ever gave him occasion to have any.'

'Did you ever tell him,' pursued Shaftesbury, 'on discourse about the Plot, that there was no kindness – or want of friendship I think it was – betwixt Mr Pepys and Sir Edmund Berry Godfrey?'

'No, my lord,' said Atkins, perceiving at last the reason for his arrest. 'I never mentioned Sir Edmund Berry Godfrey's name to him in my whole life, upon any occasion that I remember, nor ever talked with him about the Plot.'

'Do you know one Child?' interrupted Essex.

'No, my lord. I have heard of such a man's being concerned in the victualling of the navy, but to my knowledge never saw him.'

'No, no,' said Essex irritably, 'this is another sort of a man and one whom you will be found to know very well.'

'My lord,' replied Atkins composedly, 'if upon seeing him I shall so, I shall not stick to own it.'

Child was then called in and made to stand before Atkins.

'Now, pray,' said Essex, 'don't you know this man?'

'No, sir, I never saw him in my life, to my remembrance.'

'No!' echoed Essex. 'What say you, Child? Don't you know him?'

'No, my lord,' said the bewildered sailor. 'I never saw him in my life.'

Child was dismissed and Captain Atkins brought into the room.

116

The captain repeated the story he had told already to Coventry, the Privy Council and Sir Philip Howard. Samuel Atkins denied all he said.

'You know, Mr Atkins,' said the captain, directly addressing the clerk for the first time, 'this discourse was between us in the Lords Room at Derby House, in the window.'

'Captain Atkins,' said the clerk, 'God, your conscience and I know it is notoriously untrue.' He then reminded the captain that the only incident of note from their last meeting was he, the captain, asking Samuel for the loan of a crown, and the coin being willingly handed over.

'Come, come Mr Atkins,' said inquisitor Shaftesbury, 'you are a seeming hopeful young man, and for aught I see, a very ingenious one. Captain Atkins has sworn this positively against you, to whom he bears no prejudice or malice, but has acknowledged several obligations from you.' He paused and looked directly at Atkins. 'And to tell you truly,' continued the great lord, 'I do not think he has wit enough to invent such a lie. Be ingenious, pr'ythee, with us, and confess what you said.'

But Samuel was not to be moved. Then, challenged by Shaftesbury to prove the captain a rascal, he told how Captain Atkins had been relieved of his command after defying orders and surrendering his ship of war to Algerian corsairs in 1676.

Shaftesbury quickly changed the subject. 'Pray, Mr Atkins, what religion are you of?'

'A Protestant, sir, and my whole family ever so.'

'Did you ever receive the sacrament, or take the oaths?'

'No, sir, but was under an intention to do it on Sunday next.'

'It is indeed time,' struck in Essex.

'Now I am sure you won't do it,' said Shaftesbury. 'You can't forgive Captain Atkins?'

'Yes, my lord,' replied Samuel, 'I assure you I can and do. And to show it to you, I also remit to him the money he owes me, about fifty shillings, and am ready to receive the sacrament with a clean conscience. I confess I have not done it, as not thinking myself obliged by any employment I had to do it, and many thousands of my age – good Protestants – will be found not to have done it.'

'How long have you lived with Mr Pepys?' asked Shaftesbury.

'Four years last August.'

'How old are you?'

'Twenty-one years, the twenty-ninth of that month.'

'Where did you live before you came to Mr Pepys?'

'I lived, sir, formerly with Commissioner Middleton.'

'Then I am sure he was a Protestant. But now you are brought into business, and have access to St James's. 'Tis to be feared you may be otherwise, for we are apt to suspect people inclining to the sea.'

For all the old weasel's persistence, Samuel Atkins would not be budged. 'I never had temptation from within or without to alter my religion, and hope to God I never shall,' he said.

The Duke of Buckingham then moved towards him from the other side of the room. 'Well, Mr Atkins,' said the Duke, 'I never saw you before that I remember, but I swear you are an ingenious man.' He looked threateningly into Samuel's eyes, and placing a finger upon his own forehead, continued, 'I see the great workings of your brain, and would gladly, for your own sake, have you declare to us what you know of this matter.'

One after another the lords of the committee urged him to confess to the charges laid against him by Captain Atkins, stressing that a confession could only do him good, but that obstinacy could bring nothing but sorrow. But Samuel Atkins, like his master, was armed so strong in honesty that their threats passed by him as the idle wind, which he feared but respected not. Presently, both he and Captain Atkins were asked to withdraw. A short while later Samuel was called in again. Shaftesbury, doubtless imagining he would more likely get what he wanted from the young man by subtler methods than overt threats, had now assumed the role of Dutch uncle.

'Mr Atkins,' he said, 'truly we are, every lord of this committee, very sorry to be thus plain with you, but here being so positive an oath against you, we cannot answer to the Parliament the doing less than committing you to Newgate.'

Newgate! The very word made Samuel shudder.

'What your lordships please,' he said, with far greater confidence than he felt. 'If you send me to be hanged, I can say no more or otherwise.'[6]

Captain Richardson, keeper of Newgate, was summoned and handed a warrant:

> You are herewith to receive the body of Mr Samuel Atkins, for suspicion of Felony, in concealing the murder of Sir Edmundbury Godfrey, and him safely to keep, until he shall be thence delivered by due course of law: and for so doing, this shall be your warrant

sufficient. Given under our hands and seals this 1st day of Nov. 1678.

[signed] Buckingham
Winchester
P. Howard[7]

And so Atkins arrived at Newgate, where he was locked in a room of Captain Richardson's house. He was allowed neither to write nor receive visitors.[8]

On 6 November, after six days of solitary confinement, Atkins sent a message to the lords of the committee that he should like to appear before them at their next meeting. The lords wasted no time, and the prisoner was conveyed to them at their new venue in the Lord Privy Seal's chamber near the Parliament House the same day. Atkins was about to succumb, they were sure. The downfall of Pepys was in sight. The days of James as heir to the throne were numbered.[9]

'Well, Mr Atkins,' beamed Lord Halifax when Samuel entered the room, 'we hope you have considered of this business, and are ready to give us some light in it.'

'My lord, I have well indeed considered of it, and I hope am prepared to show your lordships that nothing is to be expected from me, and so my liberty will not be denied me.' He again pleaded his innocence of all that Captain Atkins accused him.

'Why, Mr Atkins,' said Lord Shaftesbury, 'Captain Atkins declares to us he has much *more* against you, and several other circumstances, by which, he says, you'll appear the worst man living.'

Samuel asked for his accuser to be sent for, which was done. After the captain had arrived, Samuel turned to the lords and asked what would happen if he perjured himself by confessing.

'Nay, nay,' said Shaftesbury, quick as a flash, 'leave us to make the use of it. Do you but confess. You shall be safe, and we'll apply it.'

But in Samuel Atkins they were dealing with a lad born in Cromwell's puritan days, brought up to regard lying as a deadly sin. 'My lord,' he said in anguish, 'I can't do it. I hope I never shall tell a lie to any man's prejudice, though I meet with ne'er so great danger.'

Shaftesbury rounded suddenly on the captain. 'Come, Captain Atkins,' he said. 'Confess truly and ingenuously. Have you belied Mr Atkins or no?'

The captain became very white, but the lords pretended not to notice. Recovering himself, the captain again swore to the truth of his statements, and Samuel was presently returned to prison.[10]

On Friday morning, 8 November, Captain Richardson entered Samuel's room with Captain Atkins. The prisoner leapt from his bed, bade them good morrow, and begged Richardson not to leave him alone with the captain lest he should swear more lies against him. But the lords had instructed Richardson to leave them alone, and he went downstairs. As the door closed behind him, Captain Atkins turned violently to Samuel, wringing his hands and crying, 'Oh! Mr Atkins, we are both undone!'*

'How undone?' asked the clerk.

'Oh, Lord! There's a man come to town last night. He lay at Mr Secretary Williamson's, was examined two hours by the King, and he has sworn positively against you that you were . . . at the murder of Sir E. Godfrey.'

'Well,' said Samuel miserably, 'God bless him.'

The captain said he did not know the stranger's name, but urged Samuel to confess and save his own life before it was too late.

'Pray,' said Samuel, 'why don't you as well ask me to forego my salvation? A thousand deaths shall not extort a lie from me.'[11]

The same afternoon, Samuel Atkins was carried once more before the lords. There, on the other side of the table, was the devil who had ridden by night to damn him.

The stranger, wearing a black periwig and a campaign coat, looked steadfastly at the prisoner. He had ridden hard to earn the £500 reward offered to the discoverer of Godfrey's murderers, and nothing so slight as the life of Samuel Atkins was going to deprive him of it.[12]

4: God Almighty on Horseback

In Victorian times, rewards for information leading to the capture of murderers were abolished because villains were committing crimes purely to betray their accomplices and claim the reward. The whole system of rewards was riddled with iniquity, and frequently large rewards attracted imaginative rogues who knew

---

* How the captain thought *he* was undone it is hard to see.

120

nothing of the crime in question but proved well able to line their purses with bogus 'discoveries'. In Godfrey's day the government had little choice but to bribe criminals with promises of a free pardon and money to turn King's Evidence. Detection of crime was in such an infant state that in many cases the only real hope of obtaining a conviction was the testimony of someone involved – or someone proficient enough in the art of lying to convince a court he had been involved.

Such a man was the stranger in the black periwig. His name, Atkins learned, was William Bedloe. Bedloe knew nothing of the real fate of Sir Edmund Berry Godfrey, but when the royal proclamations offering the small fortune of £500 reached his ears, it seemed too good an opportunity to miss. He had written to Secretary of State Henry Coventry on Wednesday, 30 October from Bristol, offering to clear up the mystery of Godfrey's murder and name the guilty parties.[1]

Bedloe had already made a brief appearance in the early scenes of the drama. It was he, along with his brother James, who had swindled Titus Oates of ten pieces of eight while the latter was at the Jesuit college at Valladolid. Bedloe was a consummate confidence trickster. He had roamed Europe cheating, robbing and living by his wits for many years. He often posed as an English army captain or travelling nobleman and had been in prison in England, France and Spain for a variety of crimes. In Normandy he had been sentenced to death for robbery, but cheated the executioner by escaping from prison before the appointed day. Shortly before the outbreak of the Plot he had been languishing in Newgate.[2]

Bedloe was a blackguard. He had a 'villainous countenance, harsh and forbidding, full of malice and revenge . . . beetle brows, hard mouth, and savage eyes'. His portrait shows him 'unscrupulous, unrelenting, as he in later life became. Dressed in finery beyond his station, his arrogance is as self-evident as his malice.' In his disregard for all values but those which served his own ends he was as black as Oates. It could indeed be argued that Oates's evil was the product of mental illness and so, perhaps, more understandable than the blatant criminality of Bedloe. But in Bedloe's character there seems more colour, more lightness and swagger than in the deadly earnest wickedness of Oates. A blackguard, yes. But at least an entertainer too.[3]

One story, never before told by chroniclers of the Godfrey case, illustrates this roguish flamboyance. It appears in a memorandum by one Colonel J. Jeffrys, among the papers of the Marquis of Ormond at Kilkenny Castle. According to Jeffrys, Bedloe was a fiddler's son from Chepstow. Shortly before his appearance in London to 'discover' Godfrey's murderers, Bedloe had been to Brecon 'in a very handsome habit and equipage'. Acting the nobleman as usual, Bedloe was royally entertained by the gentlemen of Brecon. From there he travelled into Carmarthenshire, and eventually to the house of Sir Richard Rudd. He rode up to the gate of the knight's house and, without deigning to dismount from his horse, demanded of a servant whether or not Sir Richard was at home. The servant said he was, and asked to know who would speak with him.

'Tell him,' said Bedloe, 'God Almighty is here.'

The servant, 'not a little wondring at the answer', went in to speak to his master.

> All this while the stranger sate on horseback at the gate. When Sir Richard came to the doore, Mr Beddoes [sic] told him that he had heard he was an honest hospitable gentleman, and that he was (though a stranger) come to wayte upon him. Sir Richard desired him to alight and walk in, which he did. After some time and discourse, wherein he made frequent mention of Middlesex, Rochester, and Tidley, with such a familiarity, and giveing them noe other addition to their names, as if he had been some great man of birth, chardg, and education. In the midst of their discours, Sir Rice Rudd receivs his post letters, and with them a gazzett, wherein there was an advertisement of the losse of a horse, with a description of the person who was suspected to have stolen this horse. While Sir Rice was reading this advertisement, he sometimes cast his eye upon his guest, then reads, then again takes of his eye, and observs how the character and the stranger agreed. Mr Beddoes observing this, makes an apology to goe out of doores, calls for his horses, and away he goes that night (as they heard) towards Pembrokeshire.[4]

The swindler was not heard of again by his victims in Wales until they learnt of his appearance in London, with his imaginary tale of inside knowledge about the murder of Justice Godfrey.

Bedloe's first letter to Coventry has been lost, but the next day, 31 October, he followed it up with another, also from Bristol:

> Right Hon:
> by ye last post I did give yr Hon. an account of a grate parte of this Horrid desinge [design], that it did ly in my hands to discover some of the parties which have no small part in it and some whose power is to grate [too great] to be concealed any longer. If yr Lordship will give a direction to the Mayor of Bristoll to give privitly an

order to apeare at the Councill Board where I will declare what I dare not trust in a letter. I shall always be found at Mr Jones in Broad Street in Bristoll to attend yr order and to show my self a most loyall subject to his Maiestye and yr Hon.

Most Humble servant
W^m: Bedloe

Coventry arranged for him to be brought to London, and on 7 November he was examined by the Privy Council and the King himself. His story was a gallimaufry of rumour and invention presented as personal experience. The conjecture that Godfrey had been murdered by the Papists at Somerset House, first reported on the morning after his disappearance, had become widespread. Bedloe made it the core of his pretended discovery. He had come to town with the names of three unknown Papists whom he planned to accuse. When he arrived, he heard that Samuel Atkins had been arrested and swiftly wrote him into the story. Before Atkins was brought from Newgate on the afternoon of 8 November, Bedloe gave his full story to the Lords Committee.[5]

His involvement in the case had begun, he said, about the beginning of October. Two Jesuits, Le Phaire and Walsh, had offered him £4,000 'if he would be one of the four or six that should kill a man that was a great obstacle to their design'. Bedloe had agreed. On the day before Sir Edmund had disappeared, Bedloe and Le Phaire had met about four o'clock in Grays Inn Walks, agreeing before they parted to meet again in twenty-four hours to carry out the murder. But Bedloe, 'not liking the design', had failed to turn up.[6]

On Sunday night, after the disappearance, he encountered Le Phaire by accident at the entrance to Red Lion Court off Fleet Street. The Jesuit promptly enlisted him to help 'in some other special business', and arranged to see him at the same hour on Monday night at the Palsgrave's Head tavern. Le Phaire asked him pointedly not to let them down again. Between eight and nine o'clock on Monday night, Bedloe met Le Phaire in the cloister of the court at Somerset House, having earlier left a message at the Palsgrave's Head changing their rendezvous. They waited together about half an hour, Le Phaire telling Bedloe 'how much the Church of Rome and the Pope were obliged to him, and what rewards he should have for his secrecy and fidelity to them'. At last he asked Bedloe to walk with him into the middle of the court so that he could speak without being overheard.[7]

'The person you were to have killed is killed,' he whispered. 'His body lies in Somerset House.' He then promised him half the original reward if he would help carry the body 'to a place where they had chose to lay him'.[8]

Bedloe told the committee that he had asked the names of the people who would be with him on the mission. Le Phaire named himself; Walsh; a servant of Lord Belasyse; 'one that he had often seen in the queen's chapel'; and Samuel Atkins. Then he led the informer through a dark entry into Somerset House, where he knocked softly with his finger on the door of a room. Le Phaire led Bedloe into the room, which was in darkness. Pulling a lantern from under his coat, he 'showed a small light in the room' and Bedloe saw four men. He recognized Walsh and the nameless worker in the chapel. The other two told them they were Lord Belasyse's gentleman and Mr Atkins, clerk to Mr Pepys. A dark object lay beneath a cloak on a table. The conspirators decided to carry the body out of Somerset House in a sedan chair at eleven o'clock that night and take it to the corner of Clarendon House. There they would transfer it to a coach and carry it to Primrose Hill. Then the cloak was thrown from the body.[9]

'Who is it?' asked Bedloe.

The murderers told him that it was 'an old man that belonged to a person of quality, who had taken some examinations tending to the discovery of their design'. Bedloe asked why they had not killed the person of quality himself. They said this man had Oates's depositions in his own custody, and their intention had been to steal them from him. Then, when Oates should testify again about the Popish Plot, his new story was bound to differ from the first. The murderers could then step forward with the papers they had taken from Justice Godfrey and show that Oates had lied. Bedloe was satisfied, he told the committee, and had asked the Jesuits where they had killed Godfrey. 'At Somerset House,' someone had replied.[10]

At this, he said, he had begged them to excuse him for half an hour, and so made his escape. But yet again, the next day, he encountered Le Phaire, this time in Lincoln's Inn Fields. They went together into the Greyhound tavern in Fleet Street. Le Phaire put his cane up to his nose and reproached Bedloe for not keeping his promise to return and help them. Bedloe replied that he had not been willing to help, for he knew the identity of the dead man.

'Who is it?' asked Le Phaire.

'It is Justice Godfrey,' replied Bedloe.

The Jesuit admitted that he was correct. He then said that he was prepared to forgive's Bedloe's vacillation if he now assured him of his fidelity. He then told him how the murder had been committed.[11]

Le Phaire, Walsh and the servant of Lord Belasyse had met Godfrey near the King's Head in the Strand before five o'clock on the evening of the day he disappeared. They told him that if he would 'please to go with them so far as Strand Bridge, they would bring him to a place near St Clement's Church, where there were a company met, principal plotters of that design against the King'. They told the Justice that he could march in and seize both the plotters and their papers.

But Godfrey had replied that he would not go himself, but would send a constable with a warrant. The would-be murderers had argued that delay could ruin the plan, and if he went along to Strand Bridge immediately, one of them would call a constable. Godfrey had agreed, and had walked as far as Somerset House with them. They had then suggested he should walk inside Somerset House, where he would be less likely to be seen than in the street. Two of the villains had then gone inside with Sir Edmund, and the third had pretended to go for a constable.

'And when they had walked a turn or two in the court,' continued Bedloe, 'two more persons came forth, and showed him into a room. And when they had him secure there, they held a pistol to him, threatening, if he made a noise, they would shoot him, but if he would answer their expectations they would do him no harm.'

They had asked him to send for Oates's examinations. But he could not, he had said, because he had sent them to Whitehall. He had refused to answer any further questions. Suddenly, 'they seized him, and stifled him with a pillow, and so they thought he had been dead. But coming into the room some time after, they found him struggling, and then they strangled him with a long cravat.'[12]

Bedloe asked Le Phaire why they had carried the body into the fields. He answered that they had 'made a wound in the body and laid his sword nearby so that it would seem he had committed suicide'.[13]

Bedloe's tale was patently false. But it was just the sort of testimony the Whig lords of the committee were searching for. By placing the blame so certainly upon the Papists, their political war against the Duke of York and popery in general would be enormously strengthened. Further, Bedloe had taken care to name Atkins as one of the accessories to the murder. Atkins's adamantine refusal to confess anything had hitherto been a problem. There had been, after all, only Captain Atkins's word against his. But now there was a new witness who swore the same as the worthy captain.

The Plot-mongers were in business.

5: The Alibi

Bedloe was not as brazen a liar as Oates. He always left himself freedom to manoeuvre. After Samuel Atkins entered the room at the Lord Privy Seal's house, the informer came from behind the table and approached him. He looked earnestly into the clerk's face and saluted him.[1]

'Mr Atkins,' said Lord Shaftesbury when Bedloe had returned to his former position, 'do you know this gentleman?'

'No, my lord, I don't know I ever saw him in my life.'

Bedloe was not ready to commit himself to a positive identification in case Atkins should yet claim an alibi and the £500 reward slip from his grasp.

'I believe, sir,' said Bedloe, 'I have seen you somewhere, I think, but I cannot tell where: I don't, indeed, remember your face.'

'Is this the man, Mr Bedloe?' said Buckingham, pointing to Atkins.

'My lord, I can't swear this is he. 'Twas a young man, and he told me his name was Atkins, a clerk belonging to Derby House, but I cannot swear this is the same person.'

The Bishop of London then spoke for the first time: 'Where were you, Mr Atkins, on Monday the 14th of October last, between nine and ten at night?'

'I can't well remember, my lord, but I suppose at home, for I am seldom out at that time of night.'

'Were you in the Pall Mall, or that way, that you remember?' asked the bishop.

'No, my lord,' said Atkins, 'I believe verily not.'[2]

Bedloe was then asked to withdraw. When he had gone, Shaftesbury bore down on Atkins. 'Mr Atkins,' he said, 'if you are innocent, you're the most unfortunate wretch living. Pray attend to what I say. I assure you 'tis good news for you.'[3]

Samuel looked at the old warrior. He knew he could expect no favours. My lord of Shaftesbury was

> . . . a politician
> With more heads than a beast in vision,
> And more intrigues in every one
> Than all the whores of Babylon.[4]

Atkins knew that Shaftesbury, in the Plot crisis as in all the other storms he had ridden and turned to his own advantage, would

> . . . to the utmost do his best
> To save himself and hang the rest.[5]

'There remains but one way in the world to save thy life', said Shaftesbury, 'and that I would have you make use of. And you may do it without injury to yourself, if you will. Confess all you know, and make a discovery of this matter, and your life shall be saved.'[6]

His bribes were useless. Atkins again protested his innocence and refused to utter a single lie, whatever the price of truth.

'Then I tell you what, Mr Atkins,' spat Shaftesbury. 'Since you are so gallant, I assure you, you'll either be hanged or knighted. If the Papists rise and cut our throats, you'll be knighted. If not, you'll be hanged.'[7]

He stressed how the evidence was building up against him – the testimony of Captain Atkins, the evidence of Bedloe. It was enough, Shaftesbury thought, for a jury to find him guilty. 'And another thing there is,' added the earl quickly. 'There are several others, well known to this Mr Bedloe to have been concerned in it.'

'And are here in the house in custody,' lied Buckingham.

'And,' cut in Shaftesbury, 'if one of those swear you were in it, all the world cannot save you.'

'My lord,' said Atkins in desperation, 'my prayers are and shall be that one person may but be detected who was really in the murder, and I am sure I shall be acquitted.'

'Oh, he'll confess nothing. He expects a pardon,' said Buckingham.

'I'll secure him from that, I warrant you,' said Shaftesbury. 'There's three hundred to one.'

'My lord,' said Atkins, 'I expect no pardon, but desire death when I am found to deserve it. I have nothing to trust to but my innocence, next to the goodness and justice of God Almighty, to whom I commit myself.'[8]

There was nothing more to say. Atkins was returned in irons to Newgate. He slept in Captain Richardson's house once again that Friday night, but was removed into solitary confinement in the Press Yard of Newgate on Saturday morning. Bedloe appeared before the House of Commons, and swore once again that he had seen Atkins, by the light of a dark lantern, standing over the body of Sir Edmund Godfrey at Somerset House. Atkins's leg irons were not removed until Monday, when his first accuser, Captain Atkins, paid him another visit. The captain told the prisoner of Bedloe's evidence before the Commons, and urged him again to confess.[9]

'Pray, Captain Atkins,' said Samuel with his customary politeness, 'who is this man?'

'Why,' said the captain, 'his name is Bedloe.'

'Who is he, pray? Is he a man of any good fame?'

'No,' said the perjurer. 'I think of no very good fame.'

'Do you know him, pray?'

'Yes. I have known him three or four months, but have no very great acquaintance with him.'

Samuel made a mental note that on his previous visit, the captain had told him he had seen Bedloe only once before in his life.

'I do not believe a word he says,' admitted the captain. 'They are all shams. He is certainly hired by those that did it.'

'Do you think so?'

He nodded and took his leave, pausing only to tell the hapless clerk that he would soon be called before the lords once more.[10]

On Tuesday, 12 November four of Shaftesbury's Whig followers from the Commons visited Atkins. The young clerk recognized two of them as Colonel John Birch and William Sacheverell, old enemies of Samuel Pepys. They interrogated him about his movements on 12, 13 and 14 October. He could not remember how or where he had spent that weekend, but assured them that he would cudgel his memory until the details returned.[11]

Once more alone in his cell, Atkins 'considered, and brought to my perfect remembrance, how I had passed almost every hour of those aforesaid three days'.[12]

Taking advantage of his master's absence at Newmarket, he had indulged in some loose living. On 14 October, the day Bedloe claimed to have seen him by the body at Somerset House, Atkins had sent a message to Captain Vittells, a seafaring friend whose

128

yacht the *Catherine* was moored at Greenwich. At half past four that afternoon Atkins arrived in Greenwich with two girl-friends. Captain Vittells took his guests down to his cabin and they broke a bottle of wine. As the wine was 'good and just come from beyond the seas', they refilled their glasses. They were still drinking at seven, when Atkins decided they were all having a thoroughly agreeable time, so sent away the boatman waiting for him. The debauch, details of which, beyond the drinking, were never described, continued until nearly half-past ten. By then Atkins was very drunk, and Vittells placed him and the two girls into a boat. They were all 'very much fuddled' as four of the *Catherine*'s sailors rowed them along the Thames towards home. The tide was against them, and so strong that they had to abandon a plan to land near London Bridge. Instead, the seamen deposited the reeling threesome at Billingsgate at half-past eleven. 'Much in drink', Atkins boarded a coach with the girls and spent the night in bed with one of them, Sarah Williams.[13]

Atkins, and very soon Pepys, realized that the witnesses who could be brought to testify in the clerk's favour – including Vittells, the four seamen and the two girls – would seriously shake the dubious and uncertain testimony of Bedloe and Captain Atkins. Pepys, only too well aware of the peril in which he himself would stand if things went badly for Atkins, devoted the energies earlier spent on hunting 'Godfrey' to preparing a defence for his clerk.

Atkins's solitary confinement continued until 21 November. On the 19th, he was told to dress and prepare for his trial at the King's Bench Bar, and a leg iron was attached to him. But the order was a mistake. The trial on the 19th was of William Staley, another poor victim of the raging Plot. On Thursday the 21st he was visited by his sister and a lawyer called Hayes. In his own words, they brought him 'ill news of what Bedlow had sworn against me, and the little hopes there remained of saving my life, but that they were doing all they could for me, towards the making my defence, and so shewed me a paper they had drawn up'. It was a collection of statements, obtained under the supervision of Pepys, by those very witnesses with whom Atkins had spent his time on the day in question. The statements 'agreed with what I had done in my memory in substance, and different in no essential circumstance'.[14]

He was then allowed pen and ink to prepare his own account of his doings on the three days in October. The writing was taken from him and given to the Lords Committee.[15]

Shaftesbury and his Whigs realized their dilemma. With an alibi such as Atkins's it would be near to impossible to obtain a conviction. They let the matter ride, putting off yet again the young man's trial.

On 13 December a new twist in the case diverted the Plot-mongers' attention from both Atkins and Pepys. And although Atkins remained in prison until early February, his death was no longer a necessity for the successful pursuit of the exclusion plan.[16]

A new and more useful 'discoverer' had been found.

6: Terror

Throughout Atkins's ordeal the general hysteria continued to mount. The careful management of the Plot by the Whigs, and the propaganda spread by the Green Ribboners kept the London mob at fever pitch.

On the day of Atkins's arrest there had been a proclamation ordering all recusants to depart ten miles from London. The seizure of Catholics continued all through November, with Oates and Bedloe swearing new falsehoods every day before the various Plot committees and both houses of Parliament. Bedloe had not restricted himself to the murder of Godfrey. He had also claimed knowledge of the wider conspiracy. Imitating the Saviour of the Nation himself, he claimed to have been employed as a courier by the Jesuits. By opening the conspirators' letters, he said, he had learned of an army of twenty thousand Papists which would come from Spain, and with Lord Powis at their head take Chepstow Castle. Twenty thousand more would sail to Bridlington Bay from Flanders and join Lord Belasyse. Other equally fantastic tales were fed daily to the credulous population.[1]

There was renewed panic when a second London magistrate, John Powell, disappeared from his home. No one doubted that he too had been abducted and murdered by Papists. The fact that he was soon discovered, hiding from creditors, received little public-ity.[2]

The lords examining the murder of Godfrey used the slenderest clues to keep public fury directed at the Catholics. Statements like the following are typical of those taken in all seriousness by the lords:

Margaret Jones . . . sayd that one Mrs Anne Pye, living in Shandois Street at Mr Brighams ye Kings Coach maker, told this Deponent last night that one Mrs Eliz: Crawley living over against her, ye sd Mrs An. Pye in ye same street at one Mr Turners a shoemaker, said, that a Papist told her that in a little roome behind ye Altar she saw Sr Edmund Bury Godfrey.

[signed] Margaret Jones[3]

The committee ordered the arrest of a Hackney coachman called Francis Corall after Mathias Fowler, a resident of the Half Moon Tavern in Cheapside, had come to them with a new version of the removal of Godfrey's corpse from London.[4]

Corall, driver of Hackney coach number 56, was alleged to have been approached by four gentlemen with their swords drawn near St Clement's Church in the Strand. The men asked him to go with them with his coach, 'but he told them his axle tree was broke'. They then took another Hackney coach, two of them climbing inside and two on top. One of the men on top blindfolded the driver and the other drove the coach. The coachman waylaid by the men, claimed Fowler, had later told Corall 'that he found a great weight behind his Coach and asked what it was and they asked what was that to him. He answered that it would break his coach and kill his horses. They answered they would pay for them. And if he made any noise or disturbance they would pistol him.' The body of Godfrey had then been tied behind the coach 'with sticks'. According to the third-hand story, 'the coachman was gone two hours and they gave him twelve shillings'.[5]

Nothing came of the matter. It proved useless as propaganda, and so was consigned to the growing pile of confused and confusing statements pouring in from all quarters.[6]

The examination of Edward Coleman and other Catholic prisoners continued throughout November. The gaols were now bursting with popish inmates. On 20 November a new Test Act was passed, which demanded a full denial of transubstantiation and the invocation of the saints not only by all office holders, but also by the members of both houses of Parliament. Catholics were therefore officially excluded from the Lords and Commons. Despite the furious support for the Bill in the Commons, the Lords still managed to include an amendment that excepted the Duke of York. James still had his supporters, but they were growing weaker almost by the day.

The day after the passing of the Act, the courts passed the Plot's first sentence of death. The victim was William Staley, son of a Catholic banker at Covent Garden. On the morning of 14 November Staley had been overheard talking in French at the Black Lion in King Street. As he supped ale and roast beef with his companion, an elderly Frenchman called Fromante, he was observed to become heated. 'The King,' he declared, 'is a great heretic and the greatest rogue in the world.' Then, said the man who informed against him, he had said, 'I would kill him myself.'

At the trial, Staley claimed that he had in reality said, 'I would kill myself.' Even though the difference between the two statements is a mere single letter – Je *le* tuerais moi-même instead of Je *me* tuerais moi-même – the Attorney General pointed out that a declaration of possible suicide was hardly consistent with the rest of the reported conversation. It was high treason to utter the sentiments attributed to Staley. He was found guilty and sentenced to a traitor's death.[7]

Things were going well for Oates and Bedloe. On 24 November Oates made his most daring accusation so far. The Queen of England herself, he told the King in a private audience, had been up to her neck in the conspiracy against his life. Oates claimed that during a visit to Somerset House he had overheard Catherine exclaim that 'she would not take these affronts any longer that had been done unto her, but would revenge the violation of her bed.'[8]

On the 26th William Staley was hanged, drawn and quartered at Tyburn. The method of execution in this and all the cases that followed was unvarying, and barbaric in the extreme. The condemned were dragged from their prison to the place of execution on a hurdle or rough sledge. Any abuse, physical or verbal, which the mob wished to hurl at them went uncensured. At Tyburn, where Marble Arch now stands, they were hanged by the neck, but cut down before they lost consciousness. Their genitals were then cut off and their bowels were taken out and burnt in front of their eyes. Finally, the head was severed from the body and the body cut into four quarters. After pronouncing the sentence in all its detail, the judge would add, 'And the God of infinite mercy be merciful to your soul.'[9]

Staley denied his guilt to the end.[10]

Edward Coleman was brought to the King's Bench bar on Wednesday, 27 November. The two letters containing his most indiscreet references to the ascendency of catholicism were read out, and both Oates and Bedloe gave evidence against him. Oates told the court that he had known Coleman personally, and had carried letters from him to the Jesuit college at St Omers. He had also acted as messenger between Coleman and Père La Chaise, the French King's confessor. In one letter Coleman had thanked La Chaise for a promise of £10,000 to be used in bringing about the King's murder.[11]

Coleman reminded the court that when faced with him in the Council chamber, Oates had told the King that he had never seen him before, yet 'he is extremely well acquainted with me now, and hath a world of intimacy'.[12]

Oates was unperturbed. His great mouth opened and attributed his mistake before the King and Council to the poor light in the council chamber. 'My sight was bad by candle light,' he said, 'and candle light alters the sight much. But when I heard him speak I could have sworn it was he, but it was not then my business. I cannot see a great way by candle light.'[13]

With or without Oates's testimony, the letters found in Coleman's deal box were enough to condemn him. He was found guilty and sentenced to death.[14]

At the bar of the House of Commons on Thursday, Bedloe supported Oates in his accusation of the Queen. He had been at Somerset House in October, he told members, and overheard Catherine plotting her husband's death with Coleman, Lord Belasyse, some Jesuits and two French priests. Oates then swept into the Commons. In his high, affected voice he declared, 'I, Taitus Oates, accuause Caatharane, Quain of Angland, of Haigh Traison!'[15]

The word of the two worst liars in England was enough to bring the Commons screaming for the removal of the Queen and her entire household. The Lords were asked to back the motion, but reacted less hysterically and agreed only to examine Oates and Bedloe on their latest accusation. Both discoverers appeared at the bar of the House of Lords next morning.[16]

Oates was asked to explain why he had told the Lords on 31 October that he had no one else to accuse, when he now came with this new accusation. He replied that their lordships had misunderstood him. What he had meant was that he had no further members of the House of Lords to accuse. His testimony was questioned, too, over a new allegation that Sir George Wakeman had written in a letter of the Queen's complicity in the murder plot. Why had he not mentioned this letter in his original accusation of Wakeman? Titus was surprised by the Lords' sudden incredulity. He resorted to a spur-of-the-moment excuse: at the time of the first accusation he had been so exhausted from his two nights of hunting down the popish dogs that the Queen's guilt had slipped his memory. It was a minor setback. The Lords predictably refused to countenance the Commons vote to remove the Queen. But at the instigation of their Whig members, they voted an address for the arrest of all Papists in England.[17]

Edward Coleman was hanged, drawn and quartered on 3 December. Two days later the five Catholic lords in the Tower were impeached, and on 17 December William Ireland, Thomas Pickering and John Grove were tried for conspiring to murder the King. They were found guilty and sentenced to death.[18]

7: Evil Doings at the Water-Gate

Sir Edmund Godfrey's murder was now two months old, but still no progress had been made in bringing his killers to justice.

The third great discoverer of the murder, whose appearance diverted attention from the hapless Samuel Atkins, stepped on to the scene four days before Christmas. His name was Miles Prance or Praunce, a Roman Catholic silversmith living at Covent Garden. Prance, a craftsman of repute, had received commissions from both the Jesuits and the Queen herself. He was acquainted with several of the Jesuits executed for their alleged involvement in the Plot. After the trial of Ireland, Pickering and Grove, he was heard in a coffee house to say that they 'were very honest men'. It was enough in that taut atmosphere to throw suspicion upon him. Two Protestants who shared his lodgings came forward with the story that Prance had been absent from home for three nights about the time of Godfrey's disappearance. The Privy Council issued a warrant for his arrest and he was conveyed to Whitehall.[1]

On the morning of 21 December he was taken to the lobby of the House of Commons to await examination by the Commons Plot committee. Shortly afterwards Bedloe came in. Seeing Prance, the informer called out in mock astonishment, 'This is one of the rogues that I saw with a dark lantern about the body of Sir Edmund Berry Godfrey, but he was then in a periwig.'[2]

There is little doubt that the encounter between Bedloe and Prance was engineered by the Plot-mongers. They badly needed a suspect to replace the obdurate Atkins. Here was a Papist already denounced on two counts. All that was lacking was a convincing falsehood by Bedloe to weave him into the story of Godfrey's murder. At Bedloe's order the guards dragged Prance away to interrogation by the Lords Committee. The lords saw Bedloe first. Sticking strictly to his first tale of Godfrey's murder, he neatly inserted Prance as 'the very same man that was at the carrying off of Sir E. Godfrey, whom he [Bedloe] took to be the officer that attended in the Queen's Chapel.' The gaps and uncertainties in the original story were now proving useful, allowing Bedloe to interpolate the new and apparently safe inventions as they occurred to him.[3]

Examined by the committee, Prance avowed he was a Protestant, having lately taken the Oath of Allegiance, but that he had previously been a Papist. He admitted that he had 'made several things' for Grove, Pickering and other Jesuits. He confessed that he had called them very honest men, but explained he had been drunk at the time. Realizing his danger after this indiscreet talk, he had remained indoors after dark ever since. He then made a fatal mistake. He swore that he could bring his own servants to witness that he had not stopped away from home during the previous two years, except for three nights about 12 October. This was a virtual admission of guilt of Godfrey's murder – but it was based on an error. It later transpired that Prance's absence from home had been in the week *before* Godfrey vanished. But by the time that was known, the Plot was in decline and three innocent men had been executed.[4]

In answer to Bedloe's statement that when he was standing over the magistrate's corpse he had been wearing a periwig, Prance told the committee that he had not worn a periwig 'for one hour these ten years'. His wife Mary's hair had been cut off a year before to make him a light flaxen periwig, but he had never worn it and it lay at his home.[5]

He denied knowing Le Phaire, Walsh or Pritchard, three of the men accused by Bedloe.[6]

At the end of the interrogation, Prance was sent 'close prisoner' to Newgate, where he was thrown into a horrible cell known as 'Little Ease' or the condemned hole. He remained there in irons for two days, during which he decided his best hope of survival was to join the ranks of the discoverers. He knew enough of Bedloe's story of the Somerset House murder and the ways of the Jesuits to spin a convincing yarn. He sent a message to the Lords Committee requesting a royal pardon, and promised in return 'a true and perfect discovery'. On Christmas Eve, emboldened by assurances that his life was safe, he was taken before the King and the Privy Council.[7]

Prance's story differed in almost every particular from Bedloe's. He told the council that about a fortnight before Godfrey's death an Irish priest called Gerald, who was a member of the household of the Venetian Ambassador, asked him to take part in a murder. The proposed victim was not at that stage named. About a week later Prance met with Gerald, another Irishman called Green who laid cushions in the chapel of Somerset House, and a man called Lawrence Hill. They told him the man they planned to kill was Sir Edmund Berry Godfrey, 'for that he was a great enemy to the Queen or her servants, and that he had used some Irishmen ill.' Gerald told Prance that they had been employed to do the deed by Lord Belasyse, and they had been promised a reward. Prance himself had a score to settle with Sir Edmund. About two years before, the magistrate had refused to allow his discharge after Prance had been brought before the Middlesex magistrates at Hicks' Hall for failing to carry out parish duties.* The silversmith readily agreed to help in the murder.[8]

'They had been watching him a week or a fortnight before his death,' said Prance. Green had called at Godfrey's house on the morning of his disappearance and asked the maid if he might see her master. Green, Gerald and Hill 'did dodge him from the house that morning to all the places he went to, until he came to his death'. The murder, Prance said, had taken place at Somerset House.[9]

The King ordered two privy councillors, the dukes of Monmouth and Ossory, to accompany Prance to Somerset House forthwith, so that he might relate the rest of his story in its actual setting. When they reached the palace, he took up the threads of his carefully contrived story.

Sir Edmund Godfrey had passed by St Clement's Church in the Strand about nine o'clock on the last night of his life. Gerald, Green and Hill stealthily dogged his steps as he moved along the unlighted road. Presently, the magistrate left the main thoroughfare and approached the Great Water-Gate of Somerset House. Hill had crept on ahead without Sir Edmund even suspecting his presence, and before the magistrate reached the wicket gate leading into Somerset House stable yard, Hill had dived inside. As

* See p. 32 above.

Godfrey passed moments later, Hill came out as if in search of help. Stopping Sir Edmund, he told him there were two men quarrelling within, and said they might soon desist if he intervened. He agreed, and passed through the wicket, Green and Gerald coming silently after.

'And down all went till they came to a bench that is at the bottom of the steep descent [of steps],' said Prance, indicating the very spot to the dukes.

Sitting on the bench, awaiting Godfrey's appearance, had been Prance himself, a Somerset House porter called Berry and an Irishman whose name Prance did not know. When Godfrey was about half way down the steps, Prance left the bench and ran to the wicket to keep watch. At the same moment Berry crossed from the bench to a flight of stone steps that led to the Upper Court. When Godfrey reached the bench, Green – who was close behind him – lunged forward with 'a large twisted handkerchief' in his hands. Before Godfrey could draw his sword, Green wound it around the magistrate's neck and they dragged him into a corner behind the bench. Green then 'thumped him on the breast and twisted his neck until he broke it.'

About fifteen minutes later, Prance came down from his post by the wicket and found that they had throttled Godfrey, 'but his body remained warm, and seemed hardly dead'. He later amended this part of the tale. When he laid his hand upon the corpse, he later swore, 'his legs tottered and shook, and then Green wrung his neck quite round'. Together the six men lifted the corpse and took it through a door, 'up several stairs into a long dark passage or gallery' that led to the Upper Court. They carried the body through a door in the left-hand wall of the passage. This led to a flight of eight stairs into another house adjoining the palace. The house was occupied by Dr Thomas Godden, chaplain and perceptor to the Queen. As a one-time servant of Godden, Hill also lived in the house. At the top of the eight steps they turned right into 'a little closet or square room'. There they sat the body upon the floor, its back against a bed. The body was left there for two days in Hill's care.

Prance told Monmouth and Ossory that by Monday night the murderers were so afraid of discovery that they determined to move the body. About nine or ten o'clock that night, Prance had been told later, Hill, Gerald, Green, Berry and the Irishman carried Godfrey's corpse back into Somerset House 'and into some room towards the garden'. Hill later took Prance to see the body there.

On Tuesday night it was again moved, this time 'into a room in the said gallery over against the first door, somewhat higher up towards the Court, the chamber belonging to some of the servants of Sir John Arundell'. Prance's account was impressively detailed. But then, his work had taken him frequently into Somerset House and it was an old trick to lend verisimilitude to an invented tale by setting it in places well known to the storyteller. The body remained in this chamber until nine or ten o'clock on Wednesday night, when the killers decided to take it back to the little closet where it had first been concealed. Prance arrived as the others were humping it up the eight stairs. Thinking Prance was a stranger, Hill and Berry instantly fled. Gerald, Green and the Irishman recognized him and stayed where they were. Prance helped them lift the body up the stairs to the closet.

After midnight Hill and Berry returned, now apprised of Prance's identity. Hill had obtained a sedan chair, which they placed in the long dark entry at the foot of the eight stairs. They carried the body down and sat it on the chair. Prance and Gerald carried the chair through the Upper Court, Berry the porter opening the gate and letting them out.

> And they rested not till they came to Covent Garden [said Monmouth and Ossory in their report to the Privy Council], where Greene [sic] and another Irishman took their turns, and so carried the sedan and body in it as far as the new Grecian Church in the Soho: and there Hill met them with a horse: Whereupon they took out the body, and, forcing open the legs, they set it upon the horse: Hill riding behind to keep the body up, while Greene, Gerald and the Irishman, went on to accompany him. Berry the porter did not depart from the gate: and the examinant Prance, fearing to be missed, returned home when the body was set on horseback: and the sedan, which was left in one of the new unfinished houses, they took up, and brought it home, as they came back.

Prance was 'very positive' as to the place where the murder was committed. He also led the two dukes unhesitatingly to the room in the adjoining house where, according to his version, the body was first laid. But he became confused when the lords asked him to take them to the room near the garden mentioned in his narrative:

> He led us to the corner of the piazza on the left hand, and so down a pair of stairs: and so far seemed to be assured that he had been led, and did think that he had passed through the great court below: but

when from thence we went up and down into several rooms, he seemed very doubtful, and could not ascertain the place.

He made the excuse that he had been to the room only once in his life, and on that occasion it had been dark with only Hill's lantern to cast an uncertain beam. Monmouth and Ossory made inquiries at Dr Godden's house adjoining Somerset House, which contained the closet. A maid told them that Lawrence Hill had been the doctor's servant for about seven years, and that he had continued to live there 'until Michaelmas last'.[10]

Green, Berry and Hill were arrested, Green being placed in the Gatehouse and the others in Newgate. Gerald, or Fitzgerald, or Girald, and Kelly were found to have fled. On 27 December the three prisoners were called before the Lords Committee.[11]

Hill swore that Prance's evidence was false, and that he had not seen Sir Edmund Godfrey since the latter part of August. Robert Green, a small man of 54, said that he had never known Godfrey 'dead or alive'. He denied killing anyone. Green admitted that he knew Dominic Kelly, who, he said, had gone to Wales, and also Fitzgerald. Henry Berry told the lords he was innocent, and knew no one who had been involved in the Godfrey murder. He knew Hill but not Gerald. He let no sedan chair out of Somerset House on the night Prance had said. Besides, the sentries were on duty at the entrances to the palace at that time. All three prisoners were taken to Newgate, where Sir Edmund Godfrey's brothers and servants were ordered to see them and report back to the committee if they knew any of them, or if they had ever seen any of them with Godfrey. Prance was removed from the condemned hole, into which Hill was now thrown, but Prance remained in Richardson's custody at Newgate. Before sending him back to the prison that night, the lords questioned Prance about the drops of wax on Godfrey's clothes. He replied that he had not noticed them, and had seen no wax candles in the room where the body lay. His company, he repeated, had a lantern.[12]

Despite the discrepancies between Bedloe's account of the murder and Prance's, Prance was just the man the Whigs needed. Bedloe had arrived to confirm Oates's story of the Popish Plot. Now Prance entered to confirm Bedloe's account of the Popish Murder. Nothing would serve the Catholic-haters better than 'proving' that Godfrey's murder had taken place at Somerset House. Once again, it was a short step from there to wrecking the Duke of York's hopes of succeeding to the throne.

But the path was not to be easy. Two days after the examination of Green, Berry and Hill, Prance retracted his whole story. He saw the Lords Committee on Sunday, 29 December and craved an audience with the King. He was taken before Charles and immediately fell to his knees and swore that he was innocent as were all the men he had accused. He said the same to the Privy Council the next day, and denied that anyone had influenced him in his recantation. So the lords sent him back to Newgate, where he had another change of heart. A message was soon brought to the King that Prance's recantation had been false, his original tale true. But again he denied the truth of his 'discovery' and declared that his recantation had been genuine. On 30 December the Lord Chancellor thought it would be a good idea 'to have him have the rack'. Whether mechanical torture was applied or not is almost irrelevant. Back in the sub-zero misery of Little Ease Prance was given ten days of solitary confinement under the worst conditions to reconsider his stand. On 11 January 1679 he emerged from the condemned cell for the last time, swearing upon oath that the whole of his original story had been true. In later years he finally admitted that his confession had been perjury, attributing it to 'fear and cowardice'. But by then the damage was done. Green, Berry and Hill had long since followed Godfrey on the Primrose way to the everlasting bonfire.[13]

8: The Scapegoats

Green, Berry and Hill were indicted for Godfrey's murder by the self same Middlesex Grand Jury of which Godfrey himself had once been foreman. After the frequent false hopes when Prance had pronounced them all innocent, the accused were finally brought before Mr Justice Wild at the bar of the Court of King's Bench on Wednesday, 5 February 1679. The charge of murder was formally read out, and they each pleaded not guilty in turn. Along with the names of Girald and Kelly, a new name had appeared in the charge – that of Philibert Vernatt, described like Green, Berry and Hill as a labourer. Vernatt was one that 'should have been one at the doing of it, but something happened. He could not.' He also had fled and was never to be apprehended. Wild set the trial for the following Friday, but on Thursday, 6 February Sir William Jones, the Attorney General, requested a postponement until

Monday so that the Crown's case might be better prepared. The request was granted.[1]

Long before the trial was due to begin on Monday morning, the mob descended on the court. Even now, nearly four months after the murder, public anger against the Papists was being kept at boiling point. By the time the Crier was ready to swear the twelve jurymen the courtroom was so crowded that there was no room for the jury to stand together.

'Oh Yes!' bawled the Crier on the orders of the Clerk of the Court. 'My lords the King's justices do straitly charge and command all persons that are not of the jury, to withdraw forthwith, upon pain of £100 a man.'[2]

When a space had been cleared, and the charges described in detail once again, the Attorney General rose to his feet. He was supremely confident of the prosecution case.[3]

'May it please your lordship,' he said, giving a cursory nod to the presiding judge, the infamous Lord Chief Justice Scroggs himself, 'and you gentlemen of this jury, the prisoners who stand now at the bar are indicted for murder.' He looked gravely at the twelve men. 'Murder, as it is the first, so it is the greatest crime that is prohibited in the Second Table. It is a crime of so deep stain that nothing can wash it away but the blood of the offender. And unless that be done, the land in which it is shed will continue polluted.'[4]

He turned back to the judges. 'My lord, as murder is always a very great crime, so the murder which is now to be tried before your lordship is, it may be, the most heinous and most barbarous that ever was committed. The murder was committed upon a gentleman and upon a magistrate. And I wish he had not therefore been murdered, because he was a Protestant magistrate.'[5]

Sir William Jones explained that he would not delay the proceedings by making observations in advance. 'For I that have made a strict examination into this matter,' he said, 'do find that I shall better spend my time in making observations, *and showing how the witnesses do agree*, after the evidence given, than before.'[6]

There is irony in those italics. Nothing characterized the trial of Green, Berry and Hill so much as the almost total disagreement of the two chief prosecution witnesses. A modern prosecution case in such a state, in the inconceivable situation of its reaching court, would collapse before it was half way through. But neither reason nor logic held sway in 1678, even in the courts of justice.

'My lord,' continued the Attorney General, 'upon the discovery of the late horrid Plot – '

141

'And present Plot too, Mr Attorney,' broke in Scroggs. 'But pray go on.'

'If your lordship please, you may call it so, for it is to be feared they have not yet given it over. But upon the discovery of that Plot – call it late or present – Sir Edmund Berry Godfrey, whom I suppose the jury all knew, and every man that lived thereabouts must needs remember to have been a very useful and active justice of the peace, had taken several examinations about this matter . . .'[7]

And so he continued, outlining the prosecution's story of the Plot and murder, largely based upon Prance's perjured evidence, but with greater detail than Prance had hitherto provided. He spoke of several meetings of the Jesuits at the Plough alehouse, where they had discussed ways of murdering Sir Edmund.[8]

'And they made several attempts to do it: One while they dogged him into the fields; another while they sent people to spy when he came abroad, that they might follow him into some dark alley, or other obscure or unfrequented place, and there despatch him; and at last, after many attempts, they succeeded in that wicked one, when the murder was committed.'[9]

Hill, said the Attorney General, had called on Godfrey on the morning of 12 October 'to learn whither he went that day'. Green, he said, had been there before on the same errand. He then trotted out the tale of Godfrey having been on some unknown business at a house near St Clement's Church in the Strand, of his leaving the house at seven or eight o'clock at night, and soon after being lured into the yard of Somerset House by the report that two men were fighting there.[10]

'Down he went, through the back gate into the yard, where were indeed two men scuffling together, but counterfeitly. The one was Berry, the prisoner here. The other was Kelly, the priest that is run away.'[11]

The court heard how the affray ended as soon as Godfrey appeared, how Berry had then run to the lower water-gate, and Prance, 'who was in that foul fact, but hath since repented, and hath made this discovery' had gone to the upper water-gate to keep watch. Godfrey had been set upon by Hill, Gerald and Kelly and strangled with a cravat or twisted linen cloth by Green. But when Prance returned there was still some life in the magistrate, so 'to make thorough work with him, Green . . . takes hold of his head and twists his neck round, and stamps upon his breast, the marks of which outrageous cruelty did plainly appear on his body after it was found'.[12]

The shifting of the body from chamber to chamber over the next four days and the scene witnessed by Bedloe by the light of a dark lantern, were then related by Jones. The removal of the corpse, first in a sedan chair as far as Soho, and from there to Primrose Hill on horseback with Hill riding behind, were also described. 'And there, to accomplish the last part of their design – which was to murder his reputation after they had killed his body – they took his own sword and run him through, and left him in such a manner as that (according to the weakness of their understanding) the world should conclude he had killed himself.'[13]

Prance had been told the next day all that happened after he separated from his companions at the Grecian Church at Soho, said Sir William. The murderous priests were so devoid of remorse and humanity that they even produced a written narrative of the killing, he said. 'And I doubt not, but by this time it is sent to Rome, where it finds as great approbation, and causes as great joy as their other acts of a like nature have heretofore done.'[14]

Some days after the murder, he said, some of the priests attended a meeting at the Queen's Head at Bow, a village east of London. The paper was read out amid great merriment.[15]

Addressing Scroggs directly, the Attorney General admitted that the prosecution case as he had outlined it was based chiefly on the evidence of only one man. But he was in no doubt that judges and jury would be convinced. 'I will undertake,' he said, 'before I have done, so to fortify almost every particular he delivers with a concurrent proof of other testimony. And the things will so depend upon one another, and have such a connection, that little doubt will remain in any man's mind . . . but that Sir E. Godfrey was murdered at Somerset House, and that the persons who now stand indicted for it were the murderers.'[16]

With that triumphant flourish, Sir William Jones sat down.

The prosecution's first witness was, predictably, Citizen Oates himself. The evidence he gave, partly factual, mainly the product of his rancid imagination, is valueless. He repeated what was already known about his two visits to Godfrey to swear to the truth of his depositions about the Plot. Then the lies began. He told the court how Godfrey – 'Mr Godfrey', as he often insisted on calling him – had come to him, he thought on 30 September, 'and did tell me what affronts he had received from some great persons – whose names I name not now – for being so zealous in this business'. But there were others, he said, 'who were well inclined to have the discovery made, did think that he had not been quick

143

enough in the prosecution, but had been too remiss, and did threaten him that they would complain to the Parliament, which was to sit the 21st of October following.'[17]

Then he reached the crux of his testimony. 'My lord, that week before Sir E. Godfrey was missing, he came to me and told me that several popish lords – some of whom are now in the Tower – had threatened him, and asked him what he had to do with it. My lord, I shall name their names when time shall come. My lord, this is all I can say: he was in a great fright and told me he went in fear of his life by the popish party, and that he had been dogged several days.'[18]

'Did he tell you that he was dogged?' asked the Attorney General.

'Yes he did,' said Oates. 'And I did then ask him why he did not take his man with him. He said he was a poor weak fellow. I then asked him why he did not get a good brisk fellow to attend him. But he made no great matter of it. He said he did not fear them if they came fairly to work. But yet he was often threatened and came sometimes to me to give him some encouragement. And I did give him what encouragement I could that he would suffer in a just cause, and the like. But he would often tell me he was in continual danger of being hurt by them.'[19]

Oates stepped down. Thomas Robinson, Godfrey's friend of forty years, was the next witness to take the stand. He repeated truthfully and clearly the conversation that had taken place between him and Sir Edmund over lunch less than a week before he disappeared, in which the magistrate had said he should have little thanks for his pains, that he believed he should be 'the first martyr', but that he did not fear them if they came fairly, and that he should not part with his life tamely.[20]

The prosecution's star witness, Mr Miles Prance, was then called and sworn.

'Pray, sir,' said the Attorney General, 'begin at the very beginning – the meetings you had at the Plough alehouse, and the sending to Sir Edmundbury's house, and all the story.'[21]

Prance's moment had come. After weeks of vacillation, discomfort and terror he was on his own in the witness box. The Crown case would stand or fall by what he said. The reprisals would be harsh indeed if he let the Plot-mongers down.

'My lord,' he began with impressive calm, 'it was about a fortnight or three weeks before he was murdered. We met several times at the Plough alehouse.'

144

'With whom?' asked Scroggs.

'With Mr Girald, Mr Green and Mr Kelly. Girald and Kelly did entice me in, and told me it was no sin.'

'Girald and Kelly did?' said the Recorder, Sir George Jeffreys, later to acquire infamy as the 'hanging Judge'.

'Yes, Girald and Kelly.'

'What are they?'

'Two priests. And they said it was no sin, it was a charitable act. They said he was a busy man, and had done and would do a great deal of mischief, and it was a deed of charity to do it. And so they told the rest besides.'[22]

The Recorder and the Attorney General both cross-questioned Prance on details of this preliminary meeting. He seemed confident of his story.[23]

'What discourse had you then?' asked Sir William Jones.

'There they resolved that the first that could meet with him should give notice to the rest to be ready. And so in the morning, when they went out on Saturday – '

Prance was anxious to detail the crucial events of the murder itself, but there were other points the Prosecution still wished to have covered.

'But before you come to that,' interrupted the Attorney General, 'do you know of any dogging of him into the fields?'

'Yes. It was before that I heard them say they would and had dogged him into the fields.'

'Who did you hear say so?' said Scroggs.

'Girald, Kelly and Green.'

'That Green is one of the prisoners,' said Jones, ensuring that no particle of evidence escaped the jury's notice.

'Which way did they dog him?' asked Jeffreys. 'What fields?'

'Red Lion Fields,' said Prance. 'And those by Holborn.'

'Why did they not kill him there?' This came from the Attorney General. The witness could not tell who would fire the next question. Despite this he appeared unruffled.

'Because,' he said simply, 'they had not opportunity.'

'Do you know of any sending to his house, or going to it?' pursued the Attorney General.

'One time I do know of, and that was Saturday morning. Mr Kelly came to give me notice that they were gone abroad to dog him. And afterwards they told me that Hill or Green did go to his house and ask for him. But the maid told him he was not up, and [he] then went away and said he would call by and by.'[24]

This was the first intimation that Prance was amending his evidence to accord with other witnesses. In his statement to the Lords Committee on Christmas Eve, the silversmith had stated without equivocation that it had been Green who had called on Godfrey on the morning of the twelfth.[25] But when Elizabeth Curtis, Godfrey's maid, had been faced with the three prisoners, she had selected Hill as the man who had visited Hartshorn Lane. Even Curtis's statement, given later in the trial, could not be relied upon. She had clearly been confronted with the three accused, told that one of them had been the morning caller and instructed to make her selection.[26]

'What time was that in the morning?'

The voice came from the bar. It was the first time any of the prisoners had spoken. This was Hill.

'It was about nine or ten o'clock in the morning,' said Prance, anticipating word for word the testimony of Elizabeth Curtis.

'And had we been there before or after?' asked Hill.

'You had been there before.'

'Pray stay,' said Jeffreys, addressing Hill, 'till such time as we have done with our evidence. You shall have all free liberty to ask him any question, but you must stay till we have done.'[27]

'As soon as they heard he was within,' resumed Prance, 'they came out and stayed for his coming out, and dogged him . . .'

The story of the murder in Somerset House was unfolded detail by detail and, in a dialogue entered into not only by Jones, Jeffreys and Scroggs but also by the other two judges and Serjeant Stringer, the Prance version of the shifting of the body and its eventual arrival at Primrose Hill was at last unveiled to the public. At the end of it, Sir William Jones asked Prance to tell the story of the meeting at Bow which succeeded the killing.[28]

'What was the house called you met at?' asked Jones.

'It was the sign of the Queen's Head.'

'Who was it that did meet there?'

'They were priests. I cannot so well remember their names. They are written down in this paper.' It was the first time Prance had needed to resort to his written statement.

'Look upon the paper yourself,' said Recorder Jeffreys. 'You can read, I suppose?' he added with a sneer.

'There was one Luson, a priest I think,' said Prance, ignoring the jibe.

'Where did he live?' asked Jones.

'He was with Vernatt.'

'What was the occasion of your meeting there?'

'Vernatt told me it was only to be merry there.'

'What was the man of the house his name?'

'One Casshes.'

'Did you dine there?'

'Yes.'

'What had you for dinner?'

'We had a barrel of oysters and a dish of fish. I bought the fish myself.'

'What day was it?' interposed the Lord Chief Justice.

'The Friday after the Proclamation that all Papists were to be gone out of town.'

'Tell what company you had there, and what discourse,' said Jeffreys.

'There was Mr Vernatt and I, and Mr Girald, and that other priest, and one Mr Dethicke.'

'Who sent for him?' asked the Attorney General.

'Mr Vernatt sent a note for him by a cobbler.'

'Did he come upon that note?'

'He came presently,' said Prance. 'And when he was come, then they read all the writing of the murder – for Mr Vernatt should have been one at the doing of it, but something happened. He could not.'

'Mr Vernatt,' said the Attorney General, 'was very sorrowful at the reading of it, was he not?'

It is just this sort of question, and Prance's pat response, that indicates how carefully the chief prosecution witness had been primed.

'If he was,' said Prance, 'it was because he was not there.'[29]

'How did he behave himself?' pursued Jones. 'Did he read it with any pleasure and delight?'

'We were all very merry.'

'What,' said the Attorney General, moving on, 'can you say about anybody's overhearing you?'

'There was a drawer came and listened at the door,' said Prance. 'And I hearing the door a little rustle, went to the door, and catched him listening. And said I to him, "Sirrah, I could find in my heart to kick you downstairs." And away he went.'

'Was Vernatt with you there that night he was murdered, the Saturday night?' put in Justice Wild, evidently failing to follow the details of the story.

'No,' said Prance patiently. 'There was only the six I have named.'

'You say,' said Justice Jones, 'that you met at the Plough the first night?'

'Yes.'

'And there you were told it was a very charitable act to kill Sir E. Godfrey?'

'Yes, I was so.'

'Was it agreed there that he should be killed?'

'It was agreed there. And the first that met him were to give notice to the rest.'

'Who were there?'

'Girald, Kelly, Green and I.'

'When came Hill and Berry into this cause?' struck in the Lord Chief Justice. 'How came they acquainted with it?'

'They were in it before I,' said Prance.

'Who told you they were in it?'

'Mr Girald, my lord, told me so.'

'Hill and Berry were not at the Plough,' said Justice Jones. 'Where did you first hear them speak of it?'

'Girald and I have been at Berry's house divers times,' replied Prance.

'But there were two meetings at the Plough, were there not?' said Justice Dolben.

'Yes, there were.'

'And Hill was at the last meeting, was he not?'

'Yes he was, my lord.'[30]

It was time for the prosecution's next bombshell. Mr Attorney General did not want the impetus of the unfolding narrative to be lost by needless repetition for the sake of the bench.

'Now I would ask you this question by the favour of the court,' he said, steering the dialogue back on to the prosecution's carefully plotted path. 'Was there any reward proposed by these priests for the doing of it?'

'Girald and Vernatt did speak of a great reward that was to be given for it.'

'Pray, how much?'

'I do not remember what.'

'Cannot you tell how much?' prompted the Attorney General. He was giving the rehearsed cues but Prance was not responding. Sir William was not so concerned with how much as with who from.

'There was to be a good reward,' said Prance, remembering his lines. 'From Lord Belasyse, as they said.'

148

Belasyse! One of the five popish lords now in the Tower. The Plot-mongers were consolidating their position. The Plot thickened.[31]

'You had several meetings, you say,' said Justice Dolben. 'Did you there resolve what should be the way of doing it?'

'Girald was resolved to kill him that night,' said Prance. 'And if he could not get him into a more convenient place, he would kill him with his own sword in the street that leads to his own house.'

'Who was that that resolved so?' asked the Recorder, to underline the point.

'It was Girald.'

'The priest, rather than fail, was resolved to do the act of charity himself.' The anti-popish propaganda was building up beautifully.[32]

The Attorney General now moved to the mythical similarity between the evidence of Bedloe, yet to be given in open court, and that of Prance.

'I would now ask you a question,' he said, 'which though it does not prove the persons guilty, yet it gives a great strength to the evidence. Do you know Mr Bedloe, Mr Praunce?'

'I do not know him.'

'Had you ever any conference with him before you was committed to prison?'

'Never in all my life.'

'Were you ever in his company in your life before, that you know of?'

'No, not that I remember.'

'Well, you shall see how far he will agree with you.'[33]

'Now,' said the Recorder, indicating the three prisoners, 'they may ask him any questions if they please, for we have done with him.'

'Let him if they will,' concurred Scroggs.

'My lord,' said Lawrence Hill, 'in the first place I humbly pray that Mr Praunce's evidence may not stand good against me, as being perjured by his own confession.'

It was a telling point, unexpected from one untutored in the law.

'How?' said the Lord Chief Justice, feigning ignorance.

'I suppose, my lord,' said Hill, 'it is not unknown to you that he made such an open confession before the King.'

'Look you, sir,' said Scroggs. 'I will tell you for that I do *not* know that ever he made a confession to contradict what he had said, upon his oath.'

'He was upon his oath before,' said Hill.

'Yes. He had accused you upon oath. But afterwards, you say, he confessed that it was not true. But that confession that it was not true was not upon oath. How is he then guilty of perjury?'

'My lord,' said Hill in astonishment, 'if a man can swear a thing and after deny it, he is certainly perjured.'

But heartless, ruthless Scroggs would not be outdone by the son of a shoemaker.

'If a man hath great horrors of conscience upon him,' he said, 'and is full of fears, and the guilt of such a thing disorders his mind so as to make him go back from what he had before discovered upon oath, you can't say that man is perjured if he don't forswear it.'

One humble serving man without any legal assistance was poor opposition indeed to an unscrupulous, blustering Lord Chief Justice of England.

'But I believe nobody did believe his denial,' continued Scroggs, pressing home the attack, 'because his first discovery was so particular that every man did think his general denial did only proceed from the disturbance of his mind.' He looked menacingly at Hill. 'But have you any mind to ask him any questions?'

'We can prove,' interrupted Jeffreys, 'that immediately after, he retracted his recantation.'[34]

'Try if you can trap him in any question,' said Justice Dolben. Hill gathered all his strength about him. His wife had been working hard to get together a defence and find witnesses to testify on his behalf, but only a man intimate with the labyrinth of legal form and casuistry could hope to dent the formidable opposition. Not only the prosecution but also the judges were against him, it seemed.[35]

'Pray,' he began, addressing himself to Prance, 'what hour was it that I went to Sir Edmund Berry Godfrey's?'

'About nine or ten o'clock. I am not certain in the hour.'

'No, no,' said Scroggs, 'a man cannot be precise to an hour. But prove you what you can.'

'I have a great many witnesses, beside the justice of my cause, that I was not out of my house that day,' said Hill, still imbued with an almost childlike faith in the invincibility of justice.

'You shall be heard for that,' said Scroggs. 'But the present matter is whether you will ask him any questions or no.'

'My lord,' pleaded Hill, 'it is all false that he says and I deny every word of it – and I hope it shall not be good against me.'[36]

'Well Mr Berry,' said Scroggs, passing on, 'will you ask him any questions?'

'Mr Praunce,' said Berry, 'who was in my house at the time you speak of?'

'There was your wife there and several other persons besides.'

'Who were they?' said Berry.

'There were divers people,' said Prance evasively. 'It is an alehouse.'

'But who? Can you name any of them?'

'There was Girald and Kelly and I,' said Prance. It was an aspect of the story he had not fully rehearsed. He could now only pray that the names to which he had committed himself did not in any way contradict any of his earlier statements.

'Why,' said Scroggs, 'did you not all know Mr Praunce?'

'My lord,' said Berry, 'I knew him as he passed up and down in the house.'

'Why, what answer is that?' said Scroggs. 'What do you mean by his passing up and down in the house? Did you never drink with him?'

'Drink with him, my lord? Yes.'

'Yes? Why, people don't use to drink as they go along.'

'It was in other company that [he] came to my house, no acquaintance of mine.'

'Was not Mr Praunce known by you all three?' asked Scroggs. 'Which of you can deny it? What say you, Hill?'

'My lord, I did know him.'

'What say you, Green?'

'Yes, I did know him.'[37]

The question of Prance's recantations and recanted recantations was then raised once more by the Attorney General, who called Captain Richardson, the keeper of Newgate, to describe Prance's conduct while in his custody. Richardson thought that Prance's denials had been 'only out of an apprehension that his life was not secure, that his trade would be lost among the Roman Catholics, and in case he had his pardon and were saved, he should have been in danger of being murdered by them.'[38]

Before Bedloe was called, Serjeant Stringer addressed the court, and in a speech lasting little over a minute jumbled the disparate 'facts' of Bedloe's and Prance's stories into one contrived scenario. Walsh and Le Phaire, Bedloe's culprits, were said now to be in league with Prance's men, Girald and Kelly. There was no justification whatever for this. Prance's culprits hardly featured in

Bedloe's account, and Prance at no stage mentioned the men accused by Bedloe.[39]

Bedloe, who had never at any time mentioned Green, Berry or Hill, now made a token reference to give his lies at least a tenuous link with Prance's – but then only when prompted by Justice Wild, who asked him if he had seen Hill on the night the body was carried away to Primrose Hill.

'No, my lord,' said Bedloe.

'Nor Green, nor Berry?'

'Green I did see about the court. And Berry I was told was to open the gate that Monday night.'[40]

It is helpful at this point to examine the various aspects of the two versions of the murder, misrepresented by the prosecution as independent descriptions of the same events:

MAIN POINTS	PRANCE	BEDLOE
Culprits	Green, Berry, Hill, Gerald and Kelly	Le Phaire, Walsh, Pritchard and Keynes
Motive	Godfrey an enemy to the Queen or her servants	Godfrey a great obstacle to the Papists' designs
Site of Murder	Somerset House water-gate	Upper court of Somerset House
Date of Murder	'The latter end or beginning of a week'	12 October
Time of Murder	About 9 pm	About 5 pm
Method	Strangling with a twisted handkerchief followed by wringing of neck and beating	Stifling with pillow followed by strangling with long cravat
Body disposed of on	16 October	14 October
Time of disposal	After midnight	11 pm
Method	Carried in sedan chair to Soho, and then on horseback to Primrose Hill	Carried in chair to Piccadilly, and then in coach to Primrose Hill

In spite of the assurances made in court that the witnesses agreed in every detail, the only points they did in reality agree upon were that Godfrey was murdered and that his body ended up at Primrose Hill. Beyond this, they named different murderers, different motives, different murder sites, different dates and times of day for both murder and shifting of the body, and different methods for killing and conveying the corpse to Primrose Hill.

At the end of Bedloe's evidence, Jeffreys invited the prisoners to question the witness.

'I never saw him before in my life,' said Hill.

'Do you know any of them? asked Scroggs, looking at Bedloe.

'I know Mr Berry and Green very well,' said the liar.[41]

Prance then furnished his lordship with further details about the shifting of the body and the episode of the dark lantern.[42]

'Was there no sentinel set that Monday night, that Saturday night, and that Wednesday night?' asked Scroggs.

'My lord,' said Prance, 'I am not certain. I took notice of none. If there were any they were at Berry's house, and he opened the gate when we came out with the sedan.'

'Mr Berry, I suppose, could take order with the sentinel, and give them some entertainment in his own lodge,' agreed the Attorney General.[43]

Constable John Brown and the surgeons Skillard and Cambridge then gave evidence as to the finding of the body and its condition, the surgeons repeating the opinions as to the cause of death which they had given at the inquest more than three months before.[44]

Elizabeth Curtis, Godfrey's maid, was then sworn.

'Elizabeth Curtis,' said the Attorney General, 'look upon the prisoners and tell my lord and the jury whether you know any of them or no.'

'This man that I now hear called Green, my lord, was at my master's about a fortnight before he died,' said Curtis.

'What to do?' asked Scroggs.

'I do not know, but he asked for Sir E. Godfrey.'

'What time of the day was it?'

'It was in the morning.'

'What did he say?' said the Attorney General.

'He asked for Sir E. Godfrey, and when he came to him he said, "Good morrow, sir," in English, and afterwards spoke to him in French. I could not understand him.'

'I desire she may consider well,' said Jeffreys. 'Look upon him.'

Curtis obeyed. 'That is the man,' she said.

'Upon my soul,' exclaimed Green, 'I never saw him in all my life.'

'He had a dark coloured periwig when he was there,' continued Curtis, regardless of the outburst, 'and was about a quarter of an hour talking with my master.'

'Are you sure this was the man?' asked Jones.

'Yes I am. And that other man, Hill, was there that Saturday morning, and did speak with him before he went out.'

'That you will deny too?' said Scroggs, looking at Hill.

'Yes I do,' said Hill.

'How do you know he was there?' This to the maidservant.

'I was in the parlour at that time, making up the fire.'

'Had you ever seen him before that time?'

'No, never before that time. I went into the parlour to carry my master's breakfast and brought a bunch of keys with me in, and there Hill was with him. And I went upstairs about some business, and came down again, wanting the keys, which I had left upon the table. And Hill was all that time with my master.'

'How do you know he was there?' said the Solicitor General, entering the debate for the first time.

'I was in the parlour, and stirred up the fire, and he was there a good while.'[45]

It either did not occur to the prosecution, or more likely the idea had been rejected as damaging to the Crown case, to ask Curtis what Hill and Godfrey had been speaking about. The evidence that Curtis had been 'got at' came from Godfrey's housekeeper, elderly, tall Mrs Judith Pamphlin, in a statement made several years later to Roger L'Estrange, who had a royal commission under James II to reinvestigate the case. Elizabeth Curtis had been accompanied to Newgate, to view Green, Berry and Hill as they awaited trial, by both Mrs Pamphlin and the clerk, Henry Moor. Pamphlin could not remember having seen any of them before. And Curtis, at the same time, declared that 'she had not seen any of them neither'. Pamphlin, coveniently for the prosecution, was not called to give evidence at the trial.[46] But her words are supported by a letter written by Hill to his wife while he was in prison:

On the Thursday after I came to this place, there came two grave men like Justices to examine me; they call'd me not a few rogues, and order'd me to be chain'd to boards; but was set at liberty in the night. The Monday after, they came again, and brought two women with them, which I suppose were Sir Edmund's servants. At first, when they came, they declar'd they had never seen me in their lives: and said, it was a lesser man, and had another kind of face that

154

brought the letter. So I was sent up, but immediately sent for down again, and a barber sent for to shave me, and when he had done they whisper'd; what they said God knows . . .

According to a sworn statement by Mrs Avis Warrier, wife of Green's landlord, she had spoken with Curtis while waiting to be called into court. Curtis had said then that Green had called on Sir Edmund Godfrey twice on 12 October. 'Have a care,' Mrs Warrier had said, 'for there are three men's lives at stake and there might be many more.' She had then told Curtis that Green had declared several times before he was accused that he had never seen Godfrey in his life. Curtis had replied: 'If it was not Green, 'twas Hill.' In addition, said Mrs Warrier, Curtis had told her that the caller at Hartshorn Lane had worn a black periwig. Green always wore a light reddish wig.[47]

In the middle of her examination in court, Curtis departed from the prosecution's script. The mysterious messenger who had called upon Godfrey the night before he vanished was obviously playing on her mind. Suddenly she blurted out that Hill was not 'the man that brought the note to my master'.

'What note?' asked the Attorney General.

'A note that a man brought to my master that night before.'

'What is become of that note?'

'My lord, I cannot tell. My master had it.'

'Pr'ythee tell us the story of it.'

She told of the stranger's visit, of the letter he brought, and of the state of perplexity into which it threw Sir Edmund. ' "Pr'ythee," said he, "tell him I don't know what to make of it." '

'When was that?' asked Justice Wild.

'On Friday night.'

'When? The Friday night before he was murdered?'

'Yes.'

And that was the extent of the court's examination of an episode that plainly had direct bearing upon Godfrey's disappearance and death. Despite an attempt by Curtis to resurrect the issue, the letter – which had so confused Godfrey and which had later sent him tumbling over trunks and burning masses of documents – was not referred to again. Sir William Jones quickly steered the conversation back to Hill's alleged visit to Hartshorn Lane.[48]

Two witnesses were then called to testify to the presence, at various times, of Prance, Green, Hill, Fitzgerald, Kelly and Vernatt at the Plough alehouse. Neither Hill nor Green made any bones about having drunk several times with Prance at the Plough. Hill also acknowledged that he knew Kelly by sight, but said that the only man he knew called Girald was not a priest.[49]

William Evans, a boy at the Queen's Head tavern, spoke of a group of men there two or three months before who had eaten flounders and a barrel of oysters.

'Pray give my lord an account of what you observed and heard,' said Jeffreys.

'Sir,' said Evans, 'I know nothing but that they pulled out a paper and read it, and named Sir E. Godfrey's name. And while I was at the door, somebody threatened to kick me downstairs.'

'He saith just as Mr Praunce said in every particular!' crowed the Lord Chief Justice in triumph.[50]

Sir Robert Southwell, clerk to the Privy Council, then described Prance's confident description of the events of Godfrey's murder as he conducted Monmouth, Ossory and himself about Somerset House. In all places but one he had gone 'directly and positively', but locating the room near the garden, whither he said the body had been carried, had presented him with problems.

'Then he began to stagger,' said Sir Robert, 'as if he did not know his way. But there was no way but to go on, however, and on he went. And coming across the court, we came into several rooms, and going through them we came upstairs again, and so into several other rooms again. "Sure," said he, "we were here, but I can't tell." And he was in a distraction what room he saw the body in.'[51]

But in Lord Chief Justice Scroggs's eyes this uncertainty in no way diminished Prance's credibility. On the contrary. 'His doubtfulness of the room does assert and give credit to his testimony, and confirms it to any honest man in England,' said Scroggs. 'Here, saith he, I will not be positive, but having sworn the other things which he well remembered positively, he is made the more credible for his doubtfulness of a thing which he does not remember, which a man that could swear anything would not stick at.'[52]

At length, after prolonged debate of peripheral issues, the Attorney General turned to Scroggs. 'My lord,' he said, 'we have now done with our evidence for the King, and leave it till we hear what they say.'[53]

'What have you to say for yourselves?' said Scroggs, glaring down at the prisoners. 'You shall have all the free liberty you will desire.'

156

'In the first place,' began Hill, nothing loath, 'I take God to be my witness that I am wholly innocent as to the matter that is charged upon me. And as to what is said that I dogged Sir E. Godfrey, I can prove that I went into my lodging at eight o'clock and did not stir out.'

'Come, call your witnesses,' said Scroggs.

'Mary Tilden, Catherine Lee, Mrs Broadstreet and Daniel Gray,' said Hill.

'Let them come in there,' said the Lord Chief Justice, indicating the place for witnesses.[54]

Mary Tilden, niece of Dr Thomas Godden, who had fled abroad from his house next to Somerset House because he feared, after the first statement by Prance, arrest for complicity in the murder, was the first to speak. Hill, she said, had been a trusty servant, 'never kept ill hours, always came home by eight o'clock at night'.[55]

'Always?' exclaimed Justice Dolben. 'For how long?'

'Ever since we came over last into England.'

'When was that?'

'In April last.'

'Were you there that night Sir E. Godfrey was killed?' asked Scroggs.

'I was.'

'What night was that?'

'I do not know, my lord. I heard of it in the town.'

'When did you first hear of it?'

'The Thursday that he was found.'

'Did you not hear of it on the Wednesday?'

'Yes, I did.'

'Who could tell you the Wednesday before?'

'Why, my lord, in the town it was said he was missing from Saturday, and a Thursday he was found.'

'What can you say concerning Hill, that he was not out after eight o'clock that night?'

'He was a very good servant to my uncle, and never kept ill hours, but always came in by eight o'clock or before.'

'Were you not out yourself that night?' asked Justice Dolben.

'No, not I, never out after that hour.'

'Pray,' said Scroggs, 'how can you give such an account of Mr Hill, as if he was always in your company?'

'He came in to wait at the table, and did not stir out afterwards.'

'Pray, what religion are you of?' barked Scroggs. 'Are you a Papist?'

'I know not whether I came here to make a profession of my faith.'

'*Are you a Roman Catholic?*' said Scroggs accusingly.

'Yes.'

'Have you a dispensation to eat suppers on Saturday nights?'

Before she could answer that point, Jeffreys jumped in with another. 'I hope,' he said, 'you did not keep him company after supper all night?'

'No, I did not,' said Mary Tilden. 'But he came in to wait at table at supper.'

'I thought you had kept fasting on Saturday nights,' persisted Scroggs, evidently confusing Roman Catholicism with Judaism.

'No, my lord, not on Saturday nights.'

'How many dishes of meat had you to supper,' said Justice Jones in a crude attempt at trapping the witness.

'We had no meat, though we did not fast.'

'Can you speak positively as to this night, the Saturday that he was killed?' asked Scroggs.

'He was at home that night.'

'And where was he the Sunday?'

'He was at home.'

'And you are sure he was at home every night?'

'Yes, while we were in town.'

'Where was you all that Wednesday night you speak of?'

'I was home in my lodging.'

'How is it possible,' said Justice Wild, 'for you to say that Hill, who was not your constant companion, did not go out afterwards?'

'No, he was not my constant companion.'

'How then can you charge your memory that he was at home?'

'Come, you are to speak truth, though you are not upon your oath,' said Scroggs. 'Can you charge your memory to say that he came in constantly at eight o'clock at night?'

'Yes, I can, because I saw him come in constantly. And when he came in, I always sent my maid to bar the door.'

'Maid,' said Scroggs, still addressing Tilden, 'can you say he was always at home at night?'

'I can say he never was abroad after eight at night.'

'Why, you did not watch him till he went to bed, did you?' said Jeffreys.

'We were always up till eleven o'clock at night.'

'Was he in your company all that while?' asked the Attorney General.

158

'I beg your pardon,' said Mary Tilden. 'If your lordship saw the lodgings you would say it were impossible for any to go in or out, but that they must know it within. We were constant in our hours of going to supper. Our doors were never opened after he came in to wait at supper.'[56]

The cross-examination proceeded, Scroggs and his colleagues treating the witness with undisguised contempt.

'We had never been out of our lodgings after eight o'clock since we came to town,' said Tilden.

'When were you out of town?' asked Justice Jones.

Hitherto, Mary Tilden had been a model witness, immovable in what she knew to be the truth. Now she made a single slip from which the blatantly prejudiced judges would not allow her to recover.

'In October,' she replied.

'Nay, now mistress, you have spoiled all,' said Dolben in triumph. 'For in October this business was done!'

'You have undone the man instead of saving him,' sang Justice Jones.

'Why, my lord,' said Tilden in alarm, 'I only mistook the month.'

'You, woman,' said Scroggs to Mrs Ann Broadstreet, another of Godden's servants, 'what month was it you were out of town?'

'In September,' said Mrs Broadstreet.

'It is apparent,' said Scroggs, turning to Tilden, 'you consider not what you say. Or you come hither to say anything will serve the turn.'

'No, I do not,' said Mary Tilden, 'for I was out of town in *September*, came to town the latter end of September.'

'You must remember what you said, that you came to England in April last, and from that time he was always within at eight o'clock at night.'

'Except that time we were out of town, which was in September, the summer time. And it is impossible but if the body was in the house, as Prance said it was, but I must see him, or some of us must. I used to go every day into that little room for something or other, and I must needs see him if he were there.'

'You told me just now you were not upon confession, and I tell you now so: you are not!' said Scroggs, dismissing her.[57]

Mrs Broadstreet confirmed Tilden's evidence about Hill's hours and about the impossibility of there having been a corpse in the little room at their lodgings. But the damage was irreparable.

Justice Wild's reaction to Mrs Broadstreet's statement that the people of the house had seen no body, was that it was 'very suspicious'. Both Wild and Dolben were convinced the body had been there, therefore it was well for Broadstreet that she was not indicted. Catherine Lee, another servant, gave evidence that she had not seen Hill go out of the house at night, but promptly admitted that he could have left without her knowledge.[58]

Another witness, Robert How, swore that Hill had been with him on Saturday, 12 October from nine o'clock in the morning until one in the afternoon, providing, as he mistakenly thought, an alibi for the time when Prance said he had been at Godfrey's house. But How discredited his own evidence by denying in his nervousness that he was a Papist. Prance, who knew him, soon made sure the court knew his religion. With that, Hill's alibi toppled. Three more witnesses as to Hill's movements and character, unassisted as they were by anyone trained in legal niceties, made no impression on the court.[59]

Green called his landlord, James Warrier, and Mrs Warrier to testify on his behalf. Warrier told the court that on the night of 12 October Green had been with him from half past seven until after ten o'clock. But Scroggs was on the attack and would allow nothing to hinder the prosecution case. In a long, aggressive questioning of Warrier and his wife, he undermined the reliability of their memories as to the date Green had been with them.

'Where were you on the 9th of November last?' barked Scroggs.

'Truly, I can't tell,' said a bewildered Warrier.

'Why,' mocked Scroggs, 'how came you then to recollect what you did on the 12th of October, when you did not know where you were the 9th of November?'

Mrs Warrier became so confused by the concerted attack on her testimony by the Attorney General, Scroggs and Dolben, that she was unable to challenge the dismissive statement by Dolben that she was talking about 19 October, not 12 October.[60]

Berry called three sentries who had been on guard at Somerset House on the night Prance said the body had been carried out in a sedan chair. They each testified that no sedan chair had been taken out of the palace during their periods of guard duty. This covered the period from seven o'clock on Wednesday night until four o'clock the following morning. The sentries could not be shaken from their certainty either by disparaging references to their memories, or by suggestions from the bench that they had been away from their posts at crucial moments, drinking. Only with defence witnesses were the bench doubtful as to the reliability of memories. Guilty until proven otherwise was the system under which these poor men, addressed as 'Culprits' from their earliest appearance in court, had to labour to save their lives.[61]

Berry's maid, Elizabeth Minshaw, testified that her master had been at home from dusk onwards on Wednesday, 16 October, and that he had gone to bed that night about twelve o'clock.

'And you saw him no more that night?' said Dolben.

'No, my lord. But he must go through my room to go to bed at night, and therefore I suppose he was abed.'[62]

Mrs Elizabeth Hill, the prisoner's wife, then stood up and asked that Prance should explain on oath why he had denied his confession. Rising, Prance said, 'It was because of my trade, my lord, and for fear of losing my employment from the queen and the catholics, which was the most of my business, and because I had not my pardon.'

'I desire he may swear whether he were not tortured,' said Mrs Hill.

'Answer her,' said Justice Dolben. 'Were you tortured to make this confession?'

'No, my lord. Captain Richardson hath used me as civilly as any man in England. All that time that I have been there, I have wanted for nothing.'

'It was reported about town that he was tortured,' said Mrs Hill.

'No, it was no such thing,' said Justice Jones. 'It was only the tortures of his conscience for being an actor in so great a sin.'

'There are several about the court that heard him cry out. And he knows all these things to be false as God is true. And you will see it declared hereafter, when it is too late.'[63] (The prosecution was careful not to disclose details of the Lord Chancellor's recommendation that he 'have the rack'.)

Mrs Hill could see now the utter hopelessness of her cause. 'I am dissatisfied,' she told the bench. 'My witnesses were not rightly examined. They were modest and the court laughed at them.'[64]

'The sentinels that were at the gate all night let nothing out,' put in Berry, underlining his strongest defence.

'Why,' said Scroggs in derision, 'you could open the gate yourself.'[65]

The resourceful Mrs Hill had one final card to play. The King himself had sent a representative to testify on behalf of the accused, which says a great deal about Charles's attitude to the case being argued in his name. This was his faithful servant William Chiffinch.

'Well, sir, what say you?' asked Scroggs.

'I have nothing to say,' said Chiffinch, 'but that I heard Mr Praunce deny all.'

'Why,' said Scroggs, 'he does not deny that now. Well, have you any more?'

'We have no more,' said Chiffinch.[66]*

In his summing up for the prosecution, Sir William Jones repeated the appalling lie 'that Mr Bedloe doth agree with Mr Praunce as far forth as possible.'[67]

Scroggs was thinking how to expand the point as he settled his corpulent form into its heavy robes before launching into his final address to the jury. Never was the name Lord Chief Justice less justly applied. For the period of the Popish Plot trials Scroggs represented the nation's chief *injustice*.

'It is impossible,' he told the jury in summing up the day's proceedings, 'for two men so to agree in a tale with all circumstances, if they never conversed together, but it must be true.' And again: 'If all this had been a chimera, and not really so, then Praunce must be one of the notablest inventors in the world. And there must have been the mightiest chance in the world that Mr Bedloe and he should *agree so in all things*.'[68]

After the terrible, biased words of Scroggs it would have been hard for any man to consider casting a vote of Not Guilty. Such a man would instantly have been condemned as a Papist and a supporter of the Plot. And so, after a short adjournment to consider their verdict, the jury returned. The foreman delivered their judgement on each defendant in turn.

'Guilty . . . Guilty . . . Guilty.'

'Gentlemen,' said the Lord Chief Justice with relish, 'you have found the same verdict that I would have found if I had been one with you. And if it were the last word I were to speak in this world, I should have pronounced them Guilty.'[69]

Except the prisoners and their little knot of relatives and friends, everyone in court rose and gave a great shout of applause. The following day, each of the prisoners protesting his innocence, Justice Wild passed sentence of death upon them all.[70]

---

* The shorthand note of the proceedings was evidently tailored at this point before publication. Chiffinch would hardly have appeared in court to make so innocuous a contribution.

After the scapegoats had been taken away, the court continued to sit to hear the case against Samuel Atkins 'for being accessory to the murder of Sir Edmundbury Godfrey'. But the heat was now off. The Plot-mongers had their scapegoats, and Samuel Pepys's work on Atkins's behalf had been exemplary. The clerk's night of debauchery with Captain Vittells and the two girls at Greenwich provided an unshakeable alibi, and the case was dismissed.[71]

According to Prance's final statement on the murder – his confession in 1687 that all he had spoken at the trial had been false – he was released from prison a few days after the trial of Green, Berry and Hill ended. As soon as he was at liberty, his old friend William Boyce, whom the Plot-mongers had allowed to visit him in Newgate before his final 'confession', told him that some of Sir Edmund Godfrey's relations were troubled that he was so soon free, and that they feared he would recant again before Green, Berry and Hill were executed. 'So Mr Boyce took me to his own house and watched me, and went with me wheresoever I went, till the Innocent men were executed.'[72]

Robert Green and Lawrence Hill were hanged at Tyburn on 21 February. Henry Berry, because he was a Protestant, was given the dubious consideration of having his execution deferred a week. All three maintained their cries of innocence.[73]

The great anti-popish propaganda exercise was faring well. The murder had established the existence of the Plot in men's minds. The terror that followed fuelled belief in the Plot. The executions of leading Catholics and men like Coleman strengthened the nationwide conviction that the Plot must be genuine. This in turn fired the hatred for further abominations. Now the Papists who had committed that original murder were named and given their just deserts. The terror could go on and on.

Was it not miraculous, men were saying, that in His infinite wisdom the God of Englishmen and Protestants had revealed the names of Godfrey's murderers hundreds of years ago, when he had caused men to name the place that was now Primrose Hill nothing other than Greenberry Hill.[74]

The spectre of catholicism reared up in men's minds and filled them with horror. Other more personal spectres were reported too:

About the middle of this month [February 1679], on a Sunday, about eleven in the morning, a prodigious darknesse overspread the face of the sky, the like never known, and continued about half an

163

hour. The darknesse was so great, that in severall churches, they could not proceed in divine services without candles; and 'tis said during that time the figure of Sir Edmondbury Godfrey appeared in the queen's chapell at Somerset house while masse was saying.[75]

With the imprimatur bestowed upon the Plot by the public hangings of Green, Berry and Hill, the wildest imaginings rooted themselves as deeply in men's minds as the universal fear of the devil. The Queen was now transformed into a popish witch who, with two other women, had danced three times around the body of Godfrey as it lay at Somerset House. Even that unhappy lady's royal residence was by now better known to Londoners as Godfrey Hall.[76]

Shaftesbury, the Whigs, the Green Ribboners, Peyton's Gang and all republicans were riding high. The most optimistic among them saw an Exclusion Bill at the end of the road.

PART V

Enigma Variations

Now, Edmund, where's the villain?

King Lear, II.i

The death of Sir Edmund Berry Godfrey has passed for one of the most remarkable mysteries in English history. The profound sensation which it caused, the momentous consequences which it produced, the extreme difficulty of discovering the truth, have rendered Godfrey's figure fascinating to historians. Opinion as to the nature of his end has been widely different. To the minds of Kennet, Oldmixon, and Christie the Catholics were responsible. North declared that he was murdered by the patrons of Oates, to give currency to the belief in the Plot. Sir James Fitzjames Stephen hazards that Oates himself was the murderer, and is supported by Mr Traill and Mr Sidney Lee. L'Estrange was positive that he committed suicide. Lingard and Sir George Sitwell have given the same verdict. Ralph, Hallam, Macauley, Ranke, and Klopp pronounce the problem unsolved. Hume has pronounced it insoluble. All have admitted the intricacy of the case and its importance. None has been able without fear of contradiction to answer the question, 'What was the fate of Sir Edmund Godfrey?'

Sir John Pollock, *The Popish Plot*, 1903

1: The Romish Assassins

The innocence of Green, Berry and Hill was demonstrated at their trial. The truth of this cannot be blurred by the fact that judges and jury could not or would not see it. Of all the endlessly debatable aspects of the Godfrey case, the one point every investigator seems agreed upon is the innocence of the three men executed for the murder.

But the belief that the murder was committed by Catholics has never been fully dispelled. Even a level-headed man like Pepys, faithful servant of the Duke of York, wrote on 16 November 1678 that the killing 'does by the discoveries that have since been made thereof, appear to have been committed . . . at Sumersett House'.[1]

Even after the execution of Green, Berry and Hill, alternative popish assassins continued to crop up. In September 1681 the Queen's head cook was arrested, having been accused by the doorkeeper of Her Majesty's kitchen of being an accomplice of Sir George Wakeman in the killing of Godfrey! Wakeman had already been acquitted of Oates's charge that he had agreed to kill the King, and nothing came of this isolated attempt at branding him the murderer of Godfrey. And the fate of the head cook, accused also of 'preaching the art of poisoning' and of twice poisoning the doorkeeper, 'once with broth, and another time with a frigase of eggs', is not known.[2]

An agent of Secretary of State Henry Coventry reported on 28 October 1678 that a man called Hogshead had murdered Godfrey with three accomplices. Two of these 'belonged to my Lord Bellases [sic], and the other belonged to my Lord Petre'. The agent said that before the murder, Godfrey had been tried *in absentia* by a 'Court' of Papists at Wild House. 'And there was a man like a Priest who passed the sentence of death upon him.'[3]

The Catholics never really had a motive for killing Godfrey, but various possibilities have been suggested. Macauley thought that 'some hot-headed Roman Catholic, driven to frenzy by the lies of Oates and the insults of the multitude, and not nicely distinguishing between the perjured accuser and the innocent magistrate, had taken a revenge of which the history of persecuted sects furnishes but too many examples'. A rumour current within a fortnight of the discovery of the body said that in his investigation of the Plot following Oates's revelations, Godfrey had discovered some dread popish secrets 'which hee entered in a pockett booke'. The Catholics had then murdered him to obtain the pocket book. The rumour claimed support from the 'fact' that, apart from the cravat with which he was strangled, the only item missing when the body was found was the pocket book. This detail has never been confirmed. At the trial of Lord Stafford two years after the murder, an informer called Stephen Dugdale claimed that the Duke of York himself had ordered Godfrey's assassination because he was in possession of information damaging to the Papists.[4]

Exactly what this information might have been was not stated until 1903, when Sir John Pollock, the most ardent advocate of the Romish theory in modern times, published his book *The Popish Plot*. Kenyon regards the book, incompletely reprinted in 1944, as 'a remarkable display of anti-Catholic prejudice from an educated and cultivated man in the reign of Edward VII; almost worthy of Charles II's reign.'[5]

Pollock was impressed by the consistency of Prance's version of the murder. Although he confessed, recanted, confessed again, recanted again, confessed a third time and finally swore eight years later that his entire story had been a pack of lies, it is true that his 'confession', when he stood by it, was on the whole reasonably consistent. In this he contrasted with Oates and Bedloe, whose early tales were 'loose, haphazard, inconsequent', and who later altered and rearranged their evidence to meet the needs of the moment.

> Among this rout of shifting informations the evidence of Prance offers an exception to the rule of self-contradiction. In all but a few particulars it remained constant. Other witnesses invariably put out feelers to try in what direction they had best develop their tales. The methods of Oates, Atkins and Bedloe are notorious instances of this. Prance produced the flower of his full-blown. Its bouquet was as strong when it first met the air as at any later time. The evidence which he gave to Godfrey's murder in his first confession was as decisive and consistent in form as after constant repetition, recantation and renewed asseverance.[6]

In Pollock's interpretation, the vacillating, terrified Prance becomes 'the most astute and audacious of the Jesuit agents'. The cunning plan which Pollock, without a great deal of factual support, ascribes to Prance is almost too convoluted to describe. Pollock's opening conclusion is that Prance could not have evolved a story so 'detailed, elaborate, connected and consistent' unless it had been true. A man of his station, unexpectedly thrown into a horrible prison on a false charge, could not have had the 'wealth of mental equipment' for a task of invention demanding 'phenomenal powers of memory, imagination, and coolness'. Prance, Pollock informs us, 'was in fact a party to the murder'.[7]

But he did not tell the whole truth. In order to protect the actual perpetrators of the crime, he substituted Green, Berry and Hill who 'were certainly innocent'. The men Prance was shielding, according to Pollock, were none other than Le Fevre (Le Phaire), Charles Walsh, Charles Pritchard and a servant of Belasyse called Robert Dent – the very men accused by *Bedloe*![8]

> Prance manipulated his evidence so cleverly that even the keen inquisitors who sat on the parliamentary committees never for a moment suspected that the germ of truth for which they were seeking was not contained in his but in Bedloe's information. After the appearance of Prance that was relegated to a secondary position.[9]

Why did Prance describe the murder as taking place 'on a certain Monday' and 'either at the latter end or the beginning of the week' when everyone knew that Godfrey had disappeared on Saturday? Why did he tell the Privy Council that the body had lain four days at Somerset House after the murder on Monday, and that it was removed from there on the Wednesday night, an obvious self-contradiction? Why did he tell Monmouth and Ossory that 'the body lay in Somerset House about six or seven days before it was carried out'?

Pollock does not seem to consider the obvious explanation that Prance was inventing the whole story and forgetting from day to day exact details to which he was committing himself. No, this was no imperfect memory at work but a *deliberate* inconsistency. 'It is evident,' writes Pollock, 'that he was trying to throw dust in the eyes of the investigators.' He adds disconsolately, 'These tactics were in vain.'[10]

Pollock attributes all the discrepancies between Prance's story and Bedloe's to this cunning, deliberate falsification on the part of Prance. What he does not seem to realize is that Prance, ignorant of the content of Bedloe's discovery, could not possibly have corroborated it if he had tried. And why should Bedloe's culprits have needed shielding anyway? For men known to have fled the truncated arm of Restoration law seven weeks before, Le Phaire,

Walsh and company had little to gain by the deaths of Green, Berry and Hill. As Andrew Lang points out in his investigation of the case, Pollock's argument rests on his questionable interpretation of Bedloe's knowledge: 'He [Bedloe] recognized Prance, therefore he really knew the murderers.'[11]

The motive suggested by Pollock is as doubtful as his case against his alleged killers. Oates had sworn in his infamous articles that the Jesuits had held a consult at the White Horse Tavern in the Strand on 24 April 1678, at which they had debated ways and means of killing the King. Only in the date was Oates correct. The venue for the consult had not been the White Horse Tavern but the private chambers of the Duke of York at St James's Palace. Had this become known, even though the gathering had no connection with any murder conspiracy – it was in fact the ordinary triennial meeting of Fathers of the English Province of the Society of Jesus – James would have been

> ... successfully impeached and would have been lucky to escape with his head upon his shoulders. Charles would hardly have been able to withstand the outcry for the recognition of the Protestant duke [Monmouth] as heir to the throne, the Revolution would never have come to pass, and the English throne might to this day support a bastard Stuart line instead of the legitimate Hanoverian dynasty.

It is Pollock's contention that Godfrey had discovered this great secret, and so his murder – as the only method of ensuring it remained a secret – became for them 'a cruel necessity'.[12]

While it is perfectly possible, though unlikely, that Godfrey had learned the true location of the consult, Pollock overstates the importance of the 'secret'. 'More than five years afterwards,' he writes dramatically, 'James II let out the secret to Sir John Reresby. Up to that time it had been well guarded.' This is quite untrue. As early as 1680, the tide of feeling running strongly against the Duke, there appeared a pamphlet called *A Vindication of the English Catholics*, which frankly described the meeting at St James's. Even though Shaftesbury and the Whigs were still at that date questing for a way to bring about the Duke's downfall, the damning secret was ignored. There were, after all, far greater charges against him and these had so far not secured his exclusion. It was known by everyone that he was a devoted Papist in a nation that detested Papists. It would have raised few eyebrows even if Godfrey did know about the consult, and did reveal it.[13]

Serious historians now place little value on Pollock's version of the murder. And to attribute the killing to the Jesuits for any one of several unconvincing motives is to place credence in a fiction as palpable as Hitler's assertions that the Jews were on the brink of world domination in the 1930s.

2: Creatures of the Underworld

A possible solution to Godfrey's murder, unpopular but nevertheless current at the time of the inquest, was that it had nothing to do with the Plot. The first and simplest suggestion of this sort, the origin of which is now untraceable, was that Sir Edmund had been ambushed by footpads as he walked in the country on the day of his disappearance. 'At this time,' Marks reminds us, 'there was settled near St Pancras a colony of lawless persons.'[1]

The second version of the same idea was that Bromwell and Walters, the men who first espied Godfrey's cane and gloves near the Primrose Hill ditch, had, for reasons far from clear, been responsible for his death. Both men, in fact, were thrown into prison at the end of October 1678 after being quizzed by the Lords Committee at Wallingford House. According to William Bromwell he was 'severely threatened' by Shaftesbury, who was in the chair, and committed to Newgate. About ten days later, Bromwell was sent for again. Walters had meanwhile been sent 'fettered and handcuffed' to the Gate House. Shaftesbury declared that Bromwell had been 'set on by some great Roman Catholic to find out the body . . . and if any man ever was hanged, he should be hanged if he did not discover it'. But even after nine weeks in virtual solitary confinement in Newgate, and after repeated threats and attempted bribes, Bromwell still refused to perjure himself, and was finally released. Walters, who was in prison only three days and three nights and received similar threats, likewise refused to play the Plot-mongers' game.[2]

Bromwell and Walters were both Catholics. It is inconceivable that if they had been guilty of Godfrey's murder, for motives of their own or for a purpose connected with the Plot, they would have been released. They were freed because there was no case for them to answer.

Almost a hundred years after the murder, the Scottish historian David Hume proposed the third 'non-Plot' solution: 'Any man, especially so active a magistrate as Godfrey, might, in such a city as London, have made enemies, of whom his friends and family had no suspicion.'[3]

And Kenyon, the leading contemporary authority on the Plot, has his own version of Hume's revenge theory:

> The Plot gives us occasional glimpses ... of a metropolitan underworld of crime and vice of which we know scarcely anything. For that matter we know next to nothing of the more respectable world of a skilled craftsman like Miles Prance. Yet Godfrey, as an active and conscientious magistrate, perhaps the best in London, must have known that underworld well, and it would be strange if he had not made scores of enemies amongst its inhabitants. The murder of a magistrate was an unusual thing, but assaults on them were not ... It is perfectly likely that some unknown criminal, uncaring of the Plot and perhaps not even realizing Godfrey's connection with it, gave him a thorough beating up, then realized that Godfrey had recognized him, and strangled him. He then thrust the sword through the body in a clumsy attempt at mystification, and dumped it as far from the city centre as he could get.[4]

Kenyon submits what he calls 'two frail inferential arguments' in favour of the unknown criminal theory. The first involves the £500 reward offered for information leading to the arrest and conviction of Sir Edmund's killers. This was a vast sum, worth, according to Kenyon writing in 1972, 'at least £5,000 and probably more in modern money'. Yet apart from the perjurers Bedloe and Prance, no one came forward to claim the reward. Kenyon's second argument in support of his theory is that it explains the mysterious four days during which Sir Edmund's whereabouts were unknown.

> The delay is much easier to explain if we visualize a poor man working alone, who would find it difficult to borrow a cart and horse at short notice without rousing suspicion, and had to wait for some plausible occasion. In the meanwhile, the alarm raised in the City for the missing magistrate would have made him realize the unusual danger he was in.[5]

Kenyon does his own theory an injustice elsewhere by stating, erroneously, that 'Godfrey usually walked the streets with a servant to act as a bodyguard'. He sometimes had a man to light him home from winter vestry meetings, but it is clear from the evidence of men like Burnet and Robinson that even when his life was threatened he walked alone. To have a servant always in tow, he told Robinson, was 'a clog to a man'. It was well known that Godfrey regularly walked alone. This seems, on the face of it, to make Kenyon's theory more likely: according to North, Godfrey was 'the easiest Man to be trapped of any Man living'.[6]

There is another point, not tendered by Kenyon, that would seem to strengthen the underworld theory – the known fact that Godfrey had been savagely attacked by the ruffian he had dragged from the pest house at the time of the plague. The historian Hallam was presumably unaware of the episode when, in arguing against Hume's less elaborate version of the theory, he mistakenly wrote that it was not usual for justices of the peace to incur such desperate resentment 'merely on account of the discharge of their ordinary duties'. There seems little doubt that the pest house villain would have murdered Godfrey had the latter not been so proficient with a sword.[7]

It is clear, then, that the basis of the argument is sound. Godfrey clearly did earn the enmity of certain criminals, and provided an easier target than most of his colleagues in wandering about alone. But there are several crucial points that mitigate against the Kenyon–Hume theory, and at the same time all but disprove the notion that Godfrey was murdered by footpads.

The first and most obvious is that when the body was found, it had about it seven guineas, four broad pieces, four pounds in silver and three rings. It is inconceivable that highwaymen should waylay and kill a man and then flee without stealing his valuables. They might not chance stealing the gloves and cane, which could be their undoing, but one broad piece was much the same as another. The same applies to the unknown criminal murdering for revenge. Kenyon argues that for the murderer to have robbed Godfrey, it 'would have altered the whole complexion of the crime, and set the authorities looking amongst the criminal classes from the start'. The argument is hardly convincing. Apart from the obvious temptation of such a large sum, it has to be asked why a common criminal should expect the authorities to look for a murderer anywhere else but among the criminal classes. If the murder were really unconnected with the Plot, the man responsible would be unlikely to have any inkling of a possible political motive.[8]

The theory also discounts the fact that Godfrey had received death threats, culminating in the mysterious letter. A low villain would surely lie in wait, perhaps shadow his intended victim through the streets, then strike suddenly and unexpectedly. It is likely that a revenge killing of the sort Hume and Kenyon postulate would be a spur-of-the-moment event like Godfrey's encounter with the assailant in the plague. Nor is it probable such a villain would be able to write, let alone pen a note tied with string or ribbon. The underworld theory does not take account, either, of Godfrey's statement that he was master of a dangerous secret that would be fatal to him. And finally, Godfrey himself made it clear to Richard Mulys that those who threatened him were 'very great ones', hardly a reference to a mean criminal.[9]

3: Fratricide and the Grim Reaper

In 1936 the American novelist John Dickson Carr produced a part fact, part fiction account of the Godfrey murder entitled *The Murder of Sir Edmund Godfrey*. In his introduction Carr said that the book was hardly a serious addition to the history of the case:

> To write good history is the noblest work of man, and cannot be managed here; the intent is only to amuse with a detective story built on facts.[1]

Within those parameters the book succeeds. It is a colourful, evocative story with some compelling scenes. But the combination of fact and fiction can be confusing. Kenyon wrote this of the book:

> It contains some bad history and some very doubtful characterization, but it sets out the facts as they are known, and gives an exhaustive review of the possible culprits.[2]

This review of suspects has, to a certain extent, been misunderstood. It included not only those accused by previous investigators and historians, but also two scenarios created by Dickson Carr himself. For dramatic purposes, chiefly to increase the number of possible culprits and so heighten the impact of his denouement, he invented a case against Christopher Kirkby and a case against Godfrey's own brothers. At the end of the book he demolished the two cases himself. However, as the ideas have been raised, they must be considered anew. The case for fratricide is discussed in this chapter; Kirkby's possible guilt is looked at in the next.[3]

'Murder, like charity,' wrote Carr in his case against Michael and Benjamin Godfrey, 'usually begins at home.' The premature genesis of the rumour that Godfrey had been captured and murdered by Catholics is the novelist's strongest point against the brothers. The rumour began on Saturday morning, before Godfrey had been away from home more than about three hours.[4]

> At this time not even his own household could have known that he would not come back to midday dinner in the ordinary way; he had simply gone out for his morning walk, according to custom.[5]

There are two points here which must be challenged. Firstly, even in the ordinary course of events, Godfrey's servants would not have expected him home for lunch that Saturday: he had agreed to dine at Welden's with his friend Thomas Wynnel. This would seem to support Dickson Carr's point that it was odd anyone should assume something was amiss. The second point, however, redresses the balance because it weakens his argument. By his own testimony, Henry Moor perceived something odd in Godfrey's behaviour that morning, starting with the magistrate's indecision about which coat he would wear, and continuing until he made his curious, troubled exit from the gate into the lane. This abnormal conduct, added to what they knew of his strange behaviour the night before and his erratic moods for the past three weeks, had prepared his servants for something untoward.[6]

But how did the rumour that he had been 'made away' begin?

> Mr George Welden, Godfrey's close friend . . . whose truthfulness has never been questioned, states that this report was started at noon on Saturday by Michael and Benjamin Godfrey. If they knew he had been snared, how did they know it, and why did they blurt it out so soon? – unless they were too eager to blame on the easy Catholic scapegoats a murder they meant to commit themselves.[7]

This is quite incorrect. Welden did not state that the rumour had been started by Godfrey's brothers. He said simply that the brothers had told him of it. It remains a mystery where the brothers first heard the report that Sir Edmund was missing, feared dead. The most likely source is Godfrey's own servants, who before eleven o'clock that morning told Richard Adams, 'We have

175

cause to fear Sir Edmund is made away.' By the time the brothers were creating such alarm at Welden's, well past noon, the town was buzzing with talk, and Saturday's newsletters carried the rumour into the country.[8]

It must be remembered that when the brothers were with Welden, Sir Edmund was still at liberty and walking not far from them. At one o'clock he was seen in the Strand by Radcliffe and several others. It is barely conceivable that two men about to murder their brother would begin to spread the rumour that he had been slain several hours before they commit the act. They would surely wait until after the deed was done.[9]

As Dickson Carr himself admitted, there is not a shred of evidence to incriminate the Godfrey brothers. Nor is any hint of a motive produced. The most obvious motive, greed, does not bear examination, for although the brothers doubtless gained financially from Sir Edmund's death, they were already extremely wealthy men. Even in 1678 such an allegation would never have been entertained without some form of corroboration.

One serious suggestion not considered by Dickson Carr, and which is probably more unlikely than either of his invented cases, first appeared in print in Sir George Clark's *The Later Stuarts* in 1934, and at greater length a year later in the second volume of Bryant's *Pepys* trilogy. The brainchild of Professor J. W. Williams of St Andrews University, the theory suggests that Godfrey, already a sick man, 'might have died of natural causes, precipitated by excessive anxiety, at a secret consultation with the King, the Duke of York and the Catholic chiefs at Somerset House, who thus confronted with the appalling problem of explaining his body and their own presence, hit on the clumsy device of staging a pretended suicide'.[10]

It is a thought-provoking idea, but no more, alas, than wishful thinking. There is no evidence that Godfrey was seriously ill physically. He took to his bed at the beginning of October for several days, but the evidence points to his malady's being the by-product of his mental and emotional depression. He was not a Papist – quite the opposite. In the words of Dean Lloyd, who knew him well, 'he always declared a particular hatred and detestation of Popery.' Why, then, would he be involved in clandestine discussions with the leading Catholics and the secretly Catholic King? Professor Williams's theory fails to explain the savage bruising found on Godfrey's chest and abdomen, which modern medical investigation, detailed later, shows to be crucial. Nor does it explain the marks of strangling, which could not have been produced after death. And finally, the theory does not take account of the indisputable fact that both the King and the Duke of York were at Newmarket at the time of Godfrey's disappearance and death.[11]

4: Oates or his Double

Dickson Carr's case against Christopher Kirkby is linked to the Victorian theory that Titus Oates was the killer. The Oates theory was first propounded by Sir James Fitzjames Stephen, the judge who finally lost his reason after sentencing Mrs Maybrick in 1889. He found support from men like Lord Birkenhead, Sidney Lee and H. D. Traill. The *Encyclopaedia Britannica* subscribes to the theory, and John Buchan adopted the idea in a fictional account of the murder.[1]

Oates, of course, was the chief beneficiary of the murder. He admitted as much himself in later years. Without the murder, the Plot would have died, and instead of becoming the Saviour of the Nation Titus would have found himself along with Tonge in a Newgate cell.

Birkenhead thought that 'Oates and his colleagues, or unscrupulous men behind them, may perhaps have committed the murder in order to rouse popular feeling against the Catholics.'[2]

Traill, in his biography of Shaftesbury, went further:

That there were Catholics capable of committing the crime is only a matter of more or less probable conjecture. That Oates was capable of it, or of any other atrocity, is a matter of demonstrated fact.[3]

There can be no doubt that Oates had little or no conscience. To say, however, that he was capable of any atrocity is conjecture. Those who would have him as Godfrey's killer sometimes cite his brutal attack on a woman in the latter years of his life. The woman tugged at Oates's sleeve. Enraged, he turned upon her and beat her over the head with his cane.[4]

Once again, there is no real evidence to support the case. There is, though, certain negative evidence that tells against it. Oates was a coward. And whatever other dubious qualities the murder and disposal of Sir Edmund Godfrey required, it did demand a peculiar sort of courage. His unfitness for the work is best illustrated by Dickson Carr:

> At St Omers he had a pan broken over his head, and was beaten round the playground by a much smaller boy, because he had not the courage to strike back. He owned that he could not fire a pistol or touch a sword. When he went out with the soldiers to arrest Jesuits, he hid behind a buttress when there was danger of swordplay.[5]

This is about as much as can be said in rebuttal of a case so feeble it can hardly be taken seriously.

If Oates was not the killer, hazards Dickson Carr in his second invented case, could it not have been Christopher Kirkby?

> Kirkby . . . wore a suit just like Oates's, and a fair woolly periwig like Oates's. In fact, on the important occasion of the revelation of the plot, Kirkby had been mistaken for Oates.[6]

On this and other equally tenuous statements Dickson Carr bases his suggestion that Kirkby might have been Godfrey's killer. He states, on what authority is not clear, that ever since the murder there has grown up a rumour that Oates was the assassin. From this questionable point of departure he continues:

> Suppose, then, that someone saw the murder done? And suppose that for the second time, on a critical occasion, Kirkby was mistaken for Oates?[7]

A periwig and a similar suit hardly transform a man into another's double. We are not fortunate enough to have a proper description of Kirkby, but word portraits as well as actual portraits of Oates abound. Can it be imagined that two such peculiar-looking creatures existed in England at the same time? Can it for one moment be accepted that, in the highly improbable situation that they did, the two men should be well known to each other?

The entire notion of mistaken identity is flawed. It is not true that a rumour existed at the time that Oates had been the killer. The earliest traceable accusation of Oates is Stephen's two hundred years later. And as no one ever claimed to have seen Oates commit the murder, we have no reason to believe they were really watching Kirkby do it.[8]

Dickson Carr's final argument in favour of Kirkby is based on the false idea that Godfrey had taken no food two days prior to his death. Was this because someone was trying to poison him and he knew it? Did the killer only resort to battering, strangling and stabbing when Godfrey refused to eat poisoned food? The novelist ends his case by reminding the reader that Kirkby was a chemist. This final section of his argument falls down badly when it is considered in the light of modern medical knowledge. Outlined in the last chapter of this section, below, this shows that there is no evidence to support the idea that Godfrey had been starved before his death. On the contrary: there is positive evidence that he wasn't.[9]

5: To Be or not to Be

The idea that Godfrey had committed suicide was one of many rumours that arose during the first few hours of his disappearance. It was quickly taken up by the Catholics in a hopeless bid to turn suspicion from themselves. Ten years after the murder, the suicide theory was propounded in *The Mystery of Sir E. B. Godfrey Unfolded*, the third part of L'Estrange's *A Brief History of the Times*. Since then it has been supported, with variations, by historians such as Lingard and Sir George Sitwell, and by Alfred Marks, author of *Who Killed Sir Edmund Berry Godfrey?* the single previous factual book on the case.[1]

There are two main versions of the theory:

(1) That Godfrey threw himself upon his own sword.
(2) That Godfrey hanged himself and was later found by his brothers, or by others in whose interest it was to make the suicide look like murder – perhaps Oates himself – who then ran the sword through the corpse and threw it in the ditch.

The first is the most obvious assumption, but because it fails for several reasons the second idea was conceived. That, too, can be proved false.

The motive attributed to Oates is clear: a suicide was no good to him in the development of his Plot hysteria, a murdered body was of inestimable use. The brothers' alleged motive, current in rumours at the time of the disappearance, was that the estate of a suicide was forfeit to the Crown. If they could disguise their brother's *felo de se* so that people would think him murdered, Sir Edmund's considerable wealth would not be lost. This last notion was satisfactorily disposed of by Sir Robert Southwell, clerk to the Privy Council. The brothers had expressed no suspicion that Edmund had killed himself when they saw the council on Monday and Tuesday of the week of his absence. 'Not any suspicion of self-murther, but plainly charging the Papists'. It was claimed by some that their visits to the Lord Chancellor and Lord Privy Seal were to disclose the truth about Godfrey's suicide, and recruit the help of the lords in saving the estate. But, wrote Southwell, neither the Lord Chancellor nor the Lord Privy Seal were

> . . . fitt instruments to save the estate, especially since the King was then at New Market, as he had been from Tuesday the first of October, and returned not till after the dead body was found. The proper application had been to the Secretaryes of State [which the Godfreys would have known], who were then both in towne; or rather to have posted downe to New Market, there to make friends and to have begged what was forfeited to his Majesty by the selfe-murther.[2]

But whatever the theories at the time, whatever the brothers might or might not have suspected, Sir Edmund Godfrey did not kill himself, as will be shown.

The chief foundation of the suicide theories is the fact that Sir Edmund was undoubtedly in a disturbed state in the weeks before his death. He was known to be a melancholy man, and his father, it was rumoured, had died suicidally mad. Godfrey even told Mrs Gibbon, 'Oh! Cousin, I do inherit my father's deep melancholy. I cannot get it off. I have taken away a great many ounces of blood, but I cannot get the victory.'[3]

Here is L'Estrange's version of Godfrey's last day:

> Hardly anybody set eye upon him that did not take notice of a troubled head in his very look and gait, over and above that even the course of his perambulation was not a jaunt for any man in his right mind to take. Nay, the distraction of his thoughts appeared in the wanderings and irresolution of his steps; it did not look like a walk either for pleasure or for business, but rather the whiling away of so many hours under the fluctuation of sick and doubting thoughts, and in a kind of conflict (as a man may say) between his nature and his disease. 'Tis much to be suspected that at his first setting out, he had the very thing in his eye, as well as the place, and that, if a body may gather anything either from his melancholy or from his inquiring the way thither, he went probably to those very fields, for Collins and the milkwoman saw him thereabouts, and Mason met him then at ten in the morning, coming back

again, which in a reasonable construction, was no more than to say that his heart had not served him to go through with his work that bout. After his return, we have him again in the Strand, New Market, Lincoln's-Inn-Back-Gate, the Fields, Turnstile, Red-Lion-Fields, and so forward to the very next close where the body was found.[4]

Marks thought that Godfrey found his way to the ditch, drew his sword, placed the pommel on the earth of the opposite bank, and threw himself upon it. He quotes a Dr Freyberger, to whom he had submitted information about the case, thus:

> The position in which the body was discovered in the ditch . . . is indicative of having been assumed at the moment of death. The body must have become stiff in that position. It would be impossible to give such a position to a dead body which had been brought from a considerable distance, and therefore some considerable time after death, when rigor mortis would no doubt be present, and greatly interfere with the arrangement of such a 'life-like' position; and if the body already had become limp again, such an attitude as that of the stiff right arm, which was found stretched out and resting on the bank of the ditch, could not have been produced by any amount of poising.[5]

The most contentious part of the Marks-Freyberger theory concerns the terrible bruising on Godfrey's abdomen and chest, and the marks of strangulation about his neck. The bruising, they say, was not bruising at all – it was a discoloration of the skin brought about by a condition called post mortem hypostasis. Simply, this is the draining of the blood to the lowest parts of the body after death. And the marks on the neck, they say, were not caused by any sort of strangulation, but by the magistrate's high collar, which pressed into the neck when the neck swelled up with the action of hypostasis.[6]

Freyberger talks of an 'impression in the ground near the edge of the ditch, which some witnesses held might have been produced by the pommel of the sword'. Even assuming this impression existed, what connection can it have had with the sword? Constable Brown, who gave a detailed description of the body's position, stated plainly that 'the pommel of the sword did not reach the ground beneath the body'. Clearly, if Godfrey had fallen upon his sword with enough force to drive it through his heart and shoulder blade and six inches out of his back, the pommel *wor 'd* have reached the ground. It would not only have reached, it would have been driven deep into the soft earth of the ditch. The hilt would have been caked in mud, which it was not, and the hole left in the earth would hardly have been described as an 'impression'.[7]

There is no doubt, as Marks avers, that Sir Edmund Godfrey was in a fluctuating state of depression in the days before his death. But what Marks fails to point out is the reason for the depression: Godfrey had been the victim of death threats.

'I am threatened,' he told Richard Mulys early in October, 'for having done too much.'[8]

'Upon my conscience, I believe I shall be the first martyr,' he told his friend Robinson.[9]

'Have you not heard that I am to be hanged?' he said to Mary Gibbon.[10]

And, on the night before he disappeared, he said to his friends at Colonel Welden's house that they would soon hear of the death, or murder, of someone.[11]

This was no suicide talk. This was the discourse of a man who feared death above all else. These were the words of a man who knew his life was threatened, and by whom. 'I do not fear them if they come fairly,' he said to Robinson, 'and I shall not part with my life tamely.'[12]

When it is established that Godfrey's deep depression was caused by the threats to his life, the suicide theory collapses. It is a rare man who kills himself to escape being murdered.

Marks does not mention the mysterious letter which was delivered to Godfrey on 11 October, although it was clearly of crucial importance and set him burning papers and turning over drawers and trunks.

But the real proof that Godfrey did not commit suicide is contained in the medical evidence, discussed below.

6: Post Post Mortem

Forensic medicine was in its infancy in 1678. Although the surgeons Skillard and Cambridge performed a detailed examination of Godfrey's corpse, their knowledge was so rudimentary that the meaning of many of their discoveries eluded them. Only in recent times has it been possible to draw dependable conclusions about the cause and timing of Godfrey's death, without which no solution can be reached. While other forms of clue have grown cold, the medical evidence has been awaiting the light which only modern scientific knowlege can give. Even Dr Freyberger, writing in 1905, was restricted by bounds of medical knowledge of his day, considerably narrower then than now.

I submitted all the known facts of the Godfrey post mortem examination to Britain's foremost forensic pathologist Professor C. Keith Simpson, whose opinions on the case were first given in a radio broadcast in 1952. Simpson, whose sensational discoveries have provided crucial evidence in great murder trials such as that of Haigh the acid bath killer, also examined two newly-discovered items unknown by previous chroniclers of the case. These were:

(1) a handwritten statement by Zachariah Skillard, and
(2) a page of notes by Secretary of State Williamson, recording the salient points of a conversation with coroner John Cowper.[1]

Before explaining the precise details of Godfrey's murder, it is important to dispose of several errors which began as rumour and to which constant repetition has lent apparent historicity. The first is the often repeated statement that Godfrey was kept alive for several days by his captors. Some writers have even suggested that he was not murdered until the day he was found. The second is that during this supposed captivity he was deprived of food. There was talk at the time of the inquest that the surgeons had found evidence that he had been without food for two days before his death.

In his 1952 report on the case for BBC Radio, which was based upon the generally known medical evidence, Simpson said that the evidence of starvation was open to strong criticism:

It could only be founded on the finding of an empty bowel. But liquid food or easily digested and absorbed solid food – say, milk and white bread, wine, eggs, butter and so on – would leave virtually no residue. There is evidence that Godfrey had been depressed and disturbed for some time and may, in consequence, have been eating very little.[2]

But the surgeons Skillard and Cambridge were less informed than Simpson believed them to be. Williamson's notes of his conversation with the coroner make it clear that the diagnosis of 'no food for two days' must have been made on the evidence of an empty stomach, not an empty bowel. For Williamson refers to the discovery of faeces in the bowel, and the fact that it was 'redder

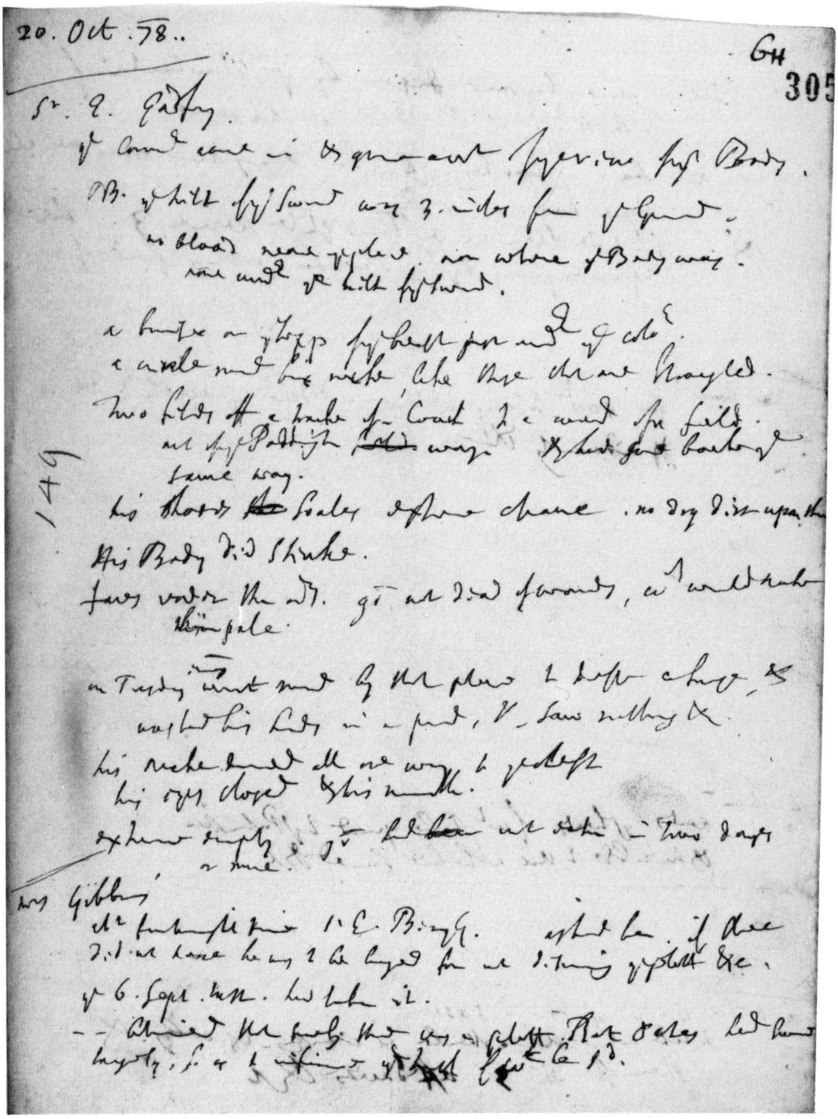

The medical evidence that lay undiscovered
for 298 years

than ordinary'. The colour of the faeces has no relevance to Godfrey's death, says Simpson. But its presence confirms that the surgeons relied for their conclusions upon an empty stomach. And the stomach, says Simpson, empties in two hours, not two days.[3]

The 'kept in captivity' theory is also easy to dismiss.

And Zachariah Skillard's previously undiscovered statement says:

> ... he had been dead five days or a week before the Coroner sate upon him for that when he [Skillard] went to open him the Lean of his body was soe putrid, that it hung upon the Insision knife . . .[4]

There was, of course, no refrigeration in 1678. The speed at which decomposition would take place would depend on the temperature on the days between Godfrey's death and the finding of the body. There is no doubt that the weather was very cold indeed on the day he disappeared – witness all the clothes he put on, including three pairs of stockings. And on the day he was found it turned to snow. Even in these cold temperatures the body was in an advanced state of decomposition by Thursday, 17 October. Simpson writes:

> The 'lean' is the muscle. If this 'was soe putrid' at the time of the post mortem, death must have occurred four or five days earlier. If Godfrey *had* been kept prisoner for several days before he was murdered, the body would have been much fresher. It is plain that he died on or about the day he disappeared.[5]

The facts about Godfrey's wounds, says Simpson, are 'wholly inconsistent with suicide'. And he is convinced that the sword wound was not the cause of death. The evidence that the magistrate died of 'asphyxia by strangulation' is overwhelming.[6]

> Sir Edmund Berry Godfrey's face was livid and his eyes intensely suffused. For such livid discoloration of eyes and face to develop, it is essential that the circulation be intact – that is, that the victim should be alive. If the sword had been driven through the body before the strangulation, the pressure in the blood vessels would have fallen during internal bleeding and the discoloration could not have developed. This suffusion of the face and eyes combined with the marks of constriction of the neck give clear evidence of strangulation. It is possible that the sword was thrust through the body *as death was taking place* – as a kind of *coup de grâce* – or afterwards.[7]

The alleged absence of bleeding was made a controversial issue at the time of the inquest, and has been heatedly debated ever since. Simpson believes it is irrelevant. The amount of blood shed, whether a great deal or none at all, is not helpful in finding whether Godfrey was alive or dead at the time the sword entered the body, he says.[8]

> A sword passed through any body, live or dead, might effectually plug the wound and prevent bleeding until it is withdrawn.[9]

There was evidence that some blood had seeped from Godfrey's body after it was deposited at the White House, but this is 'quite in keeping with the sword having been driven through the body after death.'[10]

> When a body begins to putrefy, gases form. In Godfrey's case, a certain amount of pressure would have developed with these gases. And when the sword was removed, blood accumulating internally would undoubtedly leak out through the stab holes. Rather more blood would have accumulated if the sword had transfixed the still-live body, but there is really little in this. The surgeons of the day were mistaken in attaching so much importance to bleeding. We have come to realize that blood may never clot, or it might clot and then quickly become fluid again by the action of *fibrinolysins*. Bleeding varies also with the position of the wound. I once saw a soldier who was killed by a stab wound of the heart. He bled freely *internally*, but there was scarcely a drop of blood externally even when the blade was withdrawn – because of the position of the wound.[11]

Simpson is emphatic that strangling was the cause of death. The marks on the neck provide 'unmistakeable evidence' of this. The weapon, he says, was a cloth or band. 'And as Godfrey's cravat was missing when the body was found, it is more than reasonable to suppose that it was the cravat that was used for the murder.'[12]

The theory that the magistrate hanged himself is, according to Simpson, 'quite untenable'.[13]

> The collar of his jacket had to be undone to expose the marks on the neck. They were therefore much too low to be consistent with hanging. Hanging marks lie under the lower jaw, rising under the ears. Death is caused by lifting the tongue into the back of the throat.[14]

As for the neck itself, the evidence submitted at the inquest does not prove that it was broken. The statement on which the assumption of a broken neck has been based said that 'you might have taken the chin, and have set it upon either shoulder'.[15] But,

> ... a neck might become as loose as that after the initial *rigor mortis* has disappeared, without there being any injury at all.[16]

Simpson explains the bruise under Godfrey's left ear as being 'either a knot mark, or chafing from strangling fingers during the twisting or tying of the ligature'[17]; and the Marks-Freyberger theory that the bruise marks on the chest and abdomen were the result of the blood draining to the lowest parts of the body after death, is finally dismissed:

> The bruises certainly cannot have been due to hypostasis, or extravasation, after death. The discoloration produced by the draining of the blood to the underlying parts of the body is even. It does not appear in patches. And the appearance is quite distinct from that of bruising. A cut into the skin will confirm the difference.[18]

What, then, had caused the peculiar bruising? Simpson confirms the opinion of the apothecary John Chase, who said, 'I never saw any man beaten so in my life.'[19]

> The chest and abdomen bruising are strong evidence of a 'beat-up' by fist or boot – or both. I can think of no other explanation.[20]

The attack on Godfrey, therefore, came in three separate ways: he was strangled; he was stabbed; he was beaten up. But what was the sequence?

> Bruises from a beat-up would require several minutes to develop, and *can* only develop during life. Asphyxial changes require twenty to thirty seconds, again during life. There is therefore clear evidence that the murder took place in three successive steps:
> (1) First, a beating up, lasting several minutes, by fist or boot – or both.
> (2) Second, strangling by a ligature, probably lasting no more than twenty to thirty seconds.
> (3) Third and last, the thrusting in of the sword from front to back, either at the point of death or after.
>   The beating up and the strangling occurred while Godfrey was alive, the strangling in fact causing his death.[21]

So we are looking for a peculiar sort of killer. The method is precisely set out. There cannot have been many murderers at large in London in 1678 with such a distinctive *modus operandi*.

The net is beginning to close.

PART VI

The Answer

... a mystery which, but for some
fortuitous discovery, will, doubtless,
remain unravelled until the end of all time.

Sir John Hall, *Four Famous Mysteries*, 1924

Alack, alack, Edmund, I like not this unnatural dealing.

King Lear, III. iii

1: Peyton's Gang

Of all the ingenious theories that have been devised to explain Godfrey's murder, not one has come near to providing a believable motive. Yet motive is a crucial consideration. It is of dubious value to demonstrate that A has had means and opportunity to kill B, if at the same time one cannot show that A also has a very strong reason for doing so.

'If we only knew *why* he was murdered,' mourned Kenyon, 'we would know with some certainty *who* did it.'[1]

Almost exactly three hundred years after Godfrey's murder I discovered a chain of clues that led me first to the motive, and beyond that to his killers. The first link in the chain was a secret service report in the handwriting of Secretary of State Sir Joseph Williamson. Found among the domestic state papers of King Charles II, it is a single page of notes based on information received from Colonel Thomas Blood. Blood was a veteran of numerous republican plots, including the ill-fated Yorkshire Plot of 1663. The only man ever to succeed in stealing the Crown Jewels, he had by 1677 received a royal pardon for his many infamous treasons and was working as a government spy, wheedling secrets from his former confederates in crime. In the autumn of 1677, the report shows, Blood uncovered a conspiracy by three groups of republican activists – the Fifth Monarchy Men, the Atheists and Sir Robert Peyton's Gang. The plot, seemingly the first hatched by the three groups in alliance, was a source of grave concern. This was no airy dream conceived in a bar room and likely to end, as did so many, with a few burned roofs and broken heads. It was rebellion, coolly planned. The conspirators intended to march on London with an army of supporters drawn from three counties. A great deal rested on the element of surprise. All going as planned, the Tower would be seized, the King and Duke of York would be killed, and Richard Cromwell would be set up as nominal ruler.[2]

The efficiency of Charles's spy network nipped the conspiracy in the bud. When it was realized that secret agents had infiltrated the conspirators' ranks, the rebellion was abandoned.

Peyton's Gang is the least known of the three groups involved in the conspiracy. It consisted of only twelve men, each personally selected by its leader Sir Robert Peyton, a violent opponent of the

Court and MP for Middlesex. They were hard-line Protestant supporters of the republican cause, and the more extreme supporters of Shaftesbury. Some were also members of the Green Ribbon Club. The Gang had alarmed the government with its seditious activities long before the 1677 conspiracy. Sir John Robinson, Lieutenant of the Tower Hamlets, had pressed Williamson in 1676 to root out members of the Gang holding public office. Several apart from Peyton were in positions of authority and standing. 'It is of great concern to his Majesty, the good government of the city and the adjacent parts that nobody be in commission either military or civil but such as are faithful and love and affect the government,' wrote Robinson in March 1676 in a letter that formed the second link in the chain of clues.[3]

He was taken at his word, and half of the twelve-man Gang were stripped of their public offices. 'I wish the rest were so,' prayed Robinson. But the rest, more eminent and with powerful friends, were less easily disposed of. The remarkable truth, never before disclosed, is that Sir Edmund Berry Godfrey was one of those republican conspirators dedicated to the overthrow of Charles and the setting up of Cromwell. He came of course from a strongly Protestant, doubtless Puritan, family – his father having sat in Pym's Puritan parliament in 1628–9. But it has hitherto never been intimated that Sir Edmund was anything but a staunch defender of the status quo. The idea that he was a plotter of armed rebellion would have been regarded almost as heresy by earlier chroniclers of his life and death. Yet this was so. The truth is contained on a tiny, tissue-thin slip of notepaper, the third link in the chain, among Williamson's secret papers. Written by Robinson and headed *Paitons gang*, it lists twelve names. Godfrey's is fourth from the top:[4]

> Sr Robert peyton
> Sr Reginald Foster
> Sr William Bowles
> Sr Edmund Berry Godfrey
> Georg Welch Esq
> William Barker Esq
> Richard Adams Esq
> William Hempson Esq
> Peter Sabbs Esq
> Samuell Buck Esq
> John Barker Esq
> Charles Umphreville Esq

192

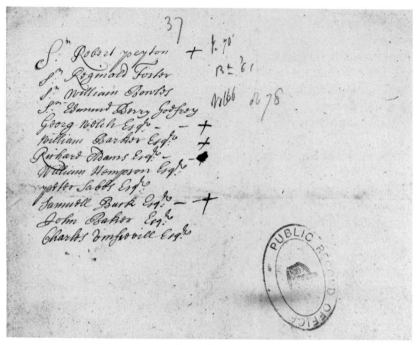

Peyton's gang

193

Sir Edmund's membership of the Gang marks him out as an extreme and active republican, and like other members of the Gang he was doubtless a Green Ribboner too. Indeed, it looks very much as if he was a founder member of that 'Club of Devils'. This is indicated by the fourth link in the chain of clues, a letter from Sir Gilbert Talbot to Williamson, dated Whitehall, 28 February 1674. Talbot refers to 'a large dinner' held for the strongly anti-popish members of the Commons at 'the Swan Tavern in King Streete'. The meeting included men like Sir Thomas Lee, Sir Eliab Harvey, Sir Nicholas Carew and William Sacheverall who, as early as 1675, were talking about the exclusion of the Duke of York. It was meetings such as this which laid the foundations for the Green Ribbon Club. This particular dinner had to be abandoned by the dissident MPs because the King suddenly prorogued Parliament and, fearing themselves in danger in the suburbs, they fled back to the city, 'some by coach, some by water'. The venue for this dinner of Opposition men is interesting. Where exactly was the Swan Tavern in King Street? Clearly it was outside London, and not far from the Thames. The only Swan that seems to fit the bill is the old Swan in King Street, Hammersmith. As his will, link number five, shows, the owner of that tavern and the host of the rebel MPs was none other than Sir Edmund Berry Godfrey.[5]

There is another twist. Godfrey's colleagues in Peyton's Gang were the 'very honourable friends' of Israel Tonge. It will be remembered that in a previously unpublished section of Tonge's journal, the sixth and final link, his reason for approaching Godfrey in the first instance was explained. He was searching for a JP before whom Oates could swear to the truth of his articles about the Plot. Having been repulsed by Williamson, Tonge was directed to Godfrey by some 'very honourable friends' with whom he consulted, and who were obviously anxious to assist in bringing the Plot to maturity. With the knowledge of Godfrey's membership of Peyton's Gang it is not difficult to see that it was the Gang whose help Tonge sought at this early stage. Both Oates and Tonge came from strongly republican backgrounds. The Fifth Monarchist Thomas Tonge, executed in 1662 for leading a republican plot to kill the king, is believed to have been a brother of Israel. Captain Oates, executed for his part in the republican Yorkshire Plot of 1663, was almost certainly a relative of Titus. Moreover, the Plot they were inventing was based on an intimate knowledge of actual republican conspiracies of earlier years.

In September 1678, then, two left-wing fanatics are in London trying to create mayhem for the hated Papists. Both are related to men of standing in the world of republican conspiracy. One of them approaches some 'very honourable friends', who without doubt are trusted contacts in the same sphere of political activity. These friends direct him to Sir Edmund Godfrey, himself secretly a member of Peyton's Gang and guilty of complicity with the Gang in at least one republican plot to murder the King and take over the country. The friends have great influence with Godfrey, prevailing upon him to commit such dereliction of duty in taking Oates's affidavit and to remain silent about it that if he were discovered could cost him his life. What republican group could hold such sway with Sir Edmund but the very one of which he was a member?

Another gap has yet to be filled. It is common knowledge that Shaftesbury, Buckingham and other leading Whigs took over the management of the Plot shortly after the death of Godfrey, and used it to whip up unparalleled hatred and as a lever to force the introduction of an Exclusion Bill. Now, thanks to the new evidence detailed, it can be seen that from as early as the beginning of September, the Whig undercover men were already assisting Oates and Tonge. Most historians have been agreed that the two perjurers received material help in the actual formulation of the eighty-one articles between 6 September and the day Oates first appeared before the Privy Council. No one has yet been able to say with certainty, though, who it was that provided the guidance and much original material for weaving into the Plot.[6]

As Peyton's Gang were supporting the inventors of the Plot from its inception, and the Gang's patrons took over the Plot in October, I suggest that it was the Gang who were nursing the Plot through its infant stage, controlling its development until such time as the great Whigs might take over. The hand of Peyton's Gang, with its notorious membership of Green Ribboners and republican plotters, is to be detected in every syllable of Oates's expanded Narrative.

The secret life and ideals of Godfrey can best be judged by looking at the individual fellow members of the Gang and their activities. Peyton himself was leader of the Green Ribbon Club and Shaftesbury's right-hand man in organizing anti-popish propaganda and spectacular republican displays such as the notorious pope-burning processions. In 1680 the club constructed a giant model of Godfrey to accompany the equally large image of the Pope. Several live cats were placed in the belly of the 'pope' so that real screams of agony issued forth when it was set ablaze. Peyton was an ardent supporter of Monmouth as the only possible successor to Charles if the monarchy must remain. During various periods of unrest he was 'talked of for Chiefe in London'. According to Sir George Sitwell, his favourite pursuits were 'preaching, praying and profligacy'. In 1680 he was expelled from the Commons and the Green Ribbon Club for secretly changing sides and allegedly acting as a spy for the Court. 'I cannot call you a fallen angel,' the Speaker snarled, 'for you have been a devil from the beginning. You were ever a profuse rolling hero, having now nothing left you but the state of man, whereby you are become nauseous to this House, and therefore they now spew you out.' But the same year Peyton was sent to the Tower for high treason, accused of having said during Charles's illness that, if the king died, he would be at the head of 20,000 men to oppose the Duke of York. If the Lord Mayor and Sheriffs proclaimed James king they would be killed, and a commonwealth declared. After his imprisonment, 'the factious personns of his gange', who had been alienated from him by his temporary adherence to James, again pledged him their allegiance. He was implicated also in the Meal Tub Plot in 1679.[7]

Another notorious member of the Gang, Charles Umphreville, was also a Green Ribboner. After the Popish Plot terror had begun to diminish, Umphreville was deeply involved in the Rye House Plot.

At the height of the Popish terror, he was one of several Gang members and Green Ribboners used by the Whigs to pack juries and make certain the desired verdicts were returned. Umphreville served on the juries at both the trial of Coleman and that of Green, Berry and Hill. Sir Reginald Forster, another member of the Gang, was foreman of the jury that convicted Coleman. The Plot-mongers contrived to pack the juries of no less than five trials arising from Oates's terror. There was little doubt about the verdicts, but to guarantee conviction there were Green Ribboners and Gangsters at the trials of Ireland, Pickering and Grove; Coleman; Whitebread, Harcourt, Fenwick, Gavan and Turner; Green, Berry and Hill; and Langhorn. All were executed. With Samuel Atkins the jury was not packed and he was acquitted.[8]

Godfrey's friendship with Richard Adams, the papist-hating lawyer of Lincoln's Inn, doubtless stemmed from their mutual complicity in seditious activities. Adams, too, was a member of the Gang. It is interesting that Adams had been imprisoned in the

Gatehouse accused of uttering treasonable words six months after Godfrey's confrontation with the King in 1669.[9] Whether it was the shoddy treatment Godfrey received from his King in the episode of the physician's bad debt that turned him so violently against the monarchy, or whether his hatred went back further, will probably never be known.

Godfrey was one of six members of Peyton's Gang not driven from office in the purges of 1676. But from that time he must have realized he was being closely watched. He was walking a tight-rope, all the time secretly active in conspiracy yet outwardly seeming the best and most conscientious JP in London. He knew that at any moment he might topple. It is noteworthy that his first recorded bout of depression descended upon him in the late summer of 1677, about the time that the regicide plot in which he was involved had to be abandoned because the government had wind of it. He prepared his will at this time, too. From that time Godfrey knew he was a marked man. At first he took an extended trip abroad, his first for many years. Then he seems to have striven hard for the next year to convince those watching him of his fidelity to the crown. There is no further hint of undercover activity, and his time was filled with public service. He was conspicuously active supervising the laying of sewers in St James's Park, responding to the demands of the parish and fulfilling with distinction all the many contrasting functions of the magistrate. In addition, he spent many weeks in detective work, interviewing witnesses, preparing a case and finally acting as public prosecutor for the summary hearing of a great murder trial in the spring of 1678. Then came Oates and Tonge, and the activities of the Gang were given a new impetus. Godfrey was still anxious not to put a foot wrong so far as the government was concerned, but at the same time he could not afford to seem desultory in the eyes of his fellow Gangsters.[10]

So reluctantly he agreed to interview Oates and Tonge at the Gang's request on 6 September. But it was not until Oates's second visit to him on 28 September that he began to show renewed signs of disturbance and alarm. Thus far he believed he had pleased the honourable friends well. Now he took a step which he knew was placing his life in peril. As from 28 September the fellow members of Peyton's Gang were no longer his very honourable friends. In a sudden and irreparable reversal of fortune they had become his very honourable foes.[11]

What was the step he took that turned the Gang so rapidly

against him? What possible motive could they have for murdering so senior and committed a member?

The answer is a single word. Betrayal. Sir Edmund Berry Godfrey was a traitor to the republican cause, a traitor to the Green Ribbon Club and a traitor to Peyton's Gang. And the key to his murder is contained in his mysterious meeting with Mr Clarke on the afternoon of the day he first saw Oates's expanded depositions. Who was the shadowy Mr Clarke whom Godfrey sent urgently to see as soon as Oates and Tonge had left him? What was it in the expanded depositions that reduced the magistrate to such panic? The answer is to be found in the manuscript statements of witnesses examined by the Lords Committee investigating the murder. Colonel Welden, at whose house Godfrey met with Clarke, was interrogated by the committee on 25 October. He told the committee how, on 28 September, a man known both to himself and Godfrey came to his house and asked for a servant to be sent to summon the magistrate. The servant was instructed to tell Godfrey, if he were not alone, 'that one Clarke would speak with him'. But Clarke, Welden revealed, was a false name to mislead outsiders. Godfrey and he both knew well that Mr Clarke was the *nom de guerre* of Edward Coleman, the intriguing, visionary secretary of the Duchess of York.

'When Mr Coleman and Sir Edmundbury were together at my house,' said Welden, 'they were reading papers.'[12]

There can be no doubt that the papers over which Godfrey and Coleman pored were the magistrate's copy of Oates's articles. The first of the new articles left with Godfrey that morning mentioned Coleman for the first time. He had not been implicated in any part of the 43 articles perused by Godfrey on 6 September. Now, in article 44, he was accused of being a prime mover in the Popish Plot. That night Coleman destroyed most of his papers and fled. If he had remembered the deal box of letters and other documents behind the fireplace, Godfrey's urgent warning would doubtless have saved his life, as it was intended to.[13]

To those who saw Godfrey as the 'honourable, upright Protestant magistrate', his intimacy with Coleman was astonishing enough. How much more baffling it is now that Godfrey's true character and activities are revealed. He was a leading member of an organization pledged to murder the King, destroy popery, and inaugurate a republic under Oliver Cromwell's son. Yet he took steps to save the life of a man who was not only a fanatical papist but who was a servant of the nation's leading Catholic, the Duke of York.

I have searched in vain all over England, and even in France, for the final evidence as to Edmund Godfrey's state of thinking, and the exact nature of his secret activities. The evidence existed for certain as late as 1744, as witnessed by a letter written that year and now among the Additional Manuscripts at the British Museum. The letter, in the hand of one Alexander Herbert Phaire, refers to 104 letters of Godfrey's. 'They contain,' wrote Phaire, 'many remarkable things, and the best and truest secret history in King Charles II's reign.' Phaire was the son of Colonel Robert Phaire, the regicide. The Colonel, an ardent republican, was a close friend of the Irish miracle healer Valentine Greatrakes, who in turn was so intimate with Godfrey that he named his son after him. It may be that in some long forgotten vault in Ireland there is deposited the final clue in the mystery of Godfrey's seditious activities.[14]*

The insertion of Coleman's name into Oates's account of the Plot was undoubtedly the work of the Gang members appointed to expand the Narrative. It was the first attempt at inaugurating the domino plan. If Coleman could be incriminated, the downfall of the Duke of York might follow. The plan failed because, at the last moment, Godfrey betrayed his fellow plotters and not only warned Coleman to destroy his papers and flee, *he also caused a copy of Oates's depositions to be sent to the Duke of York himself*, and so prepare him fully for the inevitable onslaught.

Why Godfrey took such a suicidal course, apparently so inconsistent with his own ideals, is the most enduring part of the mystery of the man and his complex motivations. Had he somehow developed a deep and intimate relationship with Coleman that surmounted even the hurdle of Coleman's hated religion? Had he, for some unknown reason, had a change of heart? When he came to the brink of destroying people rather than ideas and ideologies, did his courage fail him? Or was he, perhaps most likely of all, making a final effort to save his own life by backing those he thought most likely to be the strongest allies? His association with Coleman was not new. It is therefore likely that

---

* Professor Kenyon tells me: 'These look very much like Coleman's newsletters, which he ran as a semi-commercial operation 1674–8, and whose contents caused some scandal, though why is not clear.' He has traced them to the Carl H. Pforzheimer Library, New York.

the Gang suspected some intrigue between the two men long before their meeting of 28 September. And as it was the Gang who inserted Coleman's name in the new depositions, that tactic might have had a secondary purpose – to test Edmund Godfrey. His reaction to the contents of the expanded depositions would tell for certain if he were a traitor.

Godfrey, then, was being observed for any signs of infidelity by two opposite and irreconcilable parties – the loyalists who were the powerful men in government, and the republicans. If he made any move in either direction, he could expect reprisals from the opposite side. Yet he was in the dreadful position of having to do something. Too many conflicting influences were at work on him for it to be otherwise. He was genuinely devoted to his public work and the maintenance of law and order and social services in the community. He was, at the same time, the friend of a man who would die if he, Godfrey, did nothing. And he was a committed member of an organization in whose best interests it was that that man died.

If he betrayed the government, he could expect a judicial death. If he betrayed the Gang it would be furtive execution by hired killers.

His first choice was to remain faithful to the republicans, and for three weeks after Oates's first visit he did nothing, just as the Gang had requested. As a leading Gangster himself, he would have been well aware of the great Plot being hatched by his colleagues with Oates as their front man, and that silence at this formative stage was the best policy. So for three weeks he was, by his deliberate passivity, at last alienating himself positively from the government. This must have unnerved him considerably. He knew only too well that he had been watched constantly by government agents since the abortive conspiracy of the previous autumn. Until Oates's first visit he had managed to remain beyond the reach of the law. Then, with Oates's second visit, personalities entered into the matter. The life of his friend was at stake. How could he save it without making deadly enemies of the Gang? He could not. How could he survive, with both the government and the Gang out to kill him? He could not. But could he, by switching sides now, save both Coleman's life and his own?

He took the best of three bad choices open to him. He took the measures necessary to save Coleman, so placing himself in deadly opposition to the Gang. And to save himself he tried to buy the friendship of the government by sending a warning to the Duke of

York, and by taking his copy of the depositions, as a flag of truce, to the Lord Chief Justice. It was the best he could do, and he knew it was an appalling gamble. From that moment he fell into a state of fear and anguish.[15]

This assessment at last makes sense of all Godfrey's seemingly contradictory comments in the weeks leading up to his death, which clearly referred to a fear of death *from two distinct sources*.

By the time of his gamble, he knew what to expect from the Gang. But he could by no means be sure that the government would still not take action and have him arrested and tried for his life.

Thus, in telling Burnet and others that he should be knocked on the head, he was referring to the hired killers he expected any time to appear and execute him on behalf of the Gang.[16]

'I lie under ill circumstances,' he told Mulys. 'Some great men blame me for not having done my duty . . .' – this was a reference to the threat from the government – '. . . and I am threatened by others, and very great ones too, for having done too much' – here he was referring to the Gang and their powerful patrons.[17]

When he told Robinson he thought he should be the first martyr, but added that, 'I do not fear them if they come fairly, and shall not part with my life tamely,' he was again dwelling on the hired murderers of the Gang.[18]

'Have you not heard I am to be hanged?' Another obvious allusion to the fate he feared awaited him through the processes of law.[19]

He also informed two people, Mary Gibbon and Thomas Wynnel, that Oates had forsworn himself. Only with his secret knowledge of the Gang's real plans for the Popish Plot could he be in a position to make such a statement. To Wynnel he went on: 'There is nothing against the King. But there is a design upon the Duke of York, and this will come to a dispute among them.' Once again, he was obviously speaking of the republicans, and his own conduct had made certain of a split in their ranks.[20]

'I am master of a dangerous secret,' he said finally, 'that will be fatal to me.'[21]

Here we have the essence of the Gang's motive in ordering his death: the dangerous secret. As a prominent member of the Gang, and from his involvement in the conspiracy to take over the country by force the previous autumn, Godfrey knew a great deal about the republicans' most secret designs. In foiling the domino plan he had shown himself a traitor. The sort of knowledge he already possessed could not be trusted to a traitor.

But there is another fact that, for the honourable friends, would have made Godfrey's death even more imperative. Edward Coleman, in his intriguing with the French King's confessor, had become a trusted secret agent of the French court. As such, he had become a vital link in one of the strangest alliances in the history of the period. Shaftesbury and the Opposition hated nothing so much as France and popery. Yet, despite this, it was in the interests of both France and the Opposition to encourage civil unrest in England. To help achieve this common aim, *the Opposition leaders were secretly in the pay of their sworn enemy the King of France.*[22]

'A rough modern parallel,' wrote Hugh Ross Williamson, the historian, 'would be if the 1922 Committee of the Conservative party were in fact in the pay of Soviet Russia, accepting Communist gold to prosecute an anti-Communist policy.[23]

The man who paid the French bribes over to the Opposition was Edward Coleman.[24]

The information that republican lords and MPs were being bribed by France could not be trusted to a proven traitor. Godfrey had to be silenced. But at the same time, it was realized, his death could be useful in establishing the credibility of the Plot. It had only to be committed at the right time, in the way best contrived to create panic, and accompanied by a well-planned propaganda exercise that blamed the murder on the Papists, and the honourable friends were in business. Fortunately for the Gang, Godfrey had alienated himself from both sides. At the moment, with the government as much his enemy as the Gang, he could do little damage with his damning knowledge. The operation could be properly planned.

2: The Spy from Long Island

In April 1679 a man calling himself John Johnson arrived by ship at Folkestone. He was known to be a secret agent working against the interests of the government, and the port authorities had been alerted to look out for him some time before. Somehow he eluded the Admiralty men at Folkestone and set off on the London Road. But at Dover he was not so lucky. He was arrested on the King's warrant and sent under guard to the capital.[1]

It did not take the Admiralty Secretary, Samuel Pepys, long to discover that 'John Johnson' was his old quarry 'Mr Godfrey', whom he had pursued with such vigour as the prime suspect in Sir Edmund Berry Godfrey's murder six months before. Further inquiries revealed that 'John Johnson' was the regular pseudonym of a republican spy called Colonel John Scott, son of a Kentish miller who had lived from childhood in the New World. Even the 'Colonel' is doubtful.[2]

Scott was a blackguard of greater notoriety in America and Europe than in England. In a criminal career spanning thirty years, beginning in his youth in Long Island, New Amsterdam, he had by ingenious and minutely planned methods defrauded hundreds of people, international statesmen as well as more humble prey. In the New World he had been guilty of theft, white slavery, land swindles and a host of other crimes culminating in the murder of a man on the island of St Kitts. He was sentenced to death, but not for the first time his silver tongue saved his life, even as the noose was tightening around his neck. He was next heard of at the head of a company of soldiers in the war against France, soon after that being court-martialled for cowardice for hiding behind a rock when his men engaged the enemy. By the beginning of the 1670s he had arrived in Europe and followed a scandalous career of intrigue, violence, bigamy and fraud. In Holland he had passed as Geographer to the King of England and tricked the Dutch government into giving him command of a regiment. Having embezzled and stolen from the regiment and the people of the town where it was billeted, he had fled the country to escape the gallows. As he moved purposefully along the road to Flanders, where among other exploits he was to rob a nunnery, his furious victims back in Holland resorted to a vicarious voodoo revenge, hanging him in effigy. In France, passing under various names, he had sold dud navigation charts and useless, exploding guns to the Sun King himself.[3]

In 1677 he had arrived in England and begun spying for the republicans, travelling to and fro across the Channel, an Autolycus of espionage, selling to Shaftesbury and his cohorts whatever unconsidered trifles of anti-France, anti-popish and anti-Court party intelligence he was able to snap up. A committed anti-Catholic and opponent of the Duke of York, at least while it suited his pocket, he now openly joined the ranks of the Green Ribboners.[4]

In the summer of 1678, when Peyton and his men first began to suspect that Sir Edmund Godfrey was a traitor, Colonel Scott was lodging with Mr Payne in Cannon Street. He was Peyton's obvious choice as overseer of the murder plot. It was to be no ordinary killing that any hired assassin might perform with ease in a dark alley. It was to be precisely timed, conducted in such a way as to spread unprecedented panic, and finally to be saddled on the Papists. The execution of the plan had to progress in alignment with the gradual unveiling and maturity of Oates's Plot, so that it might appear to be a consequence of it and Plot and murder might benefit from each other. He had known Godfrey for more than ten years. With his ruthless cunning, his criminal imagination and his commitment to the Green Ribboners, Scott was Peyton's first choice. This is not idle speculation. Another of Colonel Blood's secret reports to Williamson, shortly before the unveiling of the Plot to the King, disclosed that Peyton and Scott and 'the rest of that crew' (the Gang) had been discovered plotting a murder. The intended victim Blood had not been able to find out.[5]

How, then, was it handled? Here we are on less firm ground, although there are stepping stones of solid fact. Scott himself would not commit the murder. There were others more adept in the act of killing than himself. His value was as the brains behind the operation, as organizer of those under him, and as the link man who would bring together all the various threads of the plan and prevent them from tangling. A murderer, or in modern parlance a 'hit man', was of course the first consideration. That in itself, under usual conditions, would have been no obstacle. There were hundreds of men in London who would coolly despatch an enemy for a purse of silver. But Scott had to try to make certain that the truth of the Godfrey murder would not leak out. He could not trust a hired killer who might be arrested at any time in the future on some other charge and who might then reveal the names of his paymasters for the Godfrey murder. His field was severely restricted by this consideration. He had to find a killer who could be trusted to hold his peace, a killer unlikely to be arrested for other crimes and blow the gaff to save himself. He had to find a killer who did not need to undertake other such commissions, a killer, therefore, of means. He had to find a killer sympathetic to the motivations of Peyton's Gang. In short, he had to find an experienced killer of rank within the republican circle. Next, he had to arrange the correct moment to strike, and the most effective method – from the point of view of properly publicizing the event – of disposing of the body.

There are various factors connected with Godfrey's murder which have never been explained:

(1) What was the content of the mysterious letter received by Sir Edmund on the day before he vanished?

(2) Why did he take so much money with him on the day he disappeared?

(3) Why was his body kept indoors for several days by his killers?

(4) Why did the killers choose Primrose Hill as the place to dump the body?

(5) How was it that, despite the rain and mud, his clothes were perfectly dry and his shoes were polished?

(6) How did the wax candle stains get on to the magistrate's clothing?

(7) How can the extraordinary incident of the man in the grey suit be explained?

These seven crucial points can be consistently explained in the light of new knowledge about the Gang and Colonel Scott.

The first two points are closely linked. Clearly, the letter delivered by hand to Hartshorn Lane on 11 October was the very honourable friends' way of revealing their hand at last. After receiving the letter, Godfrey knew a critical juncture had been reached. Tomorrow would make or break, kill or deliver him. In case it was to be death, which from his behaviour he truly believed, he settled all his outstanding accounts and personal debts, both of money and honour. He also destroyed an apronful of papers. It seems inescapable that part of the mysterious letter instructed him to incinerate any documents connected with his republican activities, for such a man must have held papers that would justify the seal on several death warrants. The destruction of all such papers was a vital consideration for the Gang, and they must be destroyed before the murder lest they should fall into the hands of government men searching his house after the finding of the body. No such papers were ever found. Therefore, those he burned were they. He was set a-burning by the letter.

Why would he have obeyed the injunction to destroy all dangerous documents? At this stage, he had nothing to lose and everything to gain by trying to appease the honourable friends. He had done his best for Coleman; the government, though not actually initiating any action against him, had still afforded him no protection. It was only a slender possibility that the friends would allow him to live if he co-operated at this late stage, but one he could not afford to ignore. This was the sort of psychology Scott used all the time in his swindles. Greed or self-interest provided an almost inexhaustible vein of richness for such a man to tap.

It was important for the republicans that Godfrey's death should not be attributed to footpads or highwaymen, and here we reach the second major part of the letter and the second of the unanswered questions associated with the case. Nothing would more finally destroy any possible allegations of attack by robbers than the pockets of the corpse being stuffed with gold. It is just this sort of picturesque detail that bears the stamp of Colonel John Scott. Yet having decided that Godfrey must have gold about him, Scott had to decide where that money was to come from. He would hardly use republican funds to fill Godfrey's pockets, if he could avoid it. And in deciding that Godfrey himself should supply the money, Scott was able to operate another psychological trick. He detailed a rendezvous for the following day, and ordered the magistrate to bring with him seven guineas, four broad pieces (each worth 20 shillings) and four pounds in silver. Apart from being a considerabe amount in value, it represented a fair weight to heft about the streets of London in one's pockets. On the surface, it just didn't make sense.

'Pr'ythee,' said Godfrey on reading the letter, 'tell him [the messenger] I don't know what to make of it.'[6]

Why did the honourable friends want him to take so much money with him to the confrontation? Would they rob him? Godfrey would hardly be in a position to guess the real reason. And with cruel irony, he was, by obeying the command, helping the honourable friends to make the desired use of his death. For obey them he did. Scott was certain he would. Hope of survival, as that arch swindler knew only too well, sprang eternal. Did Godfrey once again allow himself the vain hope that his life might after all be bought? It was certainly true that for lesser transgressions than his, the Green Ribbon men exacted monetary penalties for erring members. It was hopeless, but what choice had he?

The third and major function of the letter was to arrange a meeting with Godfrey on 12 October. This clause was linked in part with point four, discussed later, why the killers chose Primrose Hill as the place to dump the body. Godfrey walked into the fields north of London twice on Saturday morning. From his anxiously pressing Parsons the coachmaker to tell him the whereabouts of Paddington Woods, he made it clear that he was on no relaxed Saturday morning constitutional. The business of the coats before he left Hartshorn Lane the second time is an indication that he expected some sort of important meeting. His first inclination, bearing in mind the people he was to meet, was to don his best coat. Then, realizing the foully muddy fields in which he was to meet them, he changed his mind and put on his usual camlet coat. It is interesting that Primrose Hill was a favourite spot for duels. Did he imagine, or did Scott by subtle implication *lead* him to imagine, that it might be possible to extricate himself from his accursed position if he could only better some carefully chosen opponent with pistol or sword – as if the rift between himself and the friends were an affair of honour? Slender threads again, but Edmund Godfrey had no others to which to cling.[7]

Point three, the mystery of why Godfrey's killers kept his body for five days before disposing of it, is explained by the events of those five days. There was a concerted and successful effort by the republicans to whip up panic in that tense period of unknowing. By noon of the day he disappeared, when he was still at liberty, it was already common talk that he had been 'made away' by Papists. By the following Thursday the talk had reached screaming pitch. The appearance of his butchered corpse after this interval achieved a dramatic impact far in excess of that which would have attended the discovery of his body on the day he disappeared.

Point four concerns the killers' choice of Primrose Hill as the place to dump the body. The reason for organizing such a sensational murder, instead of a swift, stealthy stabbing, was that it might be blamed upon the Catholics. It has not yet been observed that Primrose Hill was a helpful factor in propagating this lie. The only building nearby was the White House tavern. And the White House, the Plot-mongers were soon shouting, was a hive of Catholics. It was in fact the regular meeting place of a Papist club.

The issue of the dry clothes and polished shoes, point five, proves that Godfrey's body was kept indoors until a short time before it was actually found, and that the murder had not taken place in the fields but elsewhere. If the murder had been at Primrose Hill itself, of course, the shoes would have been covered in mud. It has been argued that if Godfrey's shoes did not get dirty during his morning walks in the fields then there is no reason to suppose they would have done so when he met his killers there. But this somewhat simplistic reasoning discounts the fact that Godfrey did return to town on that cold, wet day, and that London was teeming with boot boys, any one of whom, eager to earn a groat, would call the attention of even a distracted man to the miry state of his shoes.

The presence of wax candle stains on Godfrey's clothes, point number six, was used to strengthen the case against the Papists.

Burnet pointed out that only 'persons of quality or priests' used wax candles, and that Godfrey had never used them himself. But as the case against the priests is known to be without foundation, we are left with persons of quality. There is no dispute that Peyton, his Gang and his republican comrades were all such persons.

Finally, there is point number seven, the two incidents in which the discovery of Godfrey's body was reported *before the discovery took place*. Neither of the reports was completely accurate, but the second at least contained enough obscure truth to render coincidence highly improbable. The man in the barber's shop on Tuesday morning said that Godfrey had killed himself *on Primrose Hill*. Two days later, before Bromwell and Walters saw the cane and gloves by the ditch, the young man in the grey suit was reporting that Godfrey had been found in Leicester Fields, *with his own sword run through him*. While it might be argued that the man in the barber's was simply repeating hearsay based on the knowledge of Godfrey's Saturday morning perambulations, it cannot be denied that there was something very remarkable about the man in the grey suit. He was wrong about the place, but in saying that Godfrey had been killed with his own sword he was displaying either an imperfect knowledge of the real plan to get rid of the body or an uncanny ability to see into the future. Who he was no one knows. It is unlikely ever to be discovered whether he was one of Peyton's Gang involved directly in the murder or whether (more likely, bearing in mind his youth) he was a paid *agent provocateur* who with no real knowledge spread whatever word he was fed. But it was an extraordinary occurrence for a man to be murdered with *his own* sword. The man in the grey suit must have had access to someone who knew the truth. A possible explanation for his mistake about the place is that there was a last-minute change of plan to which he was not privy. But there is another, far more likely explanation. It is clear from the testimony of Thomas Morgan, Mrs Blyth and others that the body was conveyed in daylight to the ditch. The time of the actual dumping has been isolated to a period of less than two hours after noon on the Thursday it was found. This timing is confirmed by the magistrate's dry clothing. William Griffith, who worked for Secretary of State Henry Coventry, was in a good position to know the thinking of the senior men investigating the case and to learn of clues generally unknown. He wrote that the corpse had been brought to the ditch under a load of hay on the back of a cart. To lend strong support to the hypothesis, there was nearby both scattered hay and the tracks of a cart. The presence of both was out of place in that field, and cannot otherwise be explained. The only real objection to the assertion that the body was conveyed by day is that such a task would be perilous enough in darkness, infinitely more so in daylight. In fact this is a fallacy. At night the streets were patrolled by hundreds of citizen soldiers, the trained bands; posts and chains obstructed all the main thoroughfares; and everyone was on the alert for suspicious persons and clues about the missing magistrate. Criminals commonly became active at night, therefore the watchmen, constables and guards redoubled their concentration. The senses were honed, and the general night-time quiet and lack of activity made anyone out of doors the more readily suspected. Whereas during the day, especially around noon at the height of the bustle, the streets were choked with traffic; there was noise, activity and people everywhere; the psychological comfort of daylight altered the face of the city, dulled the awareness of the guards and lent an ordinary haycart, because of the commonplace nature of such a sight, almost a cloak of invisibility. To make doubly sure of the safety of the men trundling the body through the streets leading northwards out of London, a diversion would be valuable. The man in grey was diverting the attention of all and sundry to Leicester Fields (now Leicester Square) just as the Gang's haycart would have been rumbling over the cobbles of Hog Lane or the first few hundred yards of mud on the road to Hampstead. This sort of diversionary tactic accords perfectly with Colonel John Scott's known methods of procedure. Only days later, as 'Mr Godfrey', he would employ an identical ingenuity in diverting Admiralty agents from his true escape plan.

Which members of Peyton's Gang, other than Peyton himself, were actually involved with Scott in the murder is a matter of uncertainty. One probability is Godfrey's 'friend' Richard Adams. He was not only Godfrey's second visitor on the morning of his disappearance, as early as six to seven o'clock, he was also the first to report – before eleven o'clock the same morning – the suspicion that Godfrey had been murdered. And one of the latest reports of a sighting of Sir Edmund was in the Back Court of Lincoln's Inn when it was said he was seen to make a sudden turn and go out the back door. Adams lived in Lincoln's Inn.

Precisely what followed Godfrey's trips into the country and his brief interview with Joseph Radcliffe in the Strand at lunchtime on Saturday cannot now be traced. Either by force or in obedience to some contingency instruction in Scott's letter, he came to the place selected for his murder and the storage of his body. Whatever place that was, in choosing it Scott had to be confident that it would not be searched by those conducting the search for Godfrey. Having arranged his killer, the problem of location solved itself.

A few hours after the disposal of the body, Colonel Scott took horse and fled the capital. Although he almost always used the pseudonym John Johnson, he unaccountably blurted out when challenged at Gravesend that his name was Godfrey. But he was soon on his way and, using the sort of diversionary tactics he had employed in getting rid of Sir Edmund's body, he managed to outwit even the brain-nimble Mr Pepys himself.

3: The Mighty Giant

Full investigation of the Godfrey case, especially the medical aspects, provides strong evidence as to the identity of the man selected by Scott to be the murderer. Suspicions have been raised before, but only with Professor Simpson as an expert witness is it possible to pursue the case against the mysterious 'hit man' of the honourable friends with any confidence. The motive for the murder of Godfrey is known. The identity of the very honourable friends and of the man who devised and supervised the murder is revealed. In many ways, the identity of the man they employed as their executioner is less significant than the facts already disclosed. But the naming of murderers, historically important or otherwise, provides endless fascination for students of crime.

Eight months before Godfrey's murder, another man was attacked in strikingly similar fashion. It is a present day dictum that a killer's method is a reliable indication of his identity. Simpson says that Sir Edmund was first brutally beaten with fist or boot, or both, so that his breast and abdomen were black with bruising; that he was secondly strangled and lastly stabbed. An unusual *modus operandi* to be sure, but one employed by the assailant of Philip Ricaut in February 1678 and by the same man on other occasions. Having beaten and kicked Ricaut, his attacker then tried first to strangle him and lastly to stab him with his sword. Only by luck did Ricaut escape with his life. The following day the same man attacked another gentleman called Nathaniel

Cony. Cony was first beaten about the head and thrown to the ground. Then, like Stevenson's Mr Hyde, his killer kicked and trampled upon his head, neck, breast, belly, sides and back until he was terribly bruised. He died of his injuries six days later.[1]

And so we come to the mighty giant – as he was described in a pamphlet about another of his murders, committed two years after that of Godfrey. He was, according to the historian Ogg, 'the most violent homicide of his age'. There is no exact record of all the violent crimes he committed. A pamphlet in circulation in 1680 said the talk of the coffee houses was that he had killed no less than twenty-six times. Aubrey thought him 'addicted to field sports and hospitality', and 'chiefly known for deeds of drunkenness and manslaughter'. Indeed because of the undisputed fact that he was the worst killer at large in England at the time of Godfrey's death, the mighty giant's name has been linked with the murder before. He was first presented as a suspect by the historian J. G. Muddiman in an article in *The National Review* in 1924. But Muddiman's research was so slapdash and his article so full of errors that most of his 'evidence' against the giant is useless. And the question of motive, always the stumbling block to those who rely on theorizing instead of research, is weak. Muddiman argued not only that the giant was a violent killer – 'a madman when he was sober and a homicidal lunatic when he was not' – but that he bore Godfrey a grudge, and for this reason killed him. The writer's statement that his suspect was indicted for an earlier murder in 1678 by a Grand Jury whose foreman was none other than Sir Edmund Berry Godfrey is perfectly true. But citing this as the motive for killing him seven months later is hardly plausible. What about the other eight men of the Grand Jury, among them three members of Peyton's Gang? The giant made no attempt to get his revenge upon them. Quite the reverse: he is known to have fraternized with them. The issue is also confused by Muddiman's statement, repeated as factual by almost every chronicler of the period since, that shortly after the suspect's release in April 1678, Godfrey fled abroad for several months to escape his wrath. This is completely untrue. As I have already shown, Godfrey's trip abroad was in 1677, not 1678, and he was fleeing not from a released murderer but from government agents. For the whole of 1678, except for perhaps a couple of weeks, Godfrey was in London, as the St Martin's vestry minutes prove.[2]

The mighty giant, in reality Philip Herbert, seventh Earl of Pembroke, was an ardent follower of Shaftesbury and the Opposition faction. Even though, perhaps because, his sister-in-law was the King's favourite mistress,* his sympathies lay completely with the republicans. Moreover he was a born killer. He was Scott's obvious choice as Peyton's Gang's 'hit man'. Whether his indictment by Godfrey earlier in the year played some small part in attracting him to the 'contract' on Godfrey's life will never be known. It is doubtful.[3]

They called him the Mad Peer. In *The First Satyr of Juvenal Imitated*, Lord Rochester had him as 'Boorish Pembrook brave'. He was a staunch supporter of Monmouth, and even dared defy the King by giving hospitality to Monmouth during his triumphal progress about the country in the summer of 1680. In the general election of 1681 he gave active and public support to the Whig candidates in his home county of Wiltshire. Pembroke fulfilled all the requirements of the man needed to kill Godfrey. He was a man of private means within the republican ranks. He had no need to commit crimes for a living, yet he was an experienced killer. There was little chance of his ever revealing the truth of the Godfrey execution because he was a nobleman – despite many reforms there was still in 1678 a law for the rich and a law for the poor. After one brutal murder, Pembroke was convicted of manslaughter and, on pleading benefit of clergy, was released. After another, which should in theory have brought the full fury of the law down upon him, he received a pardon from the King. In addition, he owned a large London house – in Leicester Fields – that was both close to where Godfrey was last seen alive and safe from intrusion by guards or watchmen searching for the magistrate after his disappearance.[4]

Pembroke was born at the beginning of January 1653, the son of Philip Herbert, fifth Earl of Pembroke and second Earl of Montgomery, and his second wife Catherine Villiers. He was baptized on 5 January 1653 at St Benet's, Paul's Wharf, London and created a Knight of the Bath in 1661. His half brother William, the sixth earl, died unmarried in July 1674 and he succeeded to the family title, held by the Herberts since the reign of Edward IV.[5]

Within three weeks of his investiture, he was run twice through the breast and left for dead in a duel with Bernard Howard. Pembroke was hardy, however, and as strong as he looked – he

---

* The Duchess of Portsmouth.

was indeed a giant of a man, well over six feet and powerfully built. He recovered from his wounds and continued to pay court to Henriette Mauricette, sister of the Duchess of Portsmouth, the King's French mistress. The young earl's mother was strongly against the match, and approached both the King and his mistress in a bid to scotch it. But the mighty giant was waiting only for his duelling wounds to heal. In November he presented Henriette with a diamond ring costing £900 and let it be known that as soon as he was well they should be married. The wedding took place in the week before Christmas at Westminster.[6]

In April 1675 Pembroke responded to a Parliamentary summons and took his seat in the House of Lords. In less than a month he was appointed Lord Lieutenant of Wiltshire, a post customarily held by the Earls of Pembroke.[7]

He behaved no better to members of his family that he did to outsiders. By September, with his wife pregnant and his own debauchery continuing unabated, he found himself in conflict with the Duchess of Portsmouth. The duchess told him that if he did not make proper arrangements for her sister's confinement, she would 'complain of him to the King and make known her sister's grievances', to which Pembroke replied that he would 'put her upon her head'. Despite his neglect of her, the Duchess of Pembroke was delivered of a baby girl.*[8]

The Mad Peer surrounded himself with wild animals and odious servants. At his country seat at Wilton, according to Aubrey, he had '52 mastives and 30 grey-hounds, some beares, and a lyon, and a matter of 60 fellowes more bestial than they'.[9]

There was yet another affray the following April. After one of his kinsmen had lost a lawsuit, Pembroke took it into his head to entertain the jury in a nearby tavern. He was outraged that everyone was afraid to sit next to him. At length, Sir Francis Vincent took the conspicuously empty seat near the earl. 'At last,' runs a contemporary letter reporting the episode, 'my Lord began a small health of two bottles, which Sir Francis refusing to pledge, dash went a bottle at his head, and as it is said, broke it.'† The two men were parted and Sir Francis was hustled outside to a coach. As he was about to climb in, word came that Pembroke was on his way with his sword drawn. Sir Francis refused to enter the coach,

---

* Later to marry a son of Judge Jeffreys, *Complete Peerage*.
† It is by no means clear whether it was the bottle or the head which was broken.

declaring that he had never been afraid of a naked sword in his life. In a moment Pembroke was upon him, but with one stroke broke his own sword. Scorning to take the advantage, Vincent threw away his own sword and flew fiercely at Pembroke, beating him soundly. But that was far from the end of it. Pembroke was out for the count, but Vincent found himself pursued by several of his adversary's footmen. He managed to throw one of them in the Thames, and fight off the rest with the aid of some redcoats.[10]

Pembroke was in trouble again within a week, when he wounded Sir George Hewett in the thumb and arm during a duel.[11]

In May 1676 the mighty giant met Lord Duras as the latter progressed through St James's Park one evening in his curtained sedan chair.

'Who's there?' demanded Pembroke.

'It's one,' replied Duras, failing to see why he should answer such a rude demand.

'Whoever you are, I will kill you,' stormed Pembroke, and ran his sword through the chair's drapes, just missing Duras's nose. Not pausing to see whether his unknown victim was dead or alive, the Mad Peer went his way.[12]

'Such exploits as these are usual with him,' wrote Lady Christian Hastings to her mother. 'He met Charles Bates at the playhouse, and with a box on the ear laid him dead for half an hour.'[13]

The duelling and unprovoked attacks on passers-by continued. In November 1677 he quarrelled with a man called Vaughan at Lockett's, a fashionable eating place. The following day Pembroke sent a servant to explain to Vaughan that he had been drunk and to ask him to forget what had passed. But Vaughan insisted on a duel, so they 'fought in ye moonshine behind Lockett's house'. At first Vaughan seemed to gain the upper hand, running Pembroke down. But as he moved in for the kill, one of Pembroke's unscrupulous footmen rushed at him with a sword and cut him across the hand. The stroke was so vicious it disabled him. As Vaughan staggered back with the shock and pain of the attack, Pembroke jumped to his feet and drove his sword into his belly. It is not known whether or not Vaughan died, but the last surviving report of him, on 27 November, depaired of his life.[14]

On Christmas Day 1677, Pembroke ambushed a parson and insisted he drink with him. The parson, trying to extricate himself from the giant's brutish grip, begged to be excused because he was going 'both to preach and give the blessed sacrament of the body

214

and blood of our Lord Jesus Christ'. His puzzled congregation were to be disappointed. Pembroke 'offered many outrageous blasphemies against our blessed Lord and the Virgin Mother, and forced the poore minister along with him and his crew'. They made him drink three great glasses of sack and later carried him off 'to make sport, and some talke worse things'.[15]

This time Pembroke's high birth was no immediate protection. He was seized and committed to the Tower for blasphemy. As the law stood, he had been guilty of a capital offence several times over. But his imprisonment was short-lived. On 30 January 1678 the House of Lords issued a warrant for his release on the grounds that 'the proof against him was by a single witness'. The devil was looking after his own.[16]

Within days he was in violent trouble again. On 5 February Philip Ricaut appeared before the Lords and gave them a report of Pembroke's attack upon him. The Kent gentleman said he had been visiting a friend in the Strand on the previous Saturday evening. While standing at the door taking his leave, Ricaut looked up and saw Pembroke passing by in the street. Then, without the slightest provocation, the Mad Peer struck him such a blow upon the eye 'as almost knocked it out', and then knocked him to the ground and fell upon him, grabbing his neck with his great fingers and all but choking him to death. Having almost killed his victim with blows and strangling, Pembroke then drew his sword and was about to deliver the death thrust when Ricaut scrambled into his friend's house and slammed the door shut.[17]

Beating . . . strangling . . . stabbing.

The Lords responded positively to Ricaut's appeal for protection, binding Pembroke over in the sum of two thousand pounds to keep the peace for a year. It was a technical move. The day before his appearance before the Lords on the charge of attacking Ricaut, Pembroke murdered Nathaniel Cony.[18]

Cony was a gentleman, a bit of a hypochondriac, a heavy drinker, subject to frequent fainting fits. On the night of Sunday, 3 February he dined in the City with a friend called Harry Goring. The food was good, the wine flowed and they stayed very late. At last, much in drink, they rose to go. With all the excessive politeness of the drunk, Goring offered to accompany Cony to his lodgings. But Cony, 'very ceremonious', replied that he would see his friend home. On the way they passed Long's House, a tavern in the Haymarket, and Cony suggested they drink another bottle of wine before parting finally for the night.[19]

'It was late and the door shut,' testified Goring later, 'but we knocking pretty hard for admittance did get it opened.'[20]

They reeled in, Cony making for the bar and calling for the wine. The Mad Peer, an acquaintance of Cony, was drinking with three henchmen in a private room adjoining the bar. As he walked about the room, Pembroke's attention was caught by the noisy intrusion of the two friends. Recognizing Cony, he saluted him and invited him into the room to drink.

'My lord,' said Cony, 'I am with a friend and we have some business together.'

'Pray bring your friend with you,' persisted Pembroke, at which Goring, who could hardly stand, entered the room with Cony and sat down. After several glasses, Goring suggested a game of dice.

'I will throw with you for five hundred pounds,' said Pembroke, turning to one of his men to fetch the money. But those stakes were too high for Goring and he changed his mind.

'I believe,' said Pembroke, 'you are an idle fellow that you will propose these things and not pursue them.'

'I will drink, I will play, I will fight with any man!' roared Goring.

'Who is this gentleman,' said Pembroke tauntingly, 'that I should never hear of, or know him?'

'*How?*' rejoined Goring in a sudden passion. "Sblood! Not hear of me? My name is Goring! A name and family as good as any gentleman's in England!'

'There is nobody doubts it,' replied Pembroke.

'Your *betters*,' scowled the drunken man.

Pembroke said nothing. He simply threw a glass of wine in Goring's face, took a pace back and drew his sword. Before Goring could do likewise, his blade was snatched from him by Captain Richard Savage, one of the henchmen, and broken. Savage then shoved him from the room.

'Go with your friend,' said Pembroke, waving Cony away.

'I do not know upon what account my friend is sent out,' replied Cony, at which Pembroke struck him a crushing blow on the ear, threw him to the floor, and kicked and trampled upon his torso and neck, turning it into a mass of black bruises.[21]

The injuries of which Cony died on 10 February were so similar to those sustained by Sir Edmund Godfrey eight months later that Pembroke even summoned doctors to claim that the marks on Cony's chest and abdomen were caused by blood that had drained to the lower parts of the body after death. The same hopeless attempt was to be made by Marks and Freyberger in their theory about Godfrey in 1905.

'In all natural deaths,' said a doctor on behalf of Pembroke at his subsequent trial before the House of Lords, 'there must be extravasated blood in the lower belly . . . it is a clear case.'[22]

It was of course a useless ploy. There was never any doubt that the marks on Cony were caused by the same 'obtuse weapon' as those on Godfrey – the stamping, kicking boots of the mighty giant Koorbmep. So well known was his distinctive method of attack that the phrase 'Pembroke kick' was in common usage. It was used twice at the Cony trial.[23]

The evidence was such that, in spite of his Not Guilty plea, there could be no question of an acquittal. Eighteen peers voted Not Guilty, six voted Guilty, forty found him guilty of manslaughter, for which the penalty was death. From the beginning, though, he had been secure in the knowledge that whatever the Lords' verdict, he should go free. He merely pleaded benefit of clergy, extended under Henry VII to encompass not only clerks in Holy Orders but also secular 'clerks', meaning anyone who could read. Later the benefit was accorded to any peer, literate or otherwise. And although a qualified commoner exercising the once-only privilege would be branded upon the hand, Pembroke, as a peer, escaped even this. He left the elaborately-prepared court room of West-minster Hall to kill another day. On 4 April, the day of the trial, all his lands, tenements, goods and chattels were forfeited to the Crown as an automatic result of the verdict. On 5 April they were restored to him by a warrant signed by the King.[24]

Technically, any further murders should have brought down upon his head the full vengeance of law. In practice it was different. The murder of Godfrey, of course, was never traced to him. Although the magistrate's body bore the unmistakable signs of the Pembroke kick, attention was diverted from it – another brainwave of Colonel Scott? – by Sir Edmund's own sword piercing his heart. Besides, thanks to the republican propaganda machine, the country was too occupied pursuing Catholics for the killing, for anyone to pause to consider the possible culpability of a Whig earl, whose motive for killing Godfrey nobody but a few could even imagine. In November 1678 Pembroke beat up the Earl of Dorset in a lower room at Lockett's. For a time he was confined to Wilton. But on 5 December he murdered a man at Aylesbury and went unpunished.[25]

In January 1680 there was an unsuccessful attempt on his life.

'Lord Pembroke being in a balcony in the Haymarket with other gentlemen,' says a report of the time, 'some blades passed by and fired at him, but missed and killed another.'[26]

Between eleven o'clock and midnight on Thursday, 19 August 1680, the Mad Peer was travelling with three companions in a Hackney coach between Windsor and London. At the village of Turnham Green, about five miles from the capital, a constable and his watch stopped the coach.

'Who's there?' called the constable, who like most of his fellows in the towns and shires of Charles's England was about as bright and practical as Shakespeare's Dogberry.

'It is the Lord Pembrook,' replied the coachman.

'Drive on!' bawled someone in the coach.

'They stop my horses,' the hapless coachman called back.

'They be thieves come to rob us!' shouted one of the drunken party inside the vehicle.

'We be the King's Watch,' replied the offended Dogberry, a man called William Smeeth, 'and in his name we command ye to stand, and tell us who ye be.'

'God damn 'em!' cried the passengers. 'We'll make 'em know who we are!' And with many oaths Pembroke and his thugs piled from the coach with their swords drawn. The two parties met behind the vehicle and began to fight. The affray brought people running from a nearby tavern, one of whom was one of the King's messengers who knew Pembroke well. He approached the mighty giant to persuade him to enter the coach, but before he had spoken three words Pembroke had run his sword into his belly. The messenger staggered but did not fall. He snatched a staff from one of the watchmen and felled Pembroke with a single blow. Grabbing the prostrate peer's sword, he said, 'My lord, you have killed me. I can kill you if I will, but I will not.' He stamped upon the sword and broke it, immediately falling vanquished to the ground. At the end of it the constable had been run through the side in three places, and two of the watchmen had been wounded, one of them mortally. Constable Smeeth died of his wounds five days later. After the fight, Pembroke and his louts were taken to the tavern to be held until daybreak. But they called for wine and made their guards drunk, after which they threw gold and silver about the room. While the watchmen scrambled madly one upon the other to reach the money, the villains made their escape.[27]

A second Middlesex Grand Jury indicted him for murder, but Pembroke fled to Calais before any further action could be taken

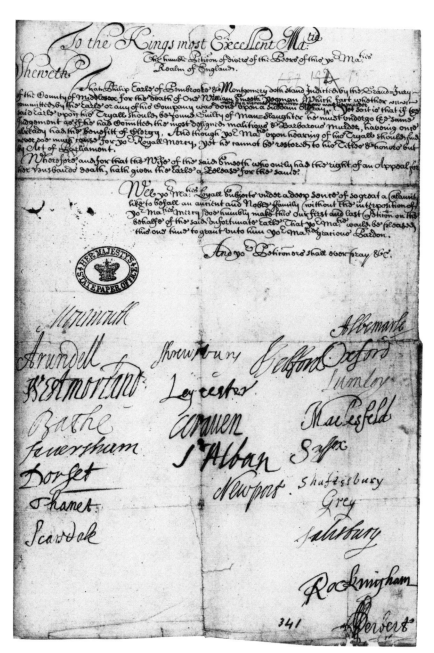

The Petition signed by twenty-two Whig peers

against him. It was not long, however, before he returned. Something told him he would be safe. That something was a secret promise that the republicans were ready to discharge the debt owed him since the Godfrey elimination. Shaftesbury, Monmouth and twenty-two other Whig peers took the unusual step of petitioning the King to pardon him. That extraordinary and telling document exists today among the State Papers. Charles granted the pardon on 22 June 1681.[28]

By May of the year 1683 life had become intolerable for ill-used Henriette Pembroke. She fled from her husband and embarked for France, where she entered a Paris monastery. Within four months of his wife's departure Pembroke, at the age of thirty, had drunk himself to death.[29]

Even as his giant frame was lugged in pomp to Wilton and laid to rest in Salisbury Cathedral, an elegy to this most savage killer of Charles II's reign was coming off the presses of Mallet, a London printer:

> But what do I hear? brave Pembrook's Dead,
> And from its Mansion, his great Soul is fled.
> Yet 'Spight of Death, his Name shall never Dye;
> Whilst others sink his shall surmount the Skie,
> Ah, Cruel Death, what made thee thus surprize
> Him who was Loyal, Noble, Just and Wise . . .
> Great Pembrook's course is ended, and now he,
> A Hero is, to all Eternity.[30]

Epilogue

The killing of Justice Godfrey achieved precisely what Scott and his paymasters intended.

Oates had made such a muck-up of everything that 'the loose and tottering fabric' of his pretended Plot was about to tumble. Even after the discovery of Coleman's papers, which brought it once more to the boil, the Plot 'began to reel and stagger again in its Credit'. When the Court returned to London from Newmarket, there seemed to be 'a damp given to that zeal wherewith the Committee had appeared to enquire into the matter . . .'[1]

Then Godfrey disappeared, and the terror-mongers went to work. By the time his body was discovered it was taken as proof absolute that a ghastly plot against the state was in progress. 'The indignation of this murder was so great abroad,' wrote Sir Robert Southwell to the Duke of Ormond, 'that 'twas found necessary to repair the neglect of doing nothing concerning it at the Council.' Southwell said the public reaction to the murder was such that it would have given credit to Oates's claims, were they 'ten times wilder and more extravagant'.[2]

Lord Chief Justice Scroggs described the murder as 'a monstrous evidence' of the existence of the plot, and Burnet thought Godfrey's death contributed 'more than any other thing' to establishing belief in Oates's wicked lies.[3]

Had Godfrey not gone his mysterious Primrose way that October, the history of Charles II's last years might have been very different. There would have been no nationwide panic, no witchhunt against the Catholics. As it was, the terror led to the eclipse of Danby and the rise to power of Shaftesbury and his Protestant country party; to the Habeas Corpus Act and the Exclusion Bill; to the torture and death of many innocent people.

Of this humble magistrate whose death has exercised fascinated minds for three hundred years, there remains no memorial save a few posthumous portraits.

One portrait, the most important because it was painted in the last year of his life, I tracked down to the basement of the National Portrait Gallery in London, a few hundred yards from where his bones lie beneath the floor of the crypt of St Martin-in-the-Fields. Above his so-sad face in elaborate gold lettering, one of his contemporaries has written his only reliable epitaph:

Sir Edmondbury Godfrey Knt. murd^{d}. A.D. 1678

APPENDICES

Appendix A: The Godfreys of Kent

Edmund's father, Thomas Godfrey, was the second son of Thomas Godfrey of Lidd (Lydd), near Rye in Kent. He had been born in the glorious days of Elizabeth on 3 January 1585.

The Godfreys were a much-respected line of long standing at Lidd. The oldest recorded mention of a direct ancestor of Edmund is another Thomas Godfrey, who rented a manor called Old Langport at Lidd as early as 1403. His will is dated 1426. He died in August 1430 and is buried in Lidd Church. Old Langport was in the hands of Edmund's grandfather when Thomas Godfrey sat down and wrote a page of notes on the history of his family about 1616.

In 1587 Mr John Hoblethwaite, Lidd Town Clerk, collected 'out of a verie antient book of Records' the names of ten Godfreys who had been Bailiffs of Lidd since 1438.

Edmund's father studied at St John's College, Cambridge and was admitted to the Middle Temple in 1604. After he had occupied 'the middle lower chamber on the left hand in Brick Court' in the Temple for about three years, he became, thanks to the recommendation of his father, gentleman in ordinary to Henry Howard, Lord Privy Seal, in which post he remained for two years.

He married Margaret Lambard, only daughter of one of the Masters of Chancery, on 5 May 1608 at St Catherine's by the Tower, and moved with her to the country. For a year they stayed with a gentleman named Robert Bowler at his house at Winchelsea, a coastal town in Sussex. It was here that their first child was born. The child, a boy named Lambard, later became Recorder of Maidstone.

In April 1609 Thomas was made a Freeman of Winchelsea and the following month he was sworn in as a Jurat, or alderman of Winchelsea Corporation. By 1610 he was Mayor's deputy and had moved with his wife and son into a house of their own in the town.

Margaret gave birth to their second child, Thomas, on 4 October 1610. He died on 8 December and was buried in the Church of St Thomas, Winchelsea.

About the middle of 1611 Thomas took a house outside St George's Gate, Canterbury. Just before the family was due to move, Margaret was taken ill and she died on 29 June. Her last words to her husband were, 'My soul is in heaven with the angels.' She was buried close to her tiny son. Even though the new house was ready, Thomas could not bring himself to move without his 'most loving wife' and he speedily disposed of it.

Eleven months later he married twenty-year-old Sarah Iles, daughter of a Yorkshire gentleman living in Hammersmith. The ceremony took place at Brandford (Brentford) in Middlesex on Thursday, 28 May 1612. Five months after, the couple moved with Lambard, now nearly four and a half, into a house close to the landing-stage of the ferry at Halling in Kent.

Sarah gave birth to two stillborn sons in July 1613, and had another miscarriage the following Christmas. Even in those days of high infant mortality, Thomas was considered an unfortunate man. It is not recorded whether any thought was given to the feelings of his wife. Yet he pursued his political career with energy and in April 1614 was elected to Parliament by the voters of Winchelsea. Soon after, the family moved to a house in Grub Street in the London parish of St Giles, Cripplegate, so that Thomas could be within easy reach of the Parliament House. Sarah had another miscarriage at her father's house at Hammersmith the following October. Of all Thomas's children conceived since 1608, only Lambard, the eldest, had survived. Finally, however, the curse seemed to lift, and a girl, Jane, was born alive in the house in Grub Street on 30 August 1615.

Another boy, Thomas, was born in October 1616. Although he survived the critical early weeks of life he was a frail creature and from the age of seven weeks suffered from constant vomiting, 'so that he could neither keep his meat nor his drink for a week togeather'.

On 2 June 1617 the family – Thomas, Sarah and the children Lambard, Jane and baby Thomas – moved out of London to the 'Godfrey country' of Kent. They stayed at Old Langport with Thomas's father until 28 July, when they moved into a house at Sellindge between Ashford and Folkestone, which Thomas the elder 'had purchased but the Michaelmas term before'.

In an age when women were allowed little fulfilment but in the bearing and rearing of children (and that whether they liked it or not), Sarah throve. A fortnight before Christmas she gave birth to her second son, Peter.

The next entry in Thomas's journal is dated 19 February, 1618:

226

I was sworne the King's servant, and a sewer of the chamber extraordinary, by warrant from William Erle of Pembroke, Lord Chamberlaine.

Although setting table, fetching and carrying dishes, tasting food and placing guests would seen a humble position to modern minds, it was, in the days of James I, an honour bestowed only upon men of Godfrey's respectable background, and preferable in his eyes to all the positions in law, local government and Parliament which he had hitherto held.

On 30 July 1618 Thomas and Sarah went on a week's holiday to France with a lady friend, Mrs Ann Whetenhall, and their old friend and neighbour from Grub Street, Edmund Harrison, the King's embroiderer. They set sail in a barque from Dover with one servant, landing at Calais. During the next few days they travelled by wagon to St Omers and Gravelines, embarking from Calais in a French barque that landed them back in England on 5 August.

Another son, Richard, was born on Thursday, 8 April 1619. The wealth of the Godfrey family at this time can be judged by the £2,000 dowry given by Thomas's father when his sister Mary married Sir John Honeywood in August that year. The dowry would be equivalent to about £75,000 today. The blight that had attended the early years of Thomas and Sarah's marriage now seemed cured. Another son, John, was born on 3 September 1620, swelling the ranks of the family to eight.

In January 1621 Thomas bought half of a stone barn and eighteen acres of marshland in West Hythe for £400, and fourteen acres of woodland at Horton. He recorded proudly in his journal, 'In all 540 pounds, which I paid at one payment'. At about the same time he bought a house and eight acres of land at Braband Lees in the parish of Smeeth, Kent, near their home at Sellindge, from his cousin John Berrie. This cost him £100, or about £3,800 at today's value.

Appendix B: Edmund's Childhood

Thomas and Sarah's next child came two days before Christmas, 1621. Thomas wrote:

> My wife was delivered of another son the 23° Decemb. 1621, between 3 and 4 of the clock in the morning, being Sunday; who was christened the 13 January, being Sunday.

Edmund Berry Godfrey was one of very few people of his time to possess three names. Thomas noted in his diary what impelled him to have his son christened thus. Edmund's godfathers were John Berrie, captain of the foot company at Lidd, and Edmund Harrison:

> They named my son Edmund Berrie, the one's name and the other's Christian name.

So far Sarah had not suckled any of her babies. Edmund was no exception. He was obviously fit, and his mother had no qualms about having him foster-fed by a nurse as she had his four brothers and his sister Jane.

Although he was the youngest member of the family, Edmund was not the feeblest. Five-year-old Thomas had not recovered from the condition that had debilitated him since he was seven weeks old. Now, wrote their father, 'he was but a liveing corpse, and the poorest carcase that (I think) was ever seen, to goe up and downe, as he did.' Yet despite his suffering he had 'a quicke eye, and a good spirit and memorie; apt to learne, and would read very prettily.'

Edmund knew little of his paternal grandfather. Before his second birthday the old man was declining rapidly. Much decayed in mind and body, he could no longer walk because of a malady that weakened his knees. Wherever he went he had to be led between two people or carried.

Between noon and one o'clock on the first day of October 1623, little Thomas Godfrey died. It was less than a month before his seventh birthday. He was buried in the chancel of Sellindge Church, next to the Godfrey family pew. In spite of her grief, Sarah gave birth without mishap to a girl on 8 December. She was named Elizabeth.

Four and a half months later Edmund's grandfather died at the house of his son Dick at New Romney in Kent, where he had been living since midsummer 1623. As Thomas wrote:

> That night he died I watched him. He had been speechless all that day, only fetched his breath very short, and when he died he did not so much as groane or strech, but put downe his eyes himself; and so his breath went out of his body without so much as stirring the candle which stood in the candlestick upon his bed.

On 24 February two-year-old Edmund travelled down to Lidd by coach with his family and saw Grandfather Godfrey laid to rest in the chancel of Lidd Church. It was a year of deaths. On 27 November Edmund's uncle Peter Godfrey died in London.

Three more sons – Michael, Thomas and Edward – were born to the Godfreys in the next three years. Six days before the birth of Edward Godfrey in the summer of 1627, part of the older section of the Godfrey house fell down. It was, recalled a perplexed Thomas, 'a fine sunn-shine day, and small wind stirring'. No one was hurt but it was apparent that the family would have to move. Fortunately there was a newer part of the house where they could live until somewhere else was found.

On the day of Edward's christening in July 1627 the weather was foul and wet, and it was thought unwise to take him out to the church. Six-year-old Edmund entered delightedly into a hurriedly-arranged baptism ceremony in the great parlour of their home, and watched as his ten-day-old brother was christened in the family's round silver basin. Edward was not a strong baby, and he was the first of Sarah's thirteen children that she breast-fed herself. She could not have bargained for the fact that he would continue to suckle for three years!

In August the family moved to a house on the estate of Hodiford in the north-west corner of Sellindge parish, which Thomas had bought from a James Cobbe.

The following February, Thomas was elected MP for New Romney in Charles I's third parliament, which sat until 1629.

Sarah, to whom Thomas was married for more than fifty-three years, thought him 'a great lover of learning and all ingenuity, which he shewed in the generous education of all his children'. Edmund's formal education began about the time of the dissolution of parliament in 1629, when he followed his two elder brothers to Westminster School, that 'Prime Nurserie and Paedagogie of Tyronick Learning'.

The Puritan third parliament of which Edmund's father had been a member had grown increasingly hostile to the King, who now strove to rule without Parliament. When it became apparent that Charles would not quickly summon a new Parliament, Thomas had no reason to remain in London. He and the family returned to Kent, leaving Edmund at Westminster. The boy's godfather, Edmund Harrison, now living at a house in Hartshorn Lane near Charing Cross, doubtless kept a paternal eye upon him.

The actual date of Edmund's election to Westminster as a King's Scholar is unknown, and no record of his showing as a student has survived. In September 1630, he travelled to Sellindge to attend the wedding of his fifteen-year-old sister Jane to Edmund Harrison.

While Edmund continued his studies at Westminster, his father was sworn in as a Justice of the Peace in February 1631. In June of the same year Edmund, now nine, received a letter from Hodiford telling him that his mother had successfully delivered a baby girl, Catherine.

The sole example of Edmund's schoolwork to have survived is a six-line poem he wrote at the age of fifteen. It forms part of a collection of complimentary verses dedicated to Charles I on the birth of his daughter Princess Anne in March 1637. Most of the verses, written while the scholars were at Chiswick, were in Latin. Only Edmund's and one other are in English. The Latin verses include efforts by his elder brothers Richard and John. Edmund's poem is somewhat prophetic, bearing in mind Charles's eventual fate:

> To his Maiestie
> No little stone, but on these happie dayes
> A Pyramid of marble lett men rayse:
> That should you chaunce to leave us, it might be
> A faithfull STEVART of your memorie.
> But if at last old age consume the same,
> Wee'le have a greater monument; your name.
>   Edmund: berry Godfrey

It is not known when Edmund left Westminster School, but he matriculated at Oxford as a commoner of Christ Church on 23 November 1638. Three days later his sister Elizabeth died at the age of fifteen at the house of Edmund Harrison and was buried in the Church of St Benet's, Paul's Wharf, London. According to

Aubrey, Edmund was during his time at Christ Church 'chamber-fellowe to my cosen W[illiam] Morgan of Wells, in Peckwater, in north-east angle'.

Appendix C: The Man with Three Names

It was rare in the early part of the seventeenth century to give a child two baptismal names. Apart from the cases of Edmund Berry Godfrey, Anthony Ashley Cooper, Robert Bruce Cotton and Thomas Pope Blount, the practice was almost unknown. This explains the consistency with which Godfrey's two Christian names were mistakenly rendered as one by his contemporaries. Historians have followed the example and rendered the name variously as Edmundbury, Edmundberry, Edmondbury, Edmondsbury.

Others less daunted by the prospect of a man with three names have tried Edmund Bury Godfrey and Edmund Berry Godfrey. A prolonged debate about the magistrate's name took place in the pages of the magazine *Notes and Queries* in the nineteenth century, and the general rule since has been to stick to Edmund Berry Godfrey.

The simple fact is, there is no true answer to the problem of Godfrey's names. He was named after one of his godfathers, John Berrie. His father referred to him as Edmund Berrie; yet in the baptismal register of Sellindge Church he is recorded thus:

Edmund=Bury Godfrey filius Thomas Godfrey

Godfrey himself always separated the names, yet spelled his second Christian name sometimes as Berry, sometimes as Bury. Spelling was a changeable thing in the 1600s. A single word would often be rendered differently in different parts of the same document, even in official publications. It is the inability of Victorian scholars, educated in the strict regimented fashion of their time, to accept this, that explains the fierce dialogue in *Notes and Queries*. Although the historians involved in the debate would never have agreed, it is true that in this case 'you pays your money and you takes your choice'.

He is referred to as Edmund Berry in this book because it was the version he used most often himself.

Appendix D: The Tankards

Almost everyone who has written at any length about Godfrey has stated that the King presented him with a silver tankard for his services during the plague and fire. This is untrue. On 17 October 1666 the Lord Chamberlain issued a warrant requesting Sir Gilbert Talbot, Master and Treasurer of His Majesty's Jewel House, 'to prepare and deliver unto Sir Edmundbury Godfrey, Knight, Eight hundred ounces of white plate as a Gift from His Majesty'.

Godfrey was not the only public servant to receive such a gift. In May 1667, Pepys wrote: 'My seeing at Sir Robert Viners, two or three great silver flagons, made with inscriptions as gifts of the King to such persons of quality as did stay in Town the late great plague for the keeping of things in order in the town.' Godfrey's friend Colonel Warcup also received a gift of plate. Godfrey's gift came not in the form of a tankard but as an engraved *oenophorum* or wine vessel. The error of historians has arisen because in about 1673 Godfrey had this magnificent object melted down, and several large flagons and tankards made from the silver, of which about eight are known to survive; there is one in the London Museum. Each are now worth between £30,000 and £40,000. Godfrey had the tankards, perhaps as many as twenty, inscribed with his own coat of arms and with the same words and designs as the original 'truly royal wine-vessel', and gave them as gifts to his closest friends.

Appendix E: The Inquest Verdict

Middlesex, ff. An Inquisition Indented; Taken the Eighteenth Day of October, In the Thirtieth Year of the Reign of our Sovereign Lord King Charles the Second: before John Cowper, one of His Majesties Coroners of the said County, upon view of the Body of Sir Edmond-Berry Godfrey Knight, then and there lying Dead; by the Oaths of

Thomas Harris,	Joseph Girle,
Phillip Wine,	John Hartwel,
John Cowsey,	William Lock,
William Collins,	John Owen,
Thomas Wollams,	Simon Standewer,
John Carvil,	Thomas Mason,
Anthony Fryer,	Paul Harding,
Christopher Jarvis,	Matthew Hains, and
Robert Trotton,	John Davis,

Good and Lawful Men, of the said Parish, and four Towns thereto near adjoyning: who were sworn, and charged to inquire, for our Sovereign Lord the King; how, when, and where the said Sir Edmond-Berry Godfrey came to his Death; who say upon their Oaths, that diverse Person to the Jurors aforesaid unknown, God not having before their Eyes; but being moved, and seduced, by the Instigation of the Devil, the twelfth day of October, Instant, with force and armes, &c. In an upon the said Sir Edmond Bury, in the peace of God, and our Sovereign Lord the King then and there, being at the Parish and County aforesaid, Felloniously, Wilfully, and of their Malice, before thought, did make an Assault, and that the said Persons, to the Jurors aforesaid unknown, a certain piece of Linnen Cloth, of no value, about the Neck of the said Sir Edmond-Bury, then and there, Felloniously, Wilfully, and of their Malice before thought, did tye and fasten; and therewith, the said Sir Edmond-Bury Godfry, Felloniously, Wilfully, and of the Malice before thought, did Suffocate and Strangle: of which said Suffocation, and Strangling, he the said Sir Edmond-Bury then, and there, Instantly Died: So that they the said Diverse Persons unknown, the said Sir Edmond-Bury Godfry, in manner and form aforesaid, Felloniously, Wilfully, and of their Malice before thought, did Kill, and Murder, against the Peace of our Sovereign Lord the King, his Crown and Dignity – And the Jurors aforesaid, upon their Oaths aforesaid, do further say, that the said Diverse Persons unknown, as soon as they the said Diverse Persons unknown, the Fellony and Murder aforesaid, in manner and form aforesaid, Felloniously, Wilfully, and of their Malice before thought, had done and committed – for that Felony and Murder, Feloniously made their Flight, and in places to the Jurors aforesaid as yet unknown, did themselves withdraw. In Witness whereof, as well the said Coroner, as the Jurors aforesaid, have to the said Inquisition, put their Hands and Seals, the day and year first above Written.

Appendix F: Godfrey's Will (1677)

IN THE NAME OF GOD AMEN. I Sr Edmund Bury Godfrey of the parish of St Martins in the Fields in the County of Middx, knight, do make this my last will and testament in manner and form following. First I desire my Executors hereafter named to cause my body to be privately buried in the meanest place of burial belonging to that parish or place wherein I shall die, but not in the Church, this to be performed without pomp or pageantry, not to be accompanied with numerous attendants either of friends or relations – the which as I asserted not in my life time I would not have imposed on me being dead. To that end and to avoid being troublesome to the world and especially to the streets when dead, I desire to be buried very early in the morning or very late at night with as much privateness as may be without any solemn invitation of my acquaintances or kindred as also without any funeral sermon or other harangue which I do hereby forbid wherein so much is oftner said than so little, also I forbid any monument or other memorial of stone or brass to be made for me hoping that my failings will be buried with me in the grave without any partial remembrance of evil or good actions if any such have been which are so called at the relator's pleasure. As for the charity which I have for some years bestowed on the poor of the parish of St Martins in the Fields aforesaid *viz.* ten shillings in bread on every Lords day or on some day at the beginning of each week my will is that my Executors hereafter named do jointly and severally take care and continue to do the same by themselves, their heirs or executors for the space of ten years from and after the time of my decease, the same to be continued and given either on the Lord's day or some time on the beginning of every week as formerly to such poor of that parish as my said Executors – or whom they shall entrust in that distribution shall judge most to stand in need thereof. And I do further will that the Charity by me given of two shillings per week in bread to the poor of the parish of Selling, being the place of my birth and is near unto the town and port of Hythe in the county of Kent, be weekly continued to be given and distributed by my Executors and heirs and their Executors in the same manner during the same time and on the like terms as are already mentioned in behalf of the poor of the parish of St Martins in the Fields aforesaid and to be continued after the determination of twenty one years on the same terms therein expressed at the discretion of my Executors, their heirs or Executors and not otherwise. Item I give unto my brother Mr Peter Godfrey if he shall be living at the time of my death and not else one hundred pounds instead of my great silver flagon once

236

intended him whereon are engraven his Majesty's Royal Arms with my own adjoined and was so given me by the order of the King and Council in memory of the service which God enabled me to perform towards the visited poor in that dreadful year of Plague sixteen hundred sixty five the which I am always to remember with humility and true thankfulness. Item I give unto my niece Amy Godfrey daughter to my brother Peter Godfrey one hundred pounds in case she shall be unmarried at the time of my death and not else. Item I will that my Executors lay out one hundred pounds and what more they shall think fit towards the education of the children of my niece Mary the wife of Edward Duke of Aylestone in the county of Kent Gent. Item my will is that my Executors do so dispose of one hundred pounds by due advice of counsel in the law learned that the product or interest thereof shall be within the power and ordering of my sister Mrs Sarah Plucknett wife to Mr Christopher Plucknett during her being under coverture of any husband whatever to be by her bestowed yearly in such act or acts of charity as she shall think fit in her own discretion and if she shall happen at any time to be a widow then my executors are hereby required to pay the said one hundred pounds to her in [illegible] whilst she continues in that condition of widowhood to do what she pleases therewith or keep it to her own use. Item my will is that my Executors do pay unto my cousin Elizabeth Jenkins, widow, daughter of Thomas Iles of Oxford, Dr in Divinity, two shillings per week during her natural life if she continue a widow so long, the same to cease whenever she shall marry. Also I will that four pounds per annum be quarterly paid by my Executors to Mrs Judith Pamplyn, widow, during her natural life if she shall so long continue a widow and not otherwise. Item I give unto my dear and honoured mother Mrs Sarah Godfrey being the last respect I can pay to her the sum of ten pounds for mourning. To my sister Mrs Jane Harrison, widow, ten pounds for mourning. To my sister Mrs Sarah Plucknett and to her husband Mr Christopher Plucknett to each of them ten pounds a piece for mourning. To my sister Mrs Katherine Godfrey the widow of my good brother Lambard Godfrey Esq ten pounds for mourning. To my brother in law Mr John Bridger, merchant, ten pounds for mourning if he shall be in England when I shall happen to die. To the worthily honoured the Lady Margaret Pratt, widow of Sr George Pratt Baronet deceased ten pounds the which I desire her to accept of and bestow on a ring. Item I give unto Valentine Greatrake of Affane [?] in the Kindome of Ireland Esq the sum of ten pounds for mourning who I am sure will truly wear it for my sake. Item I give unto my nephew Mr Thomas Godfrey, son of my brother Peter Godfrey ten pounds for mourning. Item I give unto my nephew Mr Edmund Harrison ten pounds for mourning. To my cousin Mrs Susanna Willett, widow, ten pounds for mourning or how she please otherwise to bestow it on her self. More necessarily to my cousin Mrs Frances Death, widow, five pounds to buy her a ring. Nevertheless my will and meaning is that the several legacies aforementioned or any other which shall be given by me to any particular persons herein named (except those only given to the poor of any parishes or places) shall utterly cease and be void in case that the respective legatees or persons to whom such legacies are given shall happen to die before me. To my old acquaintance and friend Mr Thomas Hercules to buy him mourning, to my servant H – Moore and his wife to each of them ten pounds a piece for mourning. Item my will is that my executors do within three months after my decease dispose of and pay the sum of one hundred pounds to such poor ministers or the widows of such poor ministers in such proportion to every of them as shall be directed under the hands of my sister Mrs Jane Harrison, widow, my sister in law Mrs Katherine Godfrey, widow, my sister Mrs Sarah Plucknett wife to Mr Christopher Plucknett or under the hands of any two of them. Item I give unto the poor of any parish wherein I shall happen to die except it be in the parish of St Martins in the Fields in the county of Middlesex for which poor I have otherwise provided, the sum of five pounds. Item I give unto the minister of the parish wherein I shall die besides all fees due to him for my burial, for no sermon the sum of twenty shillings, but if I shall happen to die in the parish of St Martins in the Fields aforesaid my will is that forty shillings be given unto the minister thereof besides other fees or dues for burial. Lastly I do hereby constitute and make my brothers Mr Michael Godfrey and Mr Benjamin Godfrey both of London, merchants, to be joint Executors of this my last will and testament and I do particularly give unto my brother Mr Michael Godfrey my great flaggon aforementioned of the King's gift. Also I do hereby give unto my said brother Michael Godfrey and his heirs for ever the Swann Inn in Hammersmith in the Parish of Fulham in the county of Middlesex with its appurtenances and all other my lands and tenements lying and being in the Parish of Stanwell within the said county of Middlesex being now or late in the occupation of Edward Jordan of the parish of Stanwell, butcher, of John Virgo and John Ivers now or late of the parish of Stanwell aforesaid, husbandmen, and in the occupation of some or one of them or their assignes. As to the residue of my lands and tenements lying and being in the parish of Stanwell aforesaid I give and bequeath them unto my brother Mr Benjamin Godfrey aforesaid to him and his heirs for ever and I do hereby revoke and make void all former wills whatsoever together with forty pounds given by my good mother and twenty pounds given by my sister Mrs Jane Harrison on the same, except widows charity. Item I will that twenty pounds be paid and laid out in such manner by my Executors whereby the interest and product thereof, being one pound four shillings, may with that sixty pounds designed by my mother and sister aforenamed be yearly employed for the buying and giving of four chalder of sea coals to the poor almswomen in my grandfather Iles almshouse built on Brock Green in the parish of Fulham on Hammersmith side so long as the said almshouse shall be kept up and the revenue thereof be continued and employed according to its first founding and institution.

Abbreviations

(As used in Notes and Sources)

Add.	Additional Manuscripts, British Museum
ADM Letters	Admiralty Letters, part of the Pepysian Manuscripts in the Pepys Library, Magdalene College, Cambridge
Ashley	*Charles II* by Maurice Ashley (*see* Bibliography)
Ayscough	Ayscough Manuscripts, British Museum
BH	*A Brief History of the Times* (*see* Bibliog.)
BL	British Library, British Museum, London
BM	British Museum, London
Bod.	Bodleian Library, Oxford
Bohun	*See* Bibliog.
Brief Lives	*See* Aubrey, Bibliog.
Bryant	*The Years of Peril* (*see* Bibliog.)
Burnet	*See* Bibliog.
Capp	*See* Bibliog.
Carr	*See* Bibliog.
CJ	*Commons Journals*
Clark	*See* Bibliog.
Clarke	*See* Bibliog.
Coventry	Coventry Papers, Longleat
CSPD	*Calendars of State Papers Domestic*
Dalrymple	*See* Bibliog.
DNB	*Dictionary of National Biography* (1973)
Dom. Chron.	The Domestic Chronicle of Thomas Godfrey, B.M. Landsdowne MS 235
EBG	Edmund Berry Godfrey
Echard	*See* Bibliog.
EHD	*English Historical Documents*, ed. A. Browning (1953)
EHR	*English Historial Review*
Evelyn	*The Diary of John Evelyn* (*See* Bibliog.)
Examen	*See* Bibliog. (North, Roger)
Gibson	Gibson Papers, Lambeth Palace Library, London

Glassey	*See* Bibliog.
GLC	Greater London Council
Haley	Haley, *The First Earl of Shaftesbury* (*see* Bibliog.)
Hallam	*See* Bibliog.
Harl.	Harleian MSS, British Museum
Hatton	Hatton Correspondence (see Bibliog.)
HMC	*Historical Manuscripts Commission*
HMC Lords	HMC House of Lords Manuscripts
HoL	House of Lords
Hume	*See* Bibliog.
Intrigues	*See* Bibliog. (Smith, William)
Jones	*The Green Ribbon Club* by J.R. Jones (*see* Bibliog.)
Kenyon	*see* Bibliog.
Kirkby	*See* Bibliog.
Lane	*See* Bibliog.
Lang	*See* Bibliog.
LCC	London County Council
Lingard	*See* Bibliog.
Lipson	*See* Bibliog.
LJ	*Lords Journals*
Lloyd	*Funeral Sermon* (*see* Bibliog.)
LTR	London Topographical Record
Luttrell	*See* Bibliog.
Macaulay	*See* Bibliog.
Marks	*See* Bibliog.
Miscellanies	Part of the Pepysian Manuscripts in the Pepys Library, Magdalene College, Cambridge
Mornamont	Pepys, *My Two Volumes of Mornamont*, Pepys Library (MSS)
Nef	*See* Bibliog.
NPG	National Portrait Gallery, London
Ogg	*See* Bibliog.
PC	Privy Council Registers, Public Record Office, London
Pepys	*The Diary of Samuel Pepys*
Pepysian	Pepysian Manuscripts, Pepysian Library
Pollock	*See* Bibliog.
Poor	Poor Rate books for St Martin's-in-the-Fields parish, Westminster City Reference Library
PRO	Public Record Office, London

Rate Books	St Martin's-in-the-Fields Rate Books, Westminster Reference Library
Rawl.	Rawlinson Manuscripts, Bodleian Library, Oxford
Reresby	*See* Bibliog.
Ross Williamson	*See* Bibliog.
Sitwell	*See* Bibliog.
SP	State Papers
ST	*See* Cobbett, bibliog.
ST (1776)	State Trials
Tanner	*See* Bibliog.
Traill	*See* Bibliog.
Treby	*See* Bibliog.
Tuke	*See* Bibliog.
Vestry	St Martin-in-the-Fields Vestry Minutes, 1666–1683 (F2004), Westminster Reference Library
Wheatley	*See* Bibliog.
Wood	*See* Bibliog.

Notes and Sources

NOTE The records of the House of Lords Committee (in MS form in the HoL Library) are far from complete. For instance, Skillard's appearance before the committee is not even noted in the committee's report book. The Lords records should be used in conjunction with the records in the Shaftesbury Papers at the PRO. Together they give a reasonably full picture.

The HMC report on the committee's proceedings says that Moyle and Mulys are one and the same. There is no evidence to support this. In fact, since Mulys (as listed in original records, not in *HMC*) speaks in connection with the Duke of Ormonde, he is almost certainly the Robert Mulys calendared as corresponding with the Earl of Ossory in *HMC* Ormonde N.S. It is possible that the Mr Moyle referred to is the Walter Moyle on the jury at the trial of Green, Berry and Hill.

Part I: The Victim and his World

1. The Man who Died

1. *England's Grand Memorial* (pamphlet, 1679).
2. Burnet I, 428; Haley, 458.
3. *See* three portraits of EBG, two at NPG, one at Guildhall; Add. 4292; Gibson IV, No. 30.
4. *Examen*, 199; Vestry, 17 April 1672; Evidence of Alexander Kennedy MD, Prof. of Psychological Medicine, University of Durham, in *Who Killed Sir Edmund Berry Godfrey?* by Nesta Pain, Broadcast on BBC Home Service 16 September 1952, R.P. ref. no. SLO 14861, Disc DLO 15411; Evelyn, *FUMIFUGIUM: or The Inconvenience of the AER and SMOAKE of LONDON, 1661*.
5. *CJ* VIII, 676; Tuke, 32; PRO Crown Office Docquet Book C231/7, 44; Middlesex County Records, *Calendars of Session Books*; Glassey, 5–6; Bohun, *passim*; Vestry, *passim*.
6. *Dom. Chron.*; *Topographer and Genealogist*, II, 450–67; Baptism Register, Sellindge Church, 1622–5; Epitaph of Thomas Godfrey, Sellindge Church.
7. Tuke, 5–6; Christchurch Archives; *Brief Lives* (EBG).
8. Tuke 6–7.
9. *Transactions of the Woodford and District Historical Society*, part XII.
10. *The Register of Admissions to Gray's Inn 1521–1889*, by Joseph Foster, Hansard Publishing Union Ltd, London, 1889; *Brief Lives* (EBG).
3. *Ibid*, 10–11.

2. Hero in the Making

1. Tuke, 8–9.
2. *Ibid*, 9.

245

3. *Ibid*, 10–11.
4. *Ibid*, 11; Nef, II, 104.
5. Tuke, 13; Poor F386; Rugge's *Diurnall*, Add. 10, 117, f. 554.
6. PRO Crown Office Docquet Book C231/7, 44.
7. Tuke, 25, 26; EBG's will, PRO B1/44.
8. Tuke, 27, 28.
9. Lloyd, 12, 13; *CSPD 1663–4*, 535.
10. Epitaph to Thomas Godfrey, Sellindge Church; Repertory Minute 70, f. 186, Guildhall R.O.

3. Plague and Fire
1. Clark, 66.
2. Nef, II, 104.
3. *CSPD 1665–6*, x (preface), 107.
4. Tuke, 44–7.
5. *Ibid*, 47–8.
6. Guy Williams, *The Age of Agony*, 68.
7. *CSPD 1665–6*, preface, 107.
8. Guy Williams, *The Age of Agony*, 68.
9. *CSPD 1665–6*, 107.
10. *Ibid*.
11. *Ibid*.
12. *Ibid*.
13. *Ibid*.
14. Greatrakes, *Account* (1723), 36, 45; EBG's will, PRO B1/44.
15. Tuke, 39–51; *DNB* VIII, 32; *The Knights of England* by William A. Shaw, London 1906, II, 242.
16. Repertory Minute 71, fo. 176, Guildhall R.O.; Pepys.
17. Repertory Minute 71, fo. 176, Guildhall R.O.
18. *DNB* VIII, 32.

4. Scandal
1. *CSPD 1665–6*, x (preface), 107.
2. *C.J.* VIII, 676; Lipson II, 146–7.
3. Nef II, 104; *The Two Grand Inquisitors of Coles*, 1653, 11–12.
4. Nef II, 104.
5. *C.J.* VIII, 676.
6. Tuke, 36–9. Tuke is mistaken in his dating of EBG's knighthood and his removal from and restoration to the Commission of the Peace; Pepys, *Diary*, 26 May 1669; *HMC 12th Report*, Appendix VII, 64; Add. 28053 f. 24, letter from Edward Boscawen to Sir Wm Godolphin, 10 June 1669; PRO Crown Office Docquet Book C231/7, 350, 391, 392.
7. *Ibid*, 391, 392; Rate Books (the rates for the house were ten shillings a year); *The Thames About 1750*, 117; LCC *Survey of London*, XVIII; Poor F400; Harl. 6850; Fuller's *Worthies* fol. 1662, 243; Wheatley II, 193; Post Office London Directory, 1885.
8. *CSPD 1673*, 176.
9. *CSP Treasury Books 1672–5*, 790; *CSPD 1673*, 176.
10. *CSPD 1678*, 587; *L.J.* XIII, 436–8.
11. Tuke, 52; *National Review*, LXXXIV, 143 (September 1924); Vestry 1677–8.
12. Mornamont II, 1187; *see also* Rawl. A. 175/53 f. 208.

Part II: Gunpowder, Treason and Plot

1. The Years of Conspiracy

1. LTR, vol. 18, 30–3; *The King's Journalist*, 22; Capp, 23–4, 199–200; *English Conspiracy and Dissent, 1660–74*, I, 504.
2. Kenyon, 54; *A Brief Narrative of that Stupendous Tragedie Late Intended to be Acted* (William Hill, 1662); Capp, 209, 211.
3. *EHD 1660–1714*, 863.
4. Ashley, 172–3.
5. Kenyon, 4–5.
6. Haley, 307–47, specifically 342–3.
7. SP 29/397, No. 7 (PRO); Sitwell, *The First Whig*; J. R. Jones, *The Green Ribbon Club*; Pepysian MSS 2875, *Miscellanies* VII, 465–91.

2. The Great Plot Unveiled

1. Vestry, 12 August 1678.
2. Buck's *View of the Thames*, 1749, GLC Publication 212.
3. Kirkby.
4. Kenyon, 45, 54.
5. Kenyon, 45.
6. *Ibid*, 45–6.
7. *Ibid*, 46; Marks, 7–8.
8. Kirkby.
9. *Ibid*; *ST* VII, 1434–51; PRO SP 29/409; Rawl. D. 720, ff 172–91.
10. PRO SP 29/409; Rawl. D. 720, ff 172–91.
11. Kirkby.
12. *Ibid*.
13. *Ibid*.
14. *Ibid*.
15. *Ibid*.
16. *Ibid*.
17. *Ibid*.
18. *Ibid*.
19. *Ibid; Examen*, 171.
20. Kirkby.
21. *Ibid*.
22. *Ibid*.
23. *Ibid*.
24. *Ibid*.
25. *Ibid*.
26. Kenyon, 53.

3. Citizen Titus

1. Lane, 17; *DNB* XIV, 741; *The Rutland Magazine and County Historical Record*, III, 3, 158; *Intrigues*, 22–3; *Florus Anglo-Bavaricus*, 200.
2. *DNB* XIV, 741; Lane 22–3; Adam Elliot M.A., *A Modest Vindication of Titus Oates the Salamanca Doctor from Perjury* (1682), 1.
3. *DNB* XIV, 741; Baker MSS, St John's College, Cambridge; Mayor, *St John's College Register*; Lane, 23.
4. Lane, 24–5.
5. *Ibid*, 63.
6. *Examen*, 225.
7. Wood II, 417; Lane 25–9.
8. Lane, 29–32.
9. *Ibid*, 34–5; Burnet I, 425; *ST* VII, 1320.
10. *DNB* XIV, 742; *ST* VII, 1321; Lane 47, 50, 51.
11. *ST* VII, 1320.
12. *Ibid*, 1906, 1320–1; Burnet I, 425; Foley, *Records of the English Province of the Society of Jesus* (7 vols, London, 1877–83), V, 12.
13. Kenyon, 48–9.
14. Lane, 56–61; Kenyon, 49.
15. *Ibid*, 49; Lane, 61–2.
16. *DNB* XIV, 741; Echard, Book II, 461.
17. *ST* VI, 1434–1451; Lane, 72–3.

4. The Forged Letters

1. Lane, 78; PRO SP 29/409 f.57.
2. Kenyon, 58; Kirkby.
3. Lane, 79; Kirkby.
4. *CSPD 1678*, 466
5. *Examen*, 172–3
6. Lingard IX, 351n; Lane 79–80.
7. Kenyon, 59; Ralph I, 385; Clarke I, 517.
8. Kenyon, 58–9.
9. BH II, 7–9; Lane, 80.
10. BH II, 7–9; Clarke I, 517.
11. *Ibid*.

5. The Very Honourable Friends

1. Vestry 4/9/78; PRO SP 29/409, f. 57.
2. *Ibid*, f. 58.
3. *Ibid*.
4. Kirkby.
5. PRO PC 2/66.
6. PRO SP 29/409, f. 58.
7. *Ibid*.
8. *Ibid*.
9. *Ibid*.
10. *Ibid*.

6. Limbo

1. Kirkby.
2. Wood II, 415; Kirkby.
3. *Ibid*.
4. Vestry, 9/9/78.
5. Kirkby; Lane, 90.
6. Burnet I, 424.
7. PRO PC 2/66.
8. Vestry 27/9/78.
9. Kirkby.

7. The Perjurers' Progress

1. Kirkby; Tonge's Journal, PRO SP 29/409, 58; both copies of the articles survive, one at the PRO (SP 29/409), the other in the Bodleian (Rawl. D. 720, ff. 172–91).
2. Kirkby; PRO SP 29/409; Rawl. D. 720, ff. 172–91; PRO PC 2/66, 392.
3. *Ibid*.
4. *Ibid*.
5. *Ibid*.
6. *Ibid*.
7. *Ibid*.
8. *Ibid*.
9. *Ibid*; PRO SP 29/409; *ST* VI, 1434–1470; *L.J.* XIII, 312–27; Oates's *True Narrative*; Oates's *Discovery*.
10. PRO PC 2/66.
11. *Ibid*.
12. *Ibid*.
13. *Ibid*.
14. John Dryden, *Absalom and Achitophel*, lines 646–9. In this satirical poem using old Testament names and references, Dryden attacks the Whigs' manoeuvrings to exclude James from the succession. Absalom is Monmouth, Achitophel, Shaftesbury.
15. PRO PC 2/66.
16. *Ibid*.
17. *Ibid*; Blundel was a Jesuit priest; Fenwick was agent for the college at St Omers; Fogarty was Oates's Catholic physician; White or Whitebread was the new English Provincial; and Ireland was procurator of the province of the Society of Jesus.
18. PRO PC 2/66; Oates's *True Narrative*, articles LX, LXVIII.
19. PRO PC 2/66.
20. Welden's evidence before Lords Committee, *HMC Lords*, 48.
21. *CSPD 1678*, 426.

8. Lo! A Damned Crew

1. PC 2/66; *CSPD 1678*, 432.

2. PC 2/66 30/9/78 afternoon.
3. PC 2/66.
4. *CSPD 1678*, 418; PC 2/66.
5. *Ibid.*
6. *Ibid.*
7. Oates's *True Narrative*, article XLIV; PC 2/66.
8. *Ibid*, 396.
9. *Ibid*; *ST* VII, 32, 33.
10. *Ibid*, 33.
11. Lingard IX, 357, 358.
12. *ST* VII, 29; PC 2/66.
13. *Ibid*; *DNB* IV, 744.
14. PC 2/66; *ST* VII, 29.
15. *Ibid*, 30.
16. *Ibid*, 30.
17. Treby; *ST* VII, 35–58; *CJ* 525–9.
18. Treby.
19. *Ibid*; *ST* VII, 56.
20. Treby; *ST* VII, 56.
21. Treby; *ST* VII, 56.
22. PC 2/66.

Part III: The Primrose Way to the Everlasting Bonfire

1. The Final Days

1. *Intrigues*, 8.
2. *BH* III, 171, deposition of Henry Moor.
3. Evelyn, II, 343–4; Burnet, I, 429.
4. Burnet I, 429; *ST* VII, 1411.
5. *BH* III, 180, 181–2, depositions of Captain Thomas Gibbon and Mary Gibbon the elder.
6. *BH* III, 181–2, deposition of Mary Gibbon the elder.
7. Burnet I, 428; Vestry, 4 October 1678.
8. *HMC Lords 1678*, 48; *CJ* IX, 520.
9. Vestry, 4 October 1678.
10. *HMC Lords 1678*, 47; the copy EBG handed to Scroggs is at PRO (SP 29/409).
11. *CJ* IX, 520; *ST* VII, 168.
12. *BH* III, 100, 180, 193–4; Rawl. A. 183, 66–8, Letters of Mary Gibbon and Captain Thomas Gibbon 6/3/81.
13. *BH* III, 324, 325.
14. Echard, Book II, 502–3; *BH III*, 101.
15. Lloyd, *Funeral Sermon*.
16. *BH* III, 180, 187, 188–90.
17. *Ibid*, 187.
18. *Ibid*, 180.
19. *Ibid*, 180.

2. The Messenger of Death

1. *HMC Lords*, 47.
2. *BH* III, 178–9.
3. *Ibid*, 178–9.
4. *Ibid*, 309.
5. *ST* VII, 187.
6. *BH* III, 301–4, 177.
7. Vestry, 236.
8. *BH* III, 177.
9. *Ibid*, 177, 301–4; Vestry, 236.
10. *BH* III, 177
11. *Ibid*, 301–4; *HMC Lords*, 48.
12. *Ibid*, 48.
13. *BH* III, 301–4.
14. *BH* III, 304.
15. *Ibid*, 303–4.
16. *Ibid*, 304.
17. *Ibid*, 304; *HMC Lords*, 48.
18. *Ibid*.
19. *BH* III, 179.
20. Wood, 11/10/78.

3. One Day in October

1. *ST* (1776), III, 515, Fisher's evidence at trial of Thompson, Pain and Farwell.
2. *ST* VII 186–7.
3. *A Letter to Miles Prance*; *BH* III, 188.

4. *Ibid*, 172–3.
5. *Ibid*, 252, 171.
6. *Ibid*, 171.
7. William Morgan's *Survey of London*, 1682; *BH* III, 252, 209.
8. *A Letter to Miles Prance*.
9. *BH* III, 188.
10. *Ibid*, 195–6.
11. *Ibid*, 174.
12. *Ibid*, 188–90; 195–6.
13. *Ibid*, 217, 300, 304; Inquest statements of Joseph and Eleanor Radcliffe, Richard Duke and Caleb Wynde; *ST* (1776) III, 509, trial of Thompson, Pain and Farwell.
14. *A Letter to Miles Prance; BH* III 217–8; 174–5.
15. *Ibid*, 175.
16. *Ibid*, 196–7.
17. *Ibid*, 200–1.

4. Suspicion, Search and Speculation
1. *BH* III, 191, 203; Burnet I, 429; EBG's will, PRO B1/44.
2. *BH* III, 191, 203–4.
3. *Ibid*, 203, 190–1.
4. *Ibid*, 200.
5. *ST*, (1776) III, 518, Affidavit of John Oakley.
6. *BH* III, 203–4.
7. *Ibid*, 203–4, 190–1.
8. *Ibid*, 192.
9. *HMC 71 Finch* II, 190–3; BM Add Mss 38015, f. 316.
10. *BH* III, 208, 209–10.
11. *Ibid*, 203–4; *HMC 71 Finch* II, 190–3; EBG's will, PRO B1/44.
12. *BH* III, 203–4.
13. *Ibid*, 203–4.
14. *HMC 71 Finch* II, 190–3; BM Add Mss 38015, f. 316.
15. *Ibid*.
16. *BH* III, 191–2.
17. *Ibid*, 205.
18. *Ibid*, 205.

19. *Ibid*, 192.
20. *Ibid*, 209; *HMC 71 Finch* II, 190–3; BM Add Mss 38015, f. 316.
21. *HMC 71 Finch* II, 190-3; Add Mss 38015, f. 316
22. *BH* III, 207–8; 293.
23. *Ibid*, 194.
24. *Ibid*, 194, 197.
25. *Ibid*, 199–200, 206–7.
26. *HMC 71 Finch* II, 190–3; Add Mss 38015, f. 316.
27. Burnet I, 429; *Examen*, 202.

5. The Man in the Grey Suit
1. *BH* III, 90–1, deposition of Wm. Goldsborough the Younger.
2. *BH* III, 88–9, 89–90, 87, depositions of Adam Angus, John Oswald, William Lloyd; Burnet I, 429.

6. I Find Murdered by Rogues
1. Tuke, 84.
2. *Old and New London*, 287; Luttrell I, 8.
3. *True and Perfect Narrative; HMC Lords*, 47
4. *BH* III, 97–100; *True and Perfect Narrative; HMC Lords*, 47.
5. *BH* III, 97–100; *True and Perfect Narrative; HMC Lords*, 47.
6. *BH* III, 97–100.
7. *Ibid*, 97–100, 212–15; *True and Perfect Narrative; A Letter to Miles Prance*, 1.
8. *BH* III, 212–15. Burnet I, 429.
9. *BH* III, 212–15.
10. *Ibid*, 212–15; *ST* VII, 184.
11. *BH* III, 212–15.
12. *Ibid*, 215–6. Deposition of John Hartwell.
13. *BH* III, 212–15; *True and Perfect Narrative; ST* VII, 185.
14. Burnet I, 429.

15. *BH* III, 212–15, 215–16.
16. *True and Perfect Narrative; ST* VII, 184, 185, 186.
17. *BH* III 212–15. Deposition of John Brown; *BH* III 200–1. Deposition of Captain Thomas Paulden.
18. *Ibid*, 200–1.
19. *Ibid*, 212–15. Deposition of Brown; EBG's will, PRO B1/44 reveals that Plucknett is married to EBG's sister Sarah.
20. *BH* III, 212–15.

7. The Inquest

1. *ST* VIII, 1384; *Old and New London*, 289; *HMC Lords 1678*, 46.
2. *Trials of the Popish Plot*, 306 (12), Sion College Library; Burnet I, 429.
3. *ST* VII, 184–5.
4. *Sir Edmundbury Godfrey's Ghost: A Letter to Miles Prance*, 2; *A Second Letter to Miles Prance*.
5. *Ibid; ST* (1776) III, 515; *ST* VII, 185; *Trials of the Popish Plot*.
6. *ST* (1776) III, 515, evidence of Fisher; *Trials of the Popish Plot*, 295; *A Letter to Miles Prance*.
7. *ST* (1776) III, 515, ; *Trials of the Popish Plot*, .

8. *Trials of the Popish Plot*, .
9. *ST* (1776) III, 515 (James Chase).
10. *ST* (1776) III, 516 (Lazinby).
11. *ST* VII, 185–6; PRO/30/24/43/6.
12. *ST* (1776) III, 505–518, the trial of Nathaniel Thompson, William Pain and John Farwell.
13. *A Second Letter to Miles Prance*, 2; Sir Edmundbury Godfrey's Ghost.
14. *ST* VII, 185–6.
15. *ST* (1776) III, 515–17, *Tracts, Tryals etc* IV (304(10)), Sion College press mark 71 H 10.
16. Depositions before coroner, *BH* III.
17. *HMC Lords 1678*, 47.
18. Depositions before coroner, *BH* III (Inquest); *BM* Ayscough MSS 4292/40; Gibson Papers (Lambeth Palace Library) Vol. 14, 942, no. 30.
19. *Ibid*, no. 30.
20. *ST* VIII, , affidavit of Forset.
21. SP 29/366, 611 (PRO); *HMC Lords 1678*, 47, *BH* III, 244.
22. *ST* (1776) III, 516 (Lazinby).
23. Gibson Papers, Vol. 14, 942, 30, Wm. Griffith to Ben Colings 19/10/78.
24. *Sir Edmundbury Godfrey's Ghost*.
25. *Ibid*.

Part IV: The Age of Discovery

1. Panic

1. *HMC Ormonde N.S.* IV, 207.
2. Finch MSS (Leicestershire R.O.), box 56.
3. *Examen*, 196.
4. *HMC Ormonde N.S.* V, 459.
5. *BH* III, 10; Burnet I, 428.
6. *Examen*, 204–5; 247. *BH* III, 199.

7. Macaulay, I, 184.
8. Somerset County R.O., DD/PH 211/85.
9. SPD King William's Chest 3, No. 68 (PRO).
10. *HMC Ormonde N.S.* IV, 461; *Printed* SP Dom, Various 12, 371 (PRO); SP Dom Entry Book 51, 59 (PRO).

11. *C.J.* IX, 516; *L.J.* XIII, 293; Reresby, 207–8.
12. *C.J.* IX, 516; *L.J.* XIII, 293–5.
13. Burnet I, 430; *The Second Part of the Growth of Popery*, 212; *Examen*, 202–3; *Notes & Queries*, 7th Series, Vol XII, 207–8, 314; *Notes & Queries*, 9th Series, Vol III, 96.
14. *CSPD* 1678, 481, 493.
15. *HMC 5th Report* Vol IV, 371.
16. Evelyn, 23 November 1679.
17. *CJ* IX, 518–66; *LJ* XIII, 335, 346; Kenyon, 83–4.
18. *LJ* XIII, 307.
19. *CSPD* 1678, 480.
20. EBG's will, PRO B1/44.
21. *Examen*, 204.
22. *Ibid*, 204–5; Evelyn, 23 November 1679.
23. Lloyd, *Funeral Sermon; Examen*, 205.
24. *Examen*, 205.

2. The Curious Flight of Mr Godfrey

1. ADM Letters VIII, 255, 6.
2. *Ibid*; Mornamont I, 113.
3. *Ibid*, 113–17; ADM Letters VIII, 256–7; 261.
4. *Ibid*, 255–7.
5. *Ibid*, 258.
6. *Ibid*, 261.
7. *Ibid*, 264–5, 267–8; Rawl. A. 172, f. 3–4.
8. *Ibid*, 264–5.

3. The Domino Plan

1. Coventry XI, f. 232; Tanner 328–9; Bryant, 158; *Florus Anglo-Bavaricus.*
2. *ST* VII, 1473; ADM Letters, VIII, 313–14; PRO SP 29/407, No. 98.
3. PRO PC 2/66.
4. *Ibid*; Coventry XI, f. 232; PRO 30/24/43/63; PRO SP 29/407, No. 98.

5. *ST* VI, 1473.
6. *Ibid*, 1473–7.
7. *Ibid*, 1478.
8. *Ibid*, 1479.
9. *Ibid*.
10. *Ibid*, 1479–82.
11. *Ibid*, 1483–4.
12. *Ibid*, 1484.

4. God Almighty on Horseback

1. *ST* VI, 1484; PRO SP 29/407/99.
2. Lane 56–61; Kenyon, 49.
3. *DNB* II, 117.
4. *HMC 6th Report*, Vol. 5, 778.
5. PRO SP 29/407/29; Add. 11055 f. 245; Coventry XI, 272–74; *ST* VI, 1486–9; *L.J.* XIII, 343.
6. *Ibid*.
7. *ST* VI, 1486.
8. *Ibid*, 1486–7.
9. *Ibid*, 1487.
10. *Ibid*, 1487.
11. *Ibid*, 1487.
12. *Ibid*, 1488.
13. *Ibid*, 1488.

5. The Alibi

1. *ST* VI, 1484.
2. *ST* VI, 1484–5.
3. *ST* VI, 1485.
4. Samuel Butler, *Hudibras*, Part III, canto. ii.
5. *Ibid*.
6. *ST* VI, 1485.
7. *ST* VI, 1485.
8. *ST* VI, 1485–6.
9. *ST* VI, 1486, 1489; *CJ* IX, 537.
10. *ST* VI, 1489.
11. *ST* VI, 1489–90.
12. *ST* VI, 1490.
13. *ST* VII, 245–7; ADM Letters Vol VIII, 313–14.
14. *ST* VI, 1490–1.

15. *Ibid*, 1490–1.
16. *ST* VI, 1491.

6. Terror
1. SP 29/407, II 244 (PRO).
2. Kenyon, 96–7; *CSPD* 1678, 540–1.
3. PRO/30/24/43/63, 109.
4. *Ibid*, 1 November 1678.
5. *Ibid*.
6. *Ibid*.
7. *ST* VI 1501–12.
8. SP 29/407, 164; *CSPD* 1678, 519, 539.
9. *ST* VI, 1510–12.
10. *ST* VI, 1501–12.
11. *ST* VII, 1–78.
12. *ST* VII, 25.
13. *Ibid*, 25.
14. *Ibid*, 70–5.
15. *CJ* IX, 549; *Examen*, 186.
16. *CJ* IX, 549; *L.J.* XIII, 388–92.
17. *Ibid*.
18. *CSPD* 1678, 552, 555, 556; *ST* VII, 78; 79–144.

7. Evil Doings at the Water-Gate
1. *HMC Lords 1678*, 51.
2. Oates's *True Narrative*, 20–21; *BH* III, 52, 53, 65; *ST* VII, 182.
3. *HMC Lords 1678*, 51.
4. *Ibid*, 51.
5. *Ibid*, 51; PC 2/67, 23 for Mrs Prance's first name.
6. *HMC Lords 1678*, 51.
7. *Ibid*, 51–2; Kenyon, 132; *LJ* XIII, 431, 436–9; *ST* VII, 183, 191.
8. *LJ* XIII, 436–8.
9. *LJ* XIII, 436.
10. *LJ* XIII, 436–8; *HMC Lords 1678*, 51; PRO SP 29 408/2/47; *ST* VII, 169–79, 210; *DNB* VIII, 28–9.
11. *LJ* XIII, 439; *HMC Lords 1678*, 52.
12. *HMC Lords 1678*, 52.

13. *Ibid*; SP 29, 407/2/17; *ST* VII, 177, 210.

8. The Scapegoats
1. *ST* VII, 159–60, 174.
2. *ST* VII, 161–2.
3. *Ibid*, 162–3.
4. *Ibid*, 163.
5. *Ibid*, 163.
6. *Ibid*, 163.
7. *Ibid*, 163.
8. *Ibid*, 163–4.
9. *Ibid*, 164.
10. *Ibid*, 164–5.
11. *Ibid*, 165.
12. *Ibid*, 165.
13. *Ibid*, 165–6.
14. *Ibid*, 166.
15. *Ibid*, 166.
16. *Ibid*, 166–7.
17. *Ibid*, 167.
18. *Ibid*, 167–8.
19. *Ibid*, 168.
20. *Ibid*, 168.
21. *Ibid*, 169.
22. *Ibid*, 169.
23. *Ibid*, 169.
24. *Ibid*, 169–70.
25. *L.J.* XIII, 436–8.
26. *ST* VII, 186–8.
27. *Ibid*, 170.
28. *Ibid*, 170–4.
29. *Ibid*, 174.
30. *Ibid*, 174–5.
31. *Ibid*, 175.
32. *Ibid*, 175.
33. *Ibid*, 175.
34. *Ibid*, 175–6.
35. *Ibid*, 176.
36. *Ibid*, 176.
37. *Ibid*, 176–7.
38. *Ibid*, 177–8.
39. *Ibid*, 178–9.
40. *Ibid*, 179–83.
41. *Ibid*, 183.
42. *Ibid*, 183–4.
43. *Ibid*, 184.
44. *Ibid*, 184–6.

45. *Ibid*, 186–7.
46. *BH* III, 141.
47. *BH* III, 142–4.
48. *ST* VII, 187–8.
49. *Ibid*, 188–9.
50. *Ibid*, 190.
51. *Ibid*, 190–2.
52. *Ibid*, 192.
53. *Ibid*, 195.
54. *Ibid*, 195.
55. *Ibid*, 195–6.
56. *Ibid*, 196–7.
57. *Ibid*, 197–8; *BH* III, 136 for Mrs Broadstreet's first name.
58. *ST* VII, 198–200.
59. *Ibid*, 201–3.
60. *Ibid*, 203–6.
61. *Ibid*, 207–9.
62. *Ibid*, 209.
63. *Ibid*, 209–10; SP 29 30/12/78, Bundle 408 (PRO).
64. *ST* VII, 210.
65. *Ibid*, 210.
66. *Ibid*, 210.
67. *Ibid*, 210–11.
68. *Ibid*, 216, 217.
69. *Ibid*, 220–1.
70. *Ibid*, 221–6.
71. *Ibid*, 231–50.
72. *BH* III, 126–32.
73. *ST* VII, 226
74. Luttrell, I, 9.
75. Luttrell, I, 8.
76. *Ibid*.

Part V: Enigma Variations

1. The Romish Assassins
1. Pepys MSS, Adm Letters VIII, 313.
2. Kenyon MSS, *HMC 14th Report*, App., Part IV, 129.
3. Coventry, XI, f. 237.
4. Macaulay, 1, 184; *ST* VII, 1319.
5. Kenyon, 266.
6. Pollock, 139.
7. *Ibid*, 139–46.
8. *Ibid*, 146–8.
9. *Ibid*, 159.
10. *Ibid*, 160–1.
11. Lang, 88.
12. Reresby, 325; Pollock 152–5.
13. Pollock, 152.

2. Creatures of the Underworld
1. Marks, 25.
2. *BH* III, 98–100.
3. Hume, Vol. 8, 68.
4. Kenyon, 269.
5. *Ibid*, 270.
6. *ST* VII, 168; *Examen*, 199.
7. Hallam, II, 292–3.
8. *HMC Lords 1678*, 47; Kenyon, 269.
9. *BH* III, 187; *CJ* IX, 520.

3. Fratricide and the Grim Reaper
1. Carr, 15.
2. Kenyon, 264n.
3. Carr, 150–74, 313–48.
4. *Ibid*, 156.
5. *Ibid*, 156–7.
6. *BH* III, 180, 195–6, 171, depositions of Thomas Wynell and Henry Moor; *HMC Lords 1678*, 48, evidence of George Welden.
7. Carr, 157.
8. *BH* III, 195–6, deposition of Thomas Wynell.
9. *BH* III, 304.
10. Clark, 94; Bryant, 219.
11. Lloyd, *Funeral Sermon*, 12.

4. Oates or his Double
1. Stephen, *History of the Criminal Law*, 393; Birkenhead, *Famous Trials*, 70; Lee's art-

icle on Oates, *DNB* XIV, 743; Traill, 128n.
2. *Famous Trials*, 70.
3. Traill, 128n.
4. Lane, 360–1.
5. Carr, 321.
6. *Ibid*, 168.
7. *Ibid*, 168–9.
8. *History of the Criminal Law*, 393.
9. Carr, 169.

5. To Be or not to Be
1. *HMC 6th Report* (Vol 5), 389; *BH* III, *passim*; Luttrell, I, 1–2 (October 1678); Lingard, 361–2; Sitwell, 38, 40, 41; Marks, 68–114.
2. Sir Robert Southwell to Lord Nottingham on the publication of *BH*, Add. 38015 f. 316–17.
3. *BH* III, 181–2, deposition of Mary Gibbon.
4. *Ibid*, 219–20.
5. *Marks, 109.*
6. *Ibid*, 110–11.
7. *Ibid*, 112; *BH* III, 212–215.
8. *CJ* IX, 520.
9. *Ibid*, 520.
10. *BH* III, 324.
11. *BH* III, 304.
12. *CJ* IX, 520; *ST* VII, 168.

6. Post Post Mortem
1. *Who Killed Sir Edmund Berry Godfrey?* by Nesta Pain, BBC Home Service, 16/9/52; PRO/30/24/43/63; SP 29/366/27241.
2. *Who Killed Sir Edmund Berry Godfrey?* (Pain).
3. SP 29/366/27241; Simpson to author 1/11/76.
4. PRO/30/24/43/63.
5. Simpson to author 1/11/76; *Who Killed Sir Edmund Berry Godfrey?* (Pain).
6. Simpson to author, 14/10/76; *Who Killed Sir Edmund Berry Godfrey?* (Pain).
7. *Ibid.*
8. *Ibid*; Simpson to author 14/10/76 and 1/11/76.
9. *Who Killed Sir Edmund Berry Godfrey?* (Pain).
10. Simpson to author, 14/10/76.
11. *Who Killed Sir Edmund Berry Godfrey?* (Pain).
12. Simpson to author, 18/10/76.
13. Simpson to author, 23/10/76.
14. *Who Killed Sir Edmund Berry Godfrey?* (Pain).
15. *ST* VII, 185, evidence of Skillard.
16. *Who Killed Sir Edmund Berry Godfrey?*(Pain).
17. *Ibid.*
18. *Ibid.*
19. *ST* (1776) III, 515.
20. *Who Killed Sir Edmund Berry Godfrey?* (Pain).
21. *Ibid.*

Part VI: The Answer

1. Peyton's Gang
1. Kenyon, 265–6.
2. PRO SP 29/397, No. 7.
3. PRO SP 29/379, f. 209.
4. *Ibid; CSPD 1676*, 11–12; PRO Crown Office Docquet Book C231/7, 508, 509, 512, 510, 517; those stripped of their offices were Peyton, Barker, Adams, Sabbs (later reinstated), Buck and Umphreville; *HMC Finch* II, 44; PRO SP 29/442, No. 37.
5. Pepysian MSS 2875, *Miscella-*

255

nies VII, 488; *Letters to Sir Joseph Williamson*, Camden Society, II, 157; *The First Earl of Shaftesbury* (Brown), 223–4; EBG's will, PRO B1/44 (published 1679).

6. Bryant, *Years of Peril*, 211.
7. B.M. Harl, 6845 f. 282; Sitwell, 198; Jones, 17; Marks, 2; Coventry XI f. 161; Williams, *A Specimen of the rhetorick* . . .
8. *Miscellanies* VII, 489; Sitwell, 198; *ST* VII, 3, 161; *ST* VII & VIII for Jurors' names.
9. PRO PC 2/62, 10.
10. Crown Office Docquet Books C231/7; Vestry, 1677–8; *CSP Treasury Books 1676–9*, 1197; *BH* III, 182–3, deposition of William Church; *L.J.* XIII, 198–200.
11. *BH* III, 192, deposition of Thomas Gibbon; *BH* III, 171, deposition of Henry Moor.
12. MSS of the House of Lords, Friday, 28 September 1678, afternoon.
13. PRO SP 29/409; Rawl. D. 720, ff. 172–91.
14. Add. 4291, f. 150.
15. MSS of the House of Lords (manuscript copies) in HoL Library, 24/10/78; *HMC Report 36, Ormonde MSS N.S.* IV, 464; Evelyn's diary entry for 21 October shows that EBG's friendship with Coleman was common knowledge before the Lords Committee's first sitting and that Carr is wrong in stating that Shaftesbury did not know of it until the first week of November.
16. Burnet I, 429; Lloyd; *BH* III, 187.
17. *C.J.* IX, 520.
18. *Ibid; ST* VII, 168.
19. *BH* III, 324.
20. *BH* III, 187, 188–90, 324.
21. *BH* III, 187.
22. Dalrymple II, 131–2.
23. Ross-Williamson, 258.
24. Hallam II, 272–3.

2. The Spy from Long Island

1. Rawl. A, 188, f. 127; Coventry XI, 393, 396.
2. Rawl. A, 194, 42–4; Coventry XI, 393; Rawl. A, 175, f. 173; *Colonel John Scott of Long Island*, 5.
3. *DNB* XVII, 979–80; *Colonel John Scott of Long Island*, *passim*.
4. *Ibid; DNB* XVII, 980; *Miscellanies* VII, 487.
5. Mornamont Vol 1, 113–17; SP 29/243, No 70; Rawl, A. 175, f.173; *CSPD 1678*, 290.
6. *ST.* VII, 187.
7. *BH* III, 293, 209.

3. The Mighty Giant

1. *HMC 9th Report* (Vol. 8), 100; *LJ* XIII, 139; *HMC 36th Report Ormonde Mss N.S.* Vol IV, 128, 361; *ST* VI, 1309–50.
2. Ogg, II, 582; *Impartial Account*, 2; *Brief Lives*, I, 317; *National Review*, Vol. 84, September 1924; *LJ* XIII, 198–200, 4 April 1678; Vestry F2004.
3. *Complete Peerage; Burke's Peerage; HMC 6th Report*, 473; Essex Papers, Camden Society, Vol. 1, 282.
4. Rochester, *The First Satyr of Juvenal Imitated* (1709 ed.); Jones, 125–6, 165; *CSPD 1679–80*, 399.
5. *Complete Peerage; Burke's Peerage; DNB* IX, 670.
6. *HMC Hastings* II, 165; *HMC*

7th Report Vol. 61, 491; HMC Ormonde NS III, 356; HMC 6th Report, 473; Essex Papers, Camden Society, Vol. 1, 282.

7. LJ XII, 652; HMC 9th Report (Vol 8), 48; CSPD 1678, 101.
8. HMC 7th Report (Vol 61), 466; Peerage and Baronetage, 2092; Complete Peerage.
9. Brief Lives, I, 317.
10. HMC Rutland II, 28; HMC 7th Report (Vol 61), 493.
11. Ibid, 467.
12. HMC Hastings II, 170.
13. Ibid, 170.
14. Hatton, I, 158–9.
15. HMC 12th Report Vol 2 appendix V, 53; HMC Finch II, 37.
16. Ibid, 37; CSPD 1678, 550, 612; LJ XIII, 131; House of Lords Calendar – HMC 9th Report (Vol. 8), 98.
17. Ibid, 100; LJ XIII, 139.
18. Ibid, 139.
19. ST VI, 1323–4.
20. Ibid, 1324.
21. Ibid, 1324, 1326–7, 1328–30.
22. Ibid, 1337, 1339–40, 1341.
23. Ibid, 1336, 1347.
24. Ibid, 1349–50; CSPD 1678, 95.
25. HMC 12th Report, app ix, 74; HMC 7th Report, (Vol 61), 495.
26. Ibid, 478.
27. A True and Sad Relation of Two Wicked and Bloody Murthers (8-page pamphlet, London, 1680).
28. CSPD 1680–1, 11.1.81; He was back by 13 Feb., see SP 29 415, No. 37 (PRO), Clarendon to Jenkins; SP 29 415, Nos 192, 196 (PRO); Luttrell, 102.
29. HMC 9th Report, 458; HMC 11th Report part V, 89.
30. An ELEGY On the Right Honourable William [sic] Earl of Pembroke who deceased on the 29th, of August, 1683 (London, 1683).

Epilogue
1. HMC 36th Report, Ormond MSS NS, Vol IV, 461, 463; Examen, 196.
2. HMC 36th Report, Ormond MSS NS, Vol IV, 461, 463.
3. ST VII, 220; Burnet I, 428.

Bibliography

ABBOTT, Wilbur Cortez   *Colonel John Scott of Long Island*
1634 (?)–1696
(1918–B.L. 10855.e.26)
English Conspiracy and Dissent,
1660–1674
The Origin of Titus Oates' Story
(EHR Vol. 25 (1910), pp 126–9 – B.L.
PP. 3408)

AKERMAN, J.Y. (ed.)   *Moneys received and paid for secret*
services of Charles II and James II
(Camden Society, London, 1851 – B.L.
Ac. 8113/52.)

ASHLEY, Maurice   *Charles II*
(London, 1971)

AUBREY, John   *'Brief Lives', chiefly of contemporaries,*
set down by John Aubrey, between the
years 1669 and 1696, Edited from the
author's MSS by Andrew Clark.
(2 vols, Clarendon Press, Oxford, 1898
– B.L. 10803.d.3.)

BEDLOE, William   *Narrative and Impartial Discovery of*
the Horrid Popish Plot
(1679 – B.L. 193.d.11.(2.))

BELLOC, Hilaire   *James the Second*
(London, 1928 – B.L. 10807.e.17.)

BELLOT, Hugh H.L.   *The Temple*
(London, 1914 – B.L. 010347.h.53.)

BESANT, Walter   *Westminster*
(London, 1895 – B.L. 010349.i.5.)

BIRKENHEAD, Lord   *See* Smith, F.

BOHUN, Edmund   *The Justice of the Peace, his calling and*
Qualifications
(London, 1693 – B.L. 884.h.7.)

BRAYLEY, Edward
Wedlake
Londiniana, or Reminiscences of the British Metropolis
(4 vols, London, 1829 – B.L. 10348. b.b.4)

BROWN, Louise Fargo
The First Earl of Shaftesbury
(1933 – B.L. Ac. 8504/16)
The Political Activities
(1912 – B.L. Ac. 8504/5)

BROWNING, Andrew
Thomas Osborne Earl of Danby
(3 vols, Glasgow, 1944–51 – B.L. 10862.c.37.)

BRYANT, Arthur
King Charles II
(London, 1931 – B.L. 10807.ee.22.)
The England of Charles II
(London, 1934 – B.L. 010352.bb.77.)
The Letters, Speeches and Declarations of Charles II
(1935 – B.L. 010920.k.37.)
Samuel Pepys: The Man in the Making
(Cambridge, 1933 – B.L. 010821.g.12.)
Samuel Pepys: The Years of Peril
(Cambridge, 1935 – B.L. 010821.g.13.)

BUTLER, Samuel
Characters and Passages from Note-Books
(Cambridge, 1908 – B.L. 12270.dd.6)

CAPP, B.S.
The Fifth Monarchy Men: A Study in Seventeenth Century Millenarianism
(London, 1972)

CARE, Henry
The History of the Damnable Popish Plot, in its Various Branches and Progress, etc
(1680 – B.L. 599.b.19.)

CARR, John Dickson
The Murder of Sir Edmund Godfrey
(1936 – B.L. 9506.df.3)

CHANCELLOR, E.
Beresford
The Annals of the Strand
(London, 1912 – B.L. 10349.ppp.1.)

CHICHELEY, Thomas — *The Case of Thomas Chicheley . . . E. Godfrey, and several persons more, who are purchasors of the Adventure Lands of those who did not pay in their taxes according to their covenant for dreyning the . . . Bedford Level, etc* (1670? – B.L. fol. 816.m.8.(15).)

CHRISTIE, William D. — *A Life of Anthony Ashley Cooper, Earl of Shaftesbury* (2 vols, 1871 – B.L. 2406.a.l.)

CLARENDON, Edward Hyde, Earl of — *Life* (3 vols, Oxford, 1759 – B.L. 683.k.4.)

CLARK, Sir George N. — *The Later Stuarts 1660–1714* (Oxford History of England, Oxford 1934 – B.L.2083.b.)

CLARKE, James Stanier — *Life of James the Second* (2 vols, 1816 – B.L.599.i.7.)

COBBETT, William (ed.) — *A Complete Collection of State Trials* (vols 6–8, 1809–26 – B.L. 6497.cc.1.)

COURSON, R. de — *The Condition of English Catholics Under Charles II* (London, 1899. B.L. appears to have only the French edition of 1898 – 4705.de.4.)

CREED, Cary — *Etchings of Statues* (1730 – B.L.786.i.18)

CREW, Albert — *The Old Bailey* (London, 1933 – B.L.6145.t.13.)

CUNNINGHAM, Peter — *The Story of Nell Gwyn: and the sayings of Charles II* (ed. H.B. Wheatley, 1892 – B.L.10825.f.32.)

DALRYMPLE, Sir John — *Memoirs of Great Britain and Ireland* (3 vols, 1771, 1773, 1778 – B.L. 598 h.9–11)

DELAUNE, Thomas — *Angliae Metropolis* (London, 1690 – B.L. 578.a.3.)

261

DE QUINCEY, Thomas	*On Murder as a Fine Art* (1924 – B.L. 012207a.2/2,23)
DRYDEN, John	*Poems and Fables* (ed. James Kinsley, OUP 1958)
EBSWORTH, Joseph Woodfall	*The Bagford Ballads* (1878 – B.L. Ac.9928/5)
ECHARD, Laurence	*History of England* (3 vols, London, 1707–18 – B.L. 9505.h.4.)
EVELYN, John	*The Diary of John Evelyn* (6 vols, 1955 – B.L. N.L.18.d.) *FUMIFUGIUM: or The Inconvenience of the AER and SMOAKE of LONDON* (1661 – B.L.1170.h.4.)
FOLEY, Helen	*Records of the English Province of the Society of Jesus* (7 vols, London, 1877–83 – B.L. 2210.c.1.)
FOSTER, Joseph	*The Register of Admissions to Gray's Inn 1521–1889* (London, Hansard Publishing Union, 1889)
FOXCROFT, Helen Charlotte	*Life and Letters of Sir George Savile, Bart, first Marquis of Halifax* (London, 1898, – B.L.10815.cc.18.)
GERARD, Rev. J.	*The Popish Plot and its Newest Historian* [on Pollock] (London, 1903 – B.L. 3940.m.11.)
GLASSEY, L.K.J.	*The Commission of the Peace 1675–1720* (Bod. Ms. D.Phil.d.5682)
GREATRAKES, Valentine	*A Brief Account* (1723 – only traceable copy is in library of The Shakespeare Centre, Stratford-upon-Avon)

GREY, Anchitel	*Debates of the House of Commons* (10 vols, London, 1769 – B.S. Ref. 10/2.)
HALEY, Kenneth H.D.	*The First Earl of Shaftesbury* (London, 1968 – B.L. X700/3084)
HALL, Sir John Richard	*The Murder of Sir Edmund Berry Godfrey* in *Four Famous Mysteries* (1922 – B.L. 09008.df.9.)
HALLAM, Henry	*Constitutional History of England* (2 vols, 1827 – B.L. 598.h.12,13.)
HAMILTON, Anthony	*Memoirs of Count Grammont* (2 vols, London, 1889 – B.L. 010661.m.44)
HARRISON, A.N.	*The Godfrey Family of Woodford* (Woodford Historical Society)
HATTON FAMILY	*Correspondence of the family of Hatton ed. by E.M. Thompson* (2 vols, Camden Society, London, 1878 – B.L. Ac.8113/115.)
HILL, William	*A Brief Narrative of that Stupendous Tragedie Late intended to be Acted* (about Thomas Tonge's plot of 1662; London, 1662 – B.L. 1132.f.38.)
HOLDSWORTH, William Searle	*History of English Law* (Vol. 9, London, 1903, – B.L. 06005.ee.47)
HOOPER, W. Eden	*History of Newgate and the Old Bailey* (London, 1935 – B.L. 06055.h.52.)
HUME, David	*History of England* (1826 – B.L. 9503.e.9.)
IRVING, H.B.	*Life of Judge Jeffreys* (London, 1898 – B.L. 2406.h.9.)
JAMES II	*The Secret History . . .* (1691 – B.L. 807.a.23.)

JEAFFRESON, John Cordy — *Middlesex County Records* (Middx County Records Soc., 1887 – B.L. Ac.8108)

JONES, James Rees — *The First Whigs* (1961 – B.L. Ac. 1342.d.(10).)

KENYON, John Phillips — *The Popish Plot* (Heinemann, 1972 – B.L. X200/7447.)

KINGSFORD, Charles Lethbridge — *Early History of Piccadilly, Soho, Leicester Square and their Neighbourhood.* (Cambridge, 1925 – B.L. 010349.k.39.)

KIRKBY, Christopher — *A Compleat and True Narrative of the Manner of the Discovery, etc* (London, 1679 – B.L. 193.d.11.(13).)

LANE, Jane — *Titus Oates* (London, 1949 – B.L. 4909.bb.28.)

LANG, Andrew — *The Mystery of Sir Edmund Berry Godfrey* in *The Valet's Tragedy* (1903 – B.L. 012355.ee.9.)

L'ESTRANGE, Sir Roger — *A Brief History of the Times* (1687, 1688 – B.L. 808.d.8.)

LINGARD, John — *History of England* (13 vols, 1839 – B.L. 9505.d.)

LIPSON, Ephraim — *Economic History of England* (2 vols, 1931 – B.L. 2238.e.14.)

LLOYD, William — *A Sermon at the Funeral of Sir Edmund-Berry Godfrey* (1678 – B.L. 694.g.12.(5).)

LUCAS, Theophilus — *Lives of the Gamesters* in *Games and Gamesters of the Restoration*, introduced by Cyril H. Hartmann. (1930 – B.L. W.P. 6666/4.)

LUTTRELL, Narcissus — *Brief Historical Relation of State Affairs From September 1678 to April 1714.* (6 vols, Oxford, 1857 – B.L. 2072.c.)

MACAULAY, Lord	*History of England* (1849 ed. Vol. 1 – B.L. 9525.d.1.) *Essays* (1885 ed. – B.L. 12272.bb.8.)
MACPHERSON, James	*The History of Great Britain from the Restoration to the Accession of the House of Hanover* (London, 1775, 2 vols – B.L. 595.m.6.) *Original Papers* (2 vols, 1775 – B.L. 2410 h. 2.)
MANCHEE, William Henry	*The Westminster City Fathers* (1924 – B.L. 010349 K. 30)
MARÉ, Eric de	*Wren's London* (Folio Society, London, 1975)
MARKS, Alfred	*Who Killed Sir Edmund Berry Godfrey?* (1905 – B.L. 9502.c.14.) *The Case of Sir Edmund Berry Godfrey* (1907 – B.L. 9010.ee.4(10).)
MILLINGTON, F.H.	*Sir Joseph Williamson* (1890 – B.L. 10803.bb.29 (6).)
MORGAN, William	*Survey of London* (1682)
MUDDIMAN, J(oseph) G(eorge)	*The King's Journalist* (1923 – B.L. 9512.eee.19) *The Mystery of Sir E.B. Godfrey* in *The National Review*, September 1924. – B.L. PP. 3611.a.b.
NEF, John Ulric the Younger	*The Rise of the British Coal Industry* (1932 – B.L. Ac. 2363/3(4).)
NORTH, Roger	*Examen: or, an enquiry into the credit and veracity of a Pretended Complete History; shewing the Perverse and Wicked Design of it, and the . . . etc* (1740 – London Library 885)
OATES, Titus	*True Narrative of the Horrid Plot*, etc (London, 1679 – B.L. 193.d.11.(1))

OGG, David | *England in the Reign of Charles II* (2 vols, Oxford, 1956 – B.L. 9506.e.21.)

PARMITER, Geoffrey V. de C. | *Reasonable Doubt* (1938 – B.L. 6496 bbb. 18.)

PEARSON, Edmund | *Masterpieces of Murder* (1964 – B.L. 5427.a.33.)

PEPYS, Samuel | *The Diary of Samuel Pepys M.A., F.R.S.* edited by Henry B. Wheatley F.S.A. (London, 1903 – B.L. 2020.g.)

PHILLIPPS, Samuel March | *A Study of the State Trials, prior to the Revolution of 1688* (1826)

PHILLIPS, Hugh | *The Thames About 1750* (Collins, 1951 – B.L. 10368.r.28.)

POLLOCK, Sir John | *The Popish Plot* (1903 – B.L. 9509.1.10.)

PRANCE, Miles | *True Narrative and Discovery of Several Very Remarkable Passages relating,* etc (London, 1679 – B.L. 515.L.19.(1.))

RANKE, Leopold von | *History of England* (6 vols, Oxford, 1875 – B.L. 9503.aaaa.1.)

REDMAYNE, J. (printer) | *The Whole Series of all that hath been Transacted in the House of Peers, concerning the Popish Plot, wherein is contained, the most Material Passages in both Houses of Parliament Relating to the full discovery thereof* (London, 1681 – B.L. 809.e.6.)

RERESBY, Sir John | *The Travels and Memoirs of Sir John Reresby, Bart* (London, 1813 – B.L. 807.e.24.)

ROBINSON, William, L.L.D. — *The History and Antiquities of the Parish of Edmonton* (1819 – B.L. 290.g.36.)

ROSS WILLIAMSON, Hugh — *Historical Enigmas* (London, 1974)

RUSSELL, Lord John — *Life of William Lord Russell* (1853 – B.L. 2406. a. 10.)

SECCOMBE, Thomas — *Titus Oates* in *Twelve Bad Men* (London, 1894 – B.L. 10803.g.14.)

SHAW, William A. — *The Knights of England* (London, 1906 – B.L. 2102.c.)

SIMS, George R. — *Two King's Pardons* (1904 – B.L. 6495.f.26.)

SITWELL, Sir George — *The First Whig* (Scarborough, 1894 – B.L. C.99.f.42.)

SMITH, Frederick Edwin, Earl of Birkenhead — *Famous Trials of History* (1926 – B.L. 06055.ee.3.)

SMITH, John — *Narrative of . . . the Popish Plot* (London, 1679 – B.L. 669.d.1(20).)

SMITH, William, M.A. — *Intrigues of the Popish Plot Laid Open* (London, 1685 – B.L. 515.1.28.)

STATE TRIALS — (1776 – B.L. 507.K.13.)

STEPHEN, Sir James Fitzjames — *A History of the Criminal Law of England* (3 vols, 1883 – B.L. 6026.K.1.)

STOWE, John — *Survey of London* (updated to 18th century by John Strype) (London, 1754 – B.L. 189.f.10.)

TANNER, J.R. (ed.) — *see:* Pepys, Samuel. *Further Correspondence of Samuel Pepys 1662–1679, from the family papers in the possession of J. Pepys Cockerell* (London, 1929 – B.L. 010902.ff.41.)

TEONGE, Rev. Henry   *Diary*
(London, 1825 – B.L. 1202.K.12)

THOMPSON, Nathaniel *A True and Perfect Narrative of the*
Late . . . Bloody Murther of Sir E.G.
who was found murthered . . . in a field
near Primrose Hill, etc.
(London, 1678 – B.L. 808.g.42)
Sir Edmundbury Godfrey's Ghost
(1682 – B.L. 1852.b.2(10).)

TIMBS, John   *Curiosities of London*
(London, 1855 – B.L. 1302.a.1.)

TRAILL, H.D.   *Shaftesbury*
(London, 1885 – B.L. 10803.de.19.)

TREBY, Sir George   *A Collection of Letters*
(1681 – contains some of Coleman's
letters – B.L. 807.g.4.)

TREVELYAN, G.M.   *England Under the Stuarts (History of*
England, Vol. 5)
(London, 1904 – B.L. W.P,12987.a/
13.)

TUKE, Richard   *Memoires of the Life and Death of Sir*
Edmondbury Godfrey
(1682 – B.L. G. 1591)

UMFREVILLE, Family *The Umfrevilles*
of   (c. 1860 – B.L. 09917 c.28.)

WALFORD, Edward   *Old and New London*
(Vol. 5, 1873 – B.L. 10348 f.12)

WELCH, Joseph   *A List of Scholars of St Peter's College,*
Westminster
(1788 – B.L. 688.h.14.)

WHEATLEY, H.B.   *Diary of John Evelyn, with Life*
(1906 – B.L. 10854.f.11.)

WILLIAMS, Guy   *The Age of Agony*
(Constable, 1975)

WILLIAMS, J.B.   *The Genesis of Oates's Plot* in *The Month*, July–December 1912 (B.L. P.P. 5534)

WILLIAMS, Sir W.   *A Specimen of the rhetorick . . . of W. Williams, Speaker of the late House of Commons . . . in his speech to Sir R. Peyton, when he expell'd him that House* (1681 – B.L. 1850.c.6.(90).)

WILLIAMSON, Sir Joseph   *Letters* (2 vols, 1874 – B.L. Ac.8113/102)

WILMOT, John   *The Works of the Earls of Rochester* (2 vols, 1731 – B.L. C.123.c.6.)

WOOD, Anthony Á   *Life and Times* (Oxford Hist. Soc., 1895 – B.L. Ac.8126/11.)

PERIODICALS

American Historical Review
Vol 14 (Oct 1908–July 1909) pp 503–28 & 696–722 – B.L. P.P.3437.baa.

Durham University Journal
1956 – B.L. 6118.n.

English Historical Review
Vol 25 (1910) *The Origin of Titus Oates's Story* by W.C. Abbott, pp 126–9 – B.L. PP3408
Vol 40 (1925) *The Journals of Edmund Warcup* 1676–84, pp 235–60 – B.L. PP3408.

The Gentleman's Magazine
Vol 63 (1793) – B.L. 2170a–71.

The National Review
1924 – PP.3611. a.b.

The Topographer and Genealogist
Vol 2 pp 450–467 – B.L. PP 8007.c.p.

An Elegy on the Rt Hon. William [sic] Earl of Pembrook
(London 1683 – B.L. Lutt.I.119.)

An Impartial Account of the Misfortune That Lately Happened to The Right Honourable Philip, Earl of Pembrooke and Montgomery
(London, 1680 – B.L. 515.1.2.(44). and 816.m.19.(48).)

A True and Sad Relation of Two Wicked and Bloody Murthers
(West Smithfield, 1680 – B.L. 1132.g.55)

Great and Bloody News from Turnham-Green
(1680 – B.L. 515.1.1.2.(45) and 816.m.19.(47).)

GREAT NEWS FROM SAXONY: or, A New and Strange Relation of the Mighty Giant KOORBMEP, of His Devouring Men, and of the great Rebellion raised by him, and his Confederates in the Midd Saxony.
(London, 20 August 1680 – B.L. 816.m.19.(46).)

Index

Absalom and Achitophel (Dryden), 39
Admiralty, 112
Adventure (ship), 49
Albemarle, Duke of, 24, 37
Algeria, 117
All Saints, Hastings, 48
Allegiance, Oath of, 135
Anabaptists, 37, 47
Anglesey, Arthur, Earl of (Lord Privy
    Seal), 60
Anglican Church, 42
Angus, Adam, curate of St Dunstan's
    in the West, 93–4
Antichrist Monarchies, 37
Arlington, 38
Arundel House, 92, 93
Arundell, Sir John, 138
Assyria, 37
Atheists, 37, 40, 191
Atkins, Captain Charles, 114–20, 127,
    129, 168
Atkins, Samuel, clerk to Pepys,
    115–21, 123, 124, 126–30, 134,
    163, 196
Aubrey, John, 213
Austria, 65
Aylesbury, 217

Back Court, Lincoln's Inn, 86, 181,
    209
Barbados, 114
Barbican, 41, 47, 49
Barillon, Paul de, French Ambassador,
    67
Barker, John, 192
Barker, Sir Richard, 42, 47, 49
Barker, William, 192
Barrow Hill – see Primrose Hill
Barwick, Dr, 86
BBC Radio, 183
Bedingfield, 60, 62, 63, 115

Bedloe, James, 50, 121
Bedloe, William, 'Captain', 50, 120–9,
    130, 132–3, 134–6, 139, 143, 149,
    151–3, 162, 168, 169, 170, 172
Belasyse, Lord, 110, 124, 130, 133,
    136, 148–9, 167
Benedictines, 110
Benefit of clergy, 217
Berry, Henry, 137–63, 167, 169, 196
Billingsgate, 129
Bills of Mortality, 28
Birch, Col. John, 128
Birkenhead, Lord, 177
Birtby, Edward, acquaintance of EBG,
    77–8
Birtby, Mrs, 77–8
Black Death, 13, 24–8
Blackwood's Magazine, 14
Blood, Col. Thomas, 38, 191, 204
Bludworth, Sir Thomas, Lord Mayor
    of London, 28–9
Blundel, Nicholas, 63
Blyth, Mrs, 103, 208
Bobbing, Kent, 48
Book of Daniel, 37
Bow village, 143, 146
Bowles, Sir William, 192
Boyce, William, 163
Bradbury, Henry, 74, 78, 80
Bread Street, ward of, 28–9
Brecon, 122
Brewer's Yard, Charing Cross, 76
Bridall, Captain, 80
Bridewell, 111
Bridgwater, Somerset, 113
Bridlington Bay, 130
Brigham, King's coachmaker, 131
Bristol, 122
Bristol, Mayor of, 122
Broad Street, Bristol, 123
Broadstreet, Ann, 157, 159

Bromwell, William, baker, discoverer of EBG's body, 94–5, 103, 171, 208
Brown, John, constable, 95–8, 153, 181
Bryant, Arthur, 176
Bubonic plague – see Great Plague
Buchan, John, 177
Buckingham, Duke of, 110, 116–19, 126, 127, 195
Buck, Samuel, 192
Buck's View of the Thames, 31
Burdet, Thomas, 87
Burial in Woollens Act (1666), 41
Burnet, Gilbert, former King's chaplain, 19, 58, 71–2, 73, 75, 92, 98, 108, 172

Caius College, Cambridge, 47
Calais, 218
Cambridge, 47, 50
Cambridge, Nicholas, surgeon, 100–1, 153, 182–3
Cannon Street, 28, 112
Canterbury, Archdeacon of, 48
Carew, Sir Nicholas, 194
Carmarthenshire, 122
Carr, John Dickson, 15, 174–8
Casshes, landlord of Queen's Head, Bow, 147
Catherine (yacht), 129
Catherine, Queen, 32, 88, 132, 133–4, 135, 136, 137, 152, 164, 167
Centre Point, 84
Chalk Farm, 94
Chalk Farm Tavern, 98
Chancellor of the Exchequer, 60
Chancery Lane, 75
Charing Cross Gardens, 84n
Charing Cross Road, 84
Charing Cross, 13, 90
Charles I, 21, 22, 42
Charles II, 27, 28, 29, 31, 37, 38, 39, 40, 42, 43, 44–6, 51–3, 55, 56, 57, 59, 60, 61, 62, 63, 64–5, 66–7, 68, 74, 98, 107, 109, 112, 113, 115, 120, 123, 125, 132, 133, 134, 136, 140, 149, 161–2, 167, 168, 170, 176–7, 191, 192, 194, 195, 196, 212, 218, 220, 221
Chase, James, 100
Chase, John, King's apothecary, 100, 187
Cheapside, 131
Chepstow, 122
Chepstow Castle, 130
Chequer Inn, 98
Chiffinch, William, 45, 162, 162n
Child, seaman, 115
Chiswell, bookseller, 93
Choqueux, royal firework-maker, 110
Christchurch, Oxford, 21
Christopher Alley, 32
City of London, 24, 28, 86, 88, 90
Civil Wars, 22–3, 42, 75
Clarendon House, 124
Clarke, Mr, 62, 64, 71, 80, 81, 85, 198
Clark, Sir George, 176
Clifford, 38
Coal, 22–3, 29–31
Cock and Pye Fields, 84
Cockpit Alley, Drury Lane, 57, 63
Cockpit, 46, 84
Coleman, Edward, secretary to Duchess of York, 64, 65–8, 74, 107, 115, 131, 132–4, 163, 196, 198, 199, 200, 202, 205, 221
Collinson, William, 88
Collins, William, 83–4, 180–1
Commons, House of, 30, 40, 93, 109, 110, 128, 131, 133–4, 196
Compton, Henry, Bishop of London, 110, 116, 126
Coniers, John or George, Benedictine monk, 63
Cony, Nathaniel, 210–11, 215–17
Cook, Lady, 84
Cooper, Anthony Ashley see Shaftesbury, First Earl of
Cooper, Richard, acquaintance of EBG, 82–3
Corall, Francis, Hackney coachman, 131
Country Party, 40, 53, 221

272

Covent Garden, 28, 132, 134
Coventry, Henry, Secretary of State (south), 59, 107, 114, 121, 122, 167, 208
Cowper, John, Middlesex coroner, 99–104, 183
Cranbrook, Essex, 76
Crawley, Elizabeth, 131
Cromwell, Oliver, 22, 42, 119, 198
Cromwell, Richard, 40, 191, 192, 198
Curtis, Elizabeth, EBG's maidservant, 78, 82, 146, 153–5

Daggers, souvenir, 109
Danby, Thomas Osborne, Earl of (Lord Treasurer), 32, 46, 51–3, 55, 57, 58–9, 60, 64–5, 93, 221
de Quincey, Thomas, 14
Dead Wall, Leicester Fields, 93
Declaration of Indulgence, 32, 38, 39
Dent, Robert, 169
Derby House (Admiralty Office), 115, 117, 126
Dewy, James, vestryman, 73
Dieppe, 114
Dolben, Justice, 148–50, 157
Dorset, Earl of, 217
Dover Castle, 49
Dover, 49, 202
Dover, Treaty of, 38, 43
Dowgate, City of London, 22, 30
Downs, the, 113
Drury Lane, 77, 78
Dryden, John, 39
Dugdale, Stephen, informer, 168
Duke, Richard, 102
Duke's coffee house, 87, 97
Duras, Lord, 214
Durham, Bishop of, 62
Dutch Wars, 30

Edgehill, Battle of, 60
Edward IV, 212
Edward VII, 168
Elizabeth I, 30, 94
Elliot, Adam, 47
Encyclopaedia Britannica, 177

Erskine Road, Chalk Farm, 98
Essex, Arthur Capel, Earl of, 110, 116–19
Essex, county of, 76
Europe, 21, 42, 43, 121
Evans, William, 156
Evelyn, John, diarist, 20, 71, 110
Exchequer, Chancellor of, 60
Exclusion Bill, 164, 195, 221

Fall, William, member of Finch's household, 92
Falmouth, Cornwall, 114
Farringdon Without, ward of, 24
Feathers Tavern, Charing Cross, 88
Fenwick, John, 63, 64, 196
Fifth Monarchists, 37, 40, 191, 194
Finch, Sir Heneage, Earl of Nottingham, Lord Chancellor, 54, 59, 60, 75, 89, 90, 92, 107, 109, 140, 161, 180
Fisher, a carpenter, 99–100
Fitzgerald – see Gerald
Flanders, 130
Fleet Street, 30, 40, 123
Flying Horse, King Street, Westminster, 57, 58
Fogerty or Fogarthy, Dr, 63
Folkestone, Kent, 114, 202
Foreign Affairs, Committee of, 59
Forset, or Fawcett, Robert, 102–3
Foster, Sir Reginald, 192, 196
Four Irish Ruffians, 52
Fowler, Mathias, 131
France, 22, 33, 38, 39, 40, 43, 50, 121, 199, 220
Frazier, Sir Alexander, 31, 60
Freeman's Yard, 92
Freyberger, Dr, 181–2, 183, 187, 217
Fromante, 132
Fuller's Rents, Holborn, 49, 50
Funeral of EBG, 111–12

Gavan, 196
George's coffee house, Freeman's Yard, 92

273

Gerald, Irish priest, 136–9, 140, 142, 145, 147, 148, 149, 155
Germany, 64
Gibbon, Mary, 72, 77, 88, 89, 90–1, 92, 102, 180, 182, 201
Girald – see Gerald
Glorious Revolution (1688), 170
Godden, Dr Thomas, 137, 139, 157, 159
Godfrey, Benjamin, 85–6, 88, 89–90, 92, 98, 174–6, 180
Godfrey Edmund Berry (EBG's son?), 21–22
Godfrey Michael, 85–6, 88, 89–90, 92, 98, 174–6, 180
Godfrey, Mr, 112–114, 203
Goldsborough, William, 93, 99
Goodwin, lawyer, 76, 84
Goring, Harry, 215–16
Gravesend, 112–13, 210
Gray's Inn Walks, 123
Gray's Inn, 22
Great Fire, 28, 30, 42
Great Plague (1665), 13, 24–8
Greatrakes, Valentine, miracle healer, 28, 199
Grecian Church, Soho, 138, 143
Greece, 37
Green, Robert, 136–63, 167, 169, 196
Green Ribbon Club, 40–41, 53, 54, 111, 112, 115, 130, 164, 192, 195, 196, 198, 204, 206
Greenberry Hill – see Primrose Hill
Greens Lane, Charing Cross, 23, 28, 87
Greenwich, 129, 163
Grey, Daniel, 157
Griffith, Captain, C-in-C of the Fleet (Portsmouth), 113–14
Griffith, William, secretary to Coventry, 102, 103, 208
Grove, John, 45, 51–2, 57, 63, 134, 135, 196
Grundy, Thomas, 86
Gunpowder Plot, 39, 110

Habeas Corpus Act, 221
Haley, Prof K. H. D., 19
Hallam, Henry, historian, 173
Hammersmith, 13, 87
Hampstead, 86, 92, 94, 209
Harcourt, 196
Harrison, Edmund, 92
Harrison, James, 22–3
Hartshorn Lane, 31, 32, 41, 56, 58, 71, 76, 77, 82, 83, 84, 85, 88, 90, 91, 94, 97, 98, 103, 108, 109, 146, 205, 206
Harvey, Sir Eliab, 194
Hastings, 47, 48, 49
Hastings, Lady Christian, 214
Hastings, Mayor of, 48
Haymarket, 215, 218
Heames, James, vestryman, 80–82
Hempson, William, 192
Henry VII, 217
Henry VIII, 42
Herbert, Philip, 5th Earl of Pembroke, 212
Herbert, Philip, 7th Earl of Pembroke, 210–220
Herbert, William 6th Earl of Pembroke, 212
Herefordshire, 42
Hewett, Sir George, 214
Hicks Hall, 32
Highgate Woods, 37
History of the Reformation (Burnet), 94
Hobbs, a surgeon, 101
Hog Lane, 84, 209
Holborn, 49, 84, 115, 145
Holland, 37, 203
Honourable Society of Gray's Inn, 22
Howard, Bernard, 212
Hudsell, Ann, 22
Hungerford Stairs, 31
Hutton, Mrs, mistress of Flying Horse, 58
Huysman, James, a painter, 86–7

Idells, Samuel, servant to Col. Welden, 63, 85

274

Innocent XI, Pope, 43
Ireland, 44
Ireland, William, 63, 64, 134, 196
Irish, 43
Ivy Lane, 93

James I, 20, 32
James II (see also James, Duke of York), 154, 170
James, Duke of York, 14, 40–41, 43, 44, 52–3, 58–9, 62, 68, 77, 93, 108, 110, 115, 119, 125, 131, 139, 168, 170, 176–7, 191, 196, 198, 201
Jeffreys, Sir George, Recorder (later Judge), 28, 145, 146, 147, 149, 153, 156, 158
Jeffreys, Col. J., 121–2
Jennings, cowkeeper, 95
Jesuit College, St Omers, 50
Jesuits, 42, 50, 51, 52, 57, 58, 59, 60–63, 64, 67, 74, 107, 109, 112, 123, 130, 133, 134, 135, 168, 170, 171, 178
Jesus, Society of – see Jesuits
Johnson, John, 202, 210
John, Don (of Austria), 65
Jones, Margaret, 131
Jones, Mr Justice, 158, 161
Jones, Mr, 123
Jones, Sir William, Attorney-General, 75–6, 100–1, 132, 140, 141–60, 162
Jonson, Ben, 32
Judaism, 158

Kelly, Dominic, 139, 142, 144, 148, 155–6
Kennel, Drury Lane, 77–8
Kent, county of, 22
Kenyon, Professor John, 14, 15, 20, 168, 172–4, 191, 199n
Keynes, 152
Kilkenny Castle, 122
King Street, Hammersmith, 194
King Street, Westminster, 57
King's Bench Bar, 129, 132
King's Head Tavern, Fleet Street, 40

King's Head Tavern, Strand, 125
King's Jewel House, 29
Kirkby, Christopher, 41–2, 43–7, 49, 51, 54–5, 56, 57–60, 71, 174, 177–9

La Chaise, Père François, confessor to Louis XIV, 65–7, 133
Lane, Jane, 48
Lang, Andrew, 170
Langhorn, Richard, lawyer, 107, 196
Lauderdale, John Maitland, Duke of, 65
Lazinby, King's surgeon, 100–1, 103
Le Phaire, Jesuit, 123–5, 135, 151, 152, 169–70
Lee, Catherine, 157, 160
Lee, Sidney, 177
Lee, Sir Thomas, 194
Leeson, Mary, 83
Leicester Fields, 93, 94, 209
L'Estrange, Sir Roger, 100, 154, 179–81
Lincoln's Inn Fields, 94, 116, 124, 181
Lincoln's Inn, 82, 86, 181, 209
Lingard, John, historian, 179
Lisbon, 113
Little Ease, Newgate, 135, 140
Lloyd, Dr William, rector of St Martin-in-the-Fields, 23, 58, 76, 94, 98, 108, 111, 176
Lloyd, servant of Danby, 51, 52, 59
Lockett's, 214, 217
Lombard Street, 92
London, Bishop of – see Compton, Henry
London Bridge, 23, 28, 37, 129
Long's House, Haymarket, 215
Lord Chamberlain, 110
Lord Chancellor – see Finch, Sir Heneage
Lord Chief Justice – see Scroggs, Sir William
Lord Mayor of London, 196
Lord Privy Seal, 59
Lord Treasurer – see Danby, Thomas

Lords, House of, 110, 131, 133–4, 213, 215, 217
Louis XIV, 38, 43, 68, 133, 202, 203
Louvre, 65
Lowen, James, Keeper of Hatfield Park, 83
Lower Chalcot Farmhouse, 98
Lucy, Sampson (Oates's pseudonym), 50
Luson, a priest, 146

Macauley, Lord, 108
Mallet, printer, 220
Marble Arch, 132
Margate, Kent, 114
Marks, Alfred, 14, 100, 171, 179, 181–2, 187, 217
Marston Moor, Battle of, 60
Mary, Duchess of York, 40, 198
Mary, Queen, 42, 68
Marylebone, 84
Mason, Thomas, 83–4, 180–1
Mauricette, Henriette, 213, 220
Maybrick, Mrs, murderer, 177
Meal Tub Plot, 196
Medals, 109
Merchant-Taylors' School, 47
Mico, Fr. Edward, secretary to Whitebread, 65
Middlesex County Sessions, 32
Middleton, Commissioner, 118
Minshaw, Elizabeth, maid, 161
Misprision of Treason, 55
Mrs Duke's coffee house – see Duke's coffeee house
Monmouth, Duke of, 60, 62, 136–9, 156, 169, 170, 196, 212, 220
Montpelier, France, 33
Moor, Henry, clerk to EBG, 13, 63–4, 71, 83, 85, 88, 89, 90, 92, 102, 154, 175
Moor, Mrs, 92
Morgan, Thomas, 103, 208
Muddiman, J. G., 14, 32–3, 211
Mulys, Richard, auditor, 73, 174, 182

Naseby, Battle of, 60
National Portrait Gallery, 221
National Review, 14, 32–3
Navy Office, 115
Nef, John Ulric, 30
New Amsterdam, 203
New Market, 181
Newcomb, printer, 90, 91
Newgate Gaol, 26, 52, 53, 58, 64, 67, 74, 107, 118, 121, 123, 128, 135, 139, 140, 151, 154, 171, 177
Newman (JP), 32
Newmarket, 59, 60, 62, 64, 67, 74, 107, 115, 128, 177, 180, 221
Newport, Earl of (Mountjoy Blount, also Lord Mountjoy), 27
Newport, Francis (Viscount Newport of Bradford in Shropshire), 60
Nicholson, 74, 80
Norfolk, Duke of, 92–3
Normandy, 121
Northumberland Avenue, 32
Northumberland House, 31, 87
Northumberland Street, 32
North, Sir Roger, 19–20, 45, 48, 111, 112, 173
Norwich, Dean of, 110
Norwich, Earl of, 48, 49
Nottingham, Earl of – see Finch

Oakham, Rutland, 47
Oakley, John, 88
Oates, Captain, 37–8, 194
Oates, Titus, 47–68, 71, 73, 74, 75, 76, 77, 104, 107–8, 110, 111, 114, 121, 124, 125, 126, 130, 132–3, 139, 143–4, 166, 167, 168, 170, 177–8, 179, 194, 195, 196, 197, 198, 199, 200, 201, 204, 221
Oath of Allegiance, 24, 39
Ofley, Widow, 92
Ogg, David, historian, 211
Old Bailey, 26
Old Palace Yard, 110
Opposition, the, 68, 108, 109, 110, 114, 115, 202, 212
Ormond, Duke of, 73, 221

Ormonde, Marquis of, 122
Ossory, Thomas Butler, Earl of,
 136–9, 156, 169
Oswald, John, minister, 93–4
Overseers of the Poor, 73–4
Oxford Street, 84
Oxford, 24, 42
Oxford , Earl of, 62

Paddington Woods, 91, 206
Paddington, 83, 84, 92
Paine, milliner, 112, 204
Pall Mall, 92, 126
Palsgrave Head tavern, 123
Pamphlin, Judith, EGB's housekeeper,
 82–5, 88, 90–91, 98, 154
Paris, 65, 220
Parker, Captain William, 48
Parker, William schoolmaster, 48
Parliament House, 110, 119
Parliament, 65, 68, 109, 130, 131
Parsons, John, coachmaker and
 churchwarden, 91, 206
Partridge, Henry, 29
Paulden, Captain Thomas, 87, 97
Pearse, James, Surgeon-General to the
 Fleet, 112, 113
Pembroke, Earls of – see Herbert
Penal Laws, 38–9, 66
Pepys, Samuel, secretary to Admiralty,
 14, 26, 31, 33, 112–14, 115–18,
 124, 128, 129, 163, 167, 202–3,
 210
Persia, 37
Petre, Lord, 110, 167
Peyton, Sir Robert, 40, 191–2, 195–6,
 203–4, 208
Peyton's Gang, 40, 111,164,
 191–202, 203–4, 208, 211
Phaire, Alexander Herbert, 199
Phaire, Colonel Robert, 199
Pheasant Inn, Holborn, 49
Pickering, Thomas, 45, 51–2, 63, 64,
 134, 135
Playhouse Theatre, Northumberland
 Avenue, 32

Plot committees, 110, 116, 134–9,
 140, 145, 171, 198
Plough Alehouse, 142, 144, 148,
 155–6
Plucknet, Christopher, surveyor of
 highways, 98
Plymouth, 114
Plymouth, Lord, 46
Pollock, Sir John, 14, 168–71
Pollution, 20
Pope-burning processions, 195–6
Popish Plot, The (Pollock), 14–15,
 168–71
Portsmouth, 113
Portsmouth, Duchess of, 212, 213
Post-mortem hypostasis, 181
Post Office, 53
Powell, John, 130
Powis, Lord, 110, 130
Prance, Mary, 135
Prance, Miles, 32, 134–40, 142–53,
 155–63, 168–76, 172
Pratt, Lady Margaret, friend of EBG,
 78, 90, 91
Press gangs, 32
Press Yard, Newgate, 128
Primrose Hill, 13, 86, 91, 93, 94–104,
 124, 143, 146, 152–3, 163, 171,
 206, 207
Pritchard, Charles, 135, 152, 169
Privy Council, 52, 55, 59, 60, 62, 63,
 64–8, 89, 90, 91, 92, 107, 115, 117,
 123, 133, 134, 136, 140, 156, 169,
 180, 195, 221
Public Record Office, 100
Pye, Ann, 131
Pym, John, 192

Queen Street, 92
Queen's Head, Bow, 143, 146, 156

Radcliffe, Eleanor, 86
Radcliffe, Joseph, oilman, 80–1, 86,
 102, 176, 209
Ramsay, Sergeant, Lord Treasurer's
 mace bearer, 97–8, 102

Rathbone, Colonel John, 38
Rawson, John, landlord of White
  House, 94–5
Red Lion Court, 123
Red Lion Fields, 84, 145, 181
Regent's Park Road, 98
Regent's Park, 94
Regicides, 23
Reresby, Sir John, 170
Restoration, 42
Rewards, 120–1, 172
Ricaut, Philip, 210–11, 215
Richardson, Captain, keeper of
  Newgate, 118–19, 120, 128, 151,
  161
Rise of the British Coal Industry, 30
Robinson, Sir John, Lieutenant of the
  Tower Hamlets, 192
Robinson, Thomas, chief
  prothonotary of the Court of
  Common Pleas, 74–5, 144, 172–3,
  182, 201
Rochester, Lord, 212
Rome, 37, 42, 143
Rooth, Sir Richard, C-in-C of the Fleet
  (Downs), 49, 113–14
Rudd, Sir Richard, 122
Rupert, Prince, 60
Rye House Plot, 196

Sabbs, Peter, 192
Sacheverell, William, 128, 194
St Andrew's University, 176
St Benet's, Paul's Wharf, 21–2, 212
St Clement's Church, 125, 131, 136,
  142
St Giles Pound, 95
St Giles's-in-the-Fields, 24
St James's Palace, 93, 118, 170
St James's Park, 44, 51–2, 73, 197,
  214
St John's College, Cambridge, 47
St Kitts, 293
St Martins Church, 73, 88, 90, 111,
  112, 222
St Martin-in-the-Fields, parish of, 21,
  28, 41, 54, 58, 59, 78

St Martin's Lane, 82, 83, 91
St Martin's vestry minutes, 33, 211
St Mary Stayning, 42, 44
St Omers, Jesuit College of, 61, 133,
  178
St Pancras, 171
St Paul's Churchyard, 93
Salisbury Cathedral, 220
Sancroft, William, Archbishop of
  Canterbury, 60
Sandhurst, Surrey, 48
Savage, Captain Richard, 216
Savoy, 90, 91, 110
Scotland, 33, 43, 47
Scott, Col. John, 203–10, 217, 221
Scroggs, Sir William, Lord Chief
  Justice, 55, 74, 77, 100, 141–62,
  201, 221
Secretaries of State – see Williamson,
  Sir Joseph, and Coventry, Henry
Sedlescombe, 47
Sellindge, Kent, 21
Shaftesbury, First Earl of, 39–41, 43,
  46, 53, 71, 110–11, 114–20, 126–8,
  130, 164, 170, 171, 192, 195, 202,
  203, 212, 220, 221
Shandois Street, 131
Shelbury, Richard, 24
Simons, Fr, 114
Simpson, Prof. C. Keith, 14, 183–7,
  210
Sitwell, Sir George, 179, 196
Skillard, Zachariah, surgeon, 100–1,
  153, 182–5
slums, 24
Smeeth, William, watchman, 218
Smith, William, Oates's schoolmaster,
  71
Snell, Thomas, 84
Soho, 138, 143, 152
Somerset House, 88, 110, 123, 124,
  125, 128, 132, 135, 136–9, 142,
  143, 146, 152, 156, 157, 164, 167,
  169, 176
Somerset Water Gate, 88, 136,
  152
Southwark, 43, 57

Southwell, Sir Robert, clerk to Privy Council, 89, 90, 91, 92, 109, 156, 180, 221
Spain, 121, 130
Speaker of the House, 60, 62, 196
Stafford, Earl of, 62, 110, 168
Staley, William, 129, 132
Stephen, Sir James Fitzjames, 177, 178
Strand Bridge, 125
Strand, the 23, 77, 86, 87, 88, 102, 110, 125, 131, 136, 142, 170, 176, 181, 209, 215
Strange, Richard, English Provincial of the Society of Jesus, 49–50, 61, 65
Stringer, Serjeant, 146, 151
Stuart, House of, 170
Suffolk, county of, 66
Swan Tavern, Hammersmith, 87, 194

Talbot, Sir Gilbert, 194
Temple Gate, 76
Test Act, (1673), 39–40, 53
Test Act (1678), 131
Thames Street, City of London, 22
Thames, River, 23, 27, 32, 43, 80, 214
The Later Stuarts (Clark), 176
The Murder of Sir Edmund Berry Godfrey (Carr), 15
Three Tobacco Pipes, Holborn, 115
Tilden, Mary, 157–9
Tonge, Dr Israel, or Ezereal, 41–7, 49, 50, 51–61, 71, 74, 75, 107, 194, 197
Tonge, Thomas, 37, 42, 194
Tottenham Court Road, 84
Tower of London, 38, 40, 110, 149, 191, 196, 215
Traill, H. D., 177
Trained bands, 110
Transubstantiation, 39–40, 131
Treaty of Dover – see Dover, Treaty of
Tuke, Richard, 32
Turner, 198
Turner, shoemaker, 131
Turnham Green village, 218
Turn-Style, 84, 181
Tyburn, 38, 58, 132, 163

Umphreville, Charles, 192, 196

Valladolid, 61, 121
Vatican, 42, 66
Vaughan, 214
Vauxhall, 41, 47, 58, 59, 60, 71
Venetian Ambassador, 136
Venner, Thomas, 37
Vernatt, Philibert, 140, 146–7, 148, 155
Victoria Embankment, 32
Villiers, Catherine, 212
Vincent, Sir Francis, 213–14
Vitells, Captain, 128, 163

Wakeman, Sir George, physician to the Queen, 44, 45, 52, 65, 107, 133, 167
Wales, 122, 139
Waller, Sir William, the 'Priest Catcher', 54
Wallingford House, 171
Walsh, Charles, Jesuit, 123–5, 135, 151, 152, 169–70
Walters, John, farrier and discoverer of EBG's body, 94–5, 103, 171, 208
Walter, Lucy, 60
Wapping, 19
Warcup, Colonel Edmund, 32
Warrier, Avis, 155
Warrier, James, 160
Welch, Georg, 192
Welden, Col. George, 63, 80, 82, 84–5, 86, 87, 89, 92, 175–6, 182, 198
Westminster Abbey, 66
Westminster City Council, 21
Westminster Hall, 217
Westminster Quarter Sessions, 74, 75
Westminster School, 21, 74
Westminster, City of, 19, 20, 23, 32, 54, 57, 81, 82, 92
Westminster, Palace of, 110
Wheeler, Richard, vestryman, 78, 91
Whigs, 130, 134, 164, 170, 195, 196, 220
White, Robert, Westminster coroner, 92

White House Tavern, Strand, 86, 94–104, 113, 170, 186, 207
Whitebread, Thomas, 50, 51, 61, 63, 65, 196
Whitehall, 28, 31, 44, 59, 60, 71, 102, 110, 125, 134, 194
Whitehall Palace, 44, 93
Whitehall, Robert, 92
Who Killed Sir Edmund Berry Godfrey? (Marks), 14
Wild House, 167
Wild, Mr Justice, 140, 147, 152, 158, 160, 162
William, Prince of Orange (later William III), 109
Williamson, Hugh Ross, historian, 202
Williamson, Sir Joseph, Secretary of State (north), 54, 59, 60, 64, 67, 120, 183–5, 191, 194
Williams, Prof. J. W., 176

Williams, Sarah, 129
Wilton, Wilts, 213, 220
Wimbledon, 57, 58
Winchelsea, 21
Winchester, Marquis of, 110, 116
Winde, Caleb, 102
Windsor, 46, 51–3, 55, 57, 218
Woolsack Inn, Ivy Lane, 93
Wooten, Lord, 99
Wynell, Thomas, 76–7, 82, 84–5, 86, 87, 175, 201

York, 38
York Buildings, 84, 85
York Water Gate, 84n
Yorkshire Plot, 37–8, 191, 194
York, Duchess of – see Mary, Duchess of York
York, Duke of – see James, Duke of York